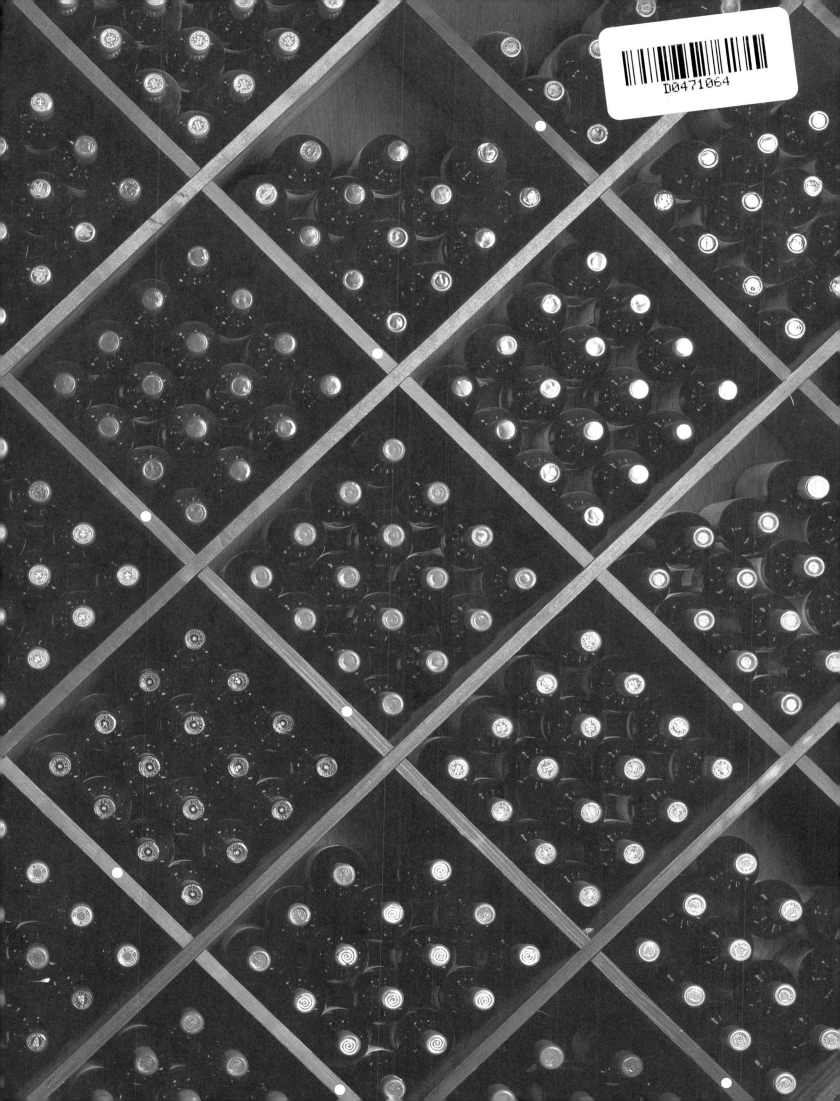

the FLAVORS of LIFE

Culinary Reflections of

MARY NELL RECK

This book was prepared by the Coronado Club to honor Mary Nell Reck and fulfill her personal goal of developing a cookbook—work which was cut short by the effects of treatment for the cancer that took her life. The Flavors of Life stands as a tribute to Mary Nell and to the special relationship she had with the Coronado Club members, staff and families.

THE CORONADO CLUB OF HOUSTON ♛ HOUSTON, TEXAS

Published in the United States by
The Coronado Club of Houston
910 Travis, 5th Floor, Houston, Texas 77002

Copyright © 2004 by The Coronado Club of Houston

Library of Congress Control Number   2004096762

ISBN 0-9760803-0-3

Printed in the United States of America by Grover Printing, a Consolidated Graphics Company

The Flavors of Life is a charitable project. All net proceeds will benefit cancer-related charities and the Culinary Scholarship Fund established in Mary Nell's honor.

Any inquiries about this book or orders for additional copies should be directed to:

Coronado Club Publications
910 Travis, 5th Floor, Houston, Texas 77002
Attn: Mary Eaton
713.659.2426
www.coronadoclub.com

First Edition

the FLAVORS of LIFE

Culinary Reflections of
MARY NELL RECK

THE CORONADO CLUB OF HOUSTON ♛ HOUSTON, TEXAS

Contents

PROFESSIONAL
CREDITS
✳

DESIGN

HILL
Strategic Brand Solutions

Chris Hill
Bobby Van Lenten

PHOTOGRAPHY

Ralph Smith Photography

PORTRAIT
PHOTOGRAPHY
(PAGE 8)

Jean Karotkin

From "Body & Soul,
The Courage and Beauty of
Breast Cancer Survivors"

Published by
Emmis Books, 2004

COPYWRITING

Jolynn Rogers

COPY EDITOR

Polly Koch

FOOD STYLING

Kat Hughes

PROP STYLING

David Lott

PRINTING

Grover Printing,
a Consolidated Graphics
Company

There's a world of difference between being a cook and a chef. Many people can be taught to cook, and cook well. A chef is more.

To be a chef requires creativity, artistry and passion, and a painstaking dedication to technique and craft. It requires knowing how to work with people and motivate them, even in the heat and rush of a busy kitchen. It takes knowing where to find the best ingredients and using them to their full measure. It takes being genuinely interested in every customer and creating meals that lift the spirits of those to whom they are served.

To be a chef calls upon the very best qualities of a person—mind, heart and hands. Mary Nell Reck was a chef.

For more than 30 years, she was a central figure in the Houston food community and on the national culinary scene. She taught cooking classes, wrote a popular cooking column, lectured, owned several restaurants and consulted for many others. She inspired thousands of people with her love of food and zest for cooking, urging them to elevate lives through the simple and beautiful act of turning common foodstuff into something precious to be given and shared.

For all of her accomplishments and honors, the culmination of her career came in the 10 years she spent as the managing director of the Coronado Club in downtown Houston. It was here that everything she was and everything she learned found their natural expression. She changed the Coronado Club and in the process was changed, too.

The Flavors of Life is a tribute to Mary Nell and to the special relationship she had with the club members and their families. It is a celebration of her joy of life – of cooking and eating and giving and sharing.

And with the publication of this book, she will continue to do so. Net proceeds from the sale of *The Flavors of Life* will go to The Rose; The Pink Ribbons Project, Dancers in Motion Against Breast Cancer; Breast Center at Baylor College of Medicine; and the Mary Nell Reck Culinary Scholarship. Her gifts and generosity of spirit are now her legacy—she continues to make a difference.

Mary Nell Reck was a true original. A spirited woman with a complex, soulful personality, she first began teaching cooking out of her house. With the popularity of her classes growing, she opened her cooking school, La Cuisine, in 1973.

During that time throughout the country, people were eating out more and entertaining more. Chefs were experimenting with fresh herbs and seasonal ingredients. Mary Nell's school, located in the Museum District, became a beacon for Houstonians. As they learned to master the subtleties of cooking, they also discovered an appreciation for the shared joy of the table.

Passionate and energetic, she brought a sense of adventure, community and possibilities to her students. And while there may have been the occasional cooking mishap, Mary Nell taught that mistakes were opportunities for learning, that disasters often turned into new dishes and that almost anything can be fixed.

By the late '70s, La Cuisine had gained a national reputation as one of the top cooking schools for culinary professionals and enthusiasts

"MARY NELL WAS AT THE FOREFRONT OF THE AMERICAN CULINARY RENAISSANCE AND A GREAT TEACHER. MILLE GRAZIE, MARY NELL!"

DAMIAN MANDOLA, FOUNDER AND OWNER OF CARRABBA'S RESTAURANTS

alike. Mary Nell's eager, inquisitive nature drove her to take on new challenges. She opened a successful restaurant, Café Moustache, with restaurateur Manfred Jachmich, launched Mary Nell's on the Square in the Theater District and later opened the Truffles and Capers restaurants. She led cooking and tasting tours through Italy, France and Mexico, and spent time in the kitchens of leading chefs Paul Bocuse, Alain Chappel, Roger Verge and Pierre Orsi. She was named one of the ten great women chefs in America by *Town and Country* magazine.

Active in food and wine groups and trade associations, Mary Nell was a founding member of the International Association of Cooking Professionals. She also received many honors, including the prestigious Chaine des Rotisseurs Maitre d'Honneur from the world's oldest gourmet society. The award is shared with only four other chefs in the United States.

For 14 years, Mary Nell wrote the popular "Cooking Lessons" column for the *Houston Post*, which was as much about living well as eating well. To this day, in homes throughout Houston are stacks of yellowed clippings of her columns and individuals whose eyes soften when they reminisce about recipes.

When Mary Nell and the Coronado Club found each other, it was a blessing in timing. After almost 20 years of a very public career, she wanted a lower profile and simpler lifestyle. Mary Nell was brought in as a consultant, and when her year was up, she was invited to stay.

"It was a culmination of everything I've ever done," she once said. "I found a place where I could follow my culinary dream."

As a longtime club member put it, "From the beginning, Mary Nell and the Coronado Club fell in love with each other, and it was a love affair ever since."

With tact, grace and dedication, and a will of steel beneath her smile, she set about reinvigorating the nearly 40-year-old establishment. Carefully, she began revamping the menus and recreating old favorites, like meat loaf, crabmeat

"I LOVED MARY NELL'S
SENSIBILITY IN HER
APPROACH TO FOOD.
IT WAS NATURAL AND
FLUID, NOTHING
FORCED OR CONTRIVED."

BEN BERRYHILL,
EXECUTIVE CHEF, CAFÉ ANNIE

remick and short ribs. She added light, bright flavorful foods that used the freshest, highest quality ingredients—wild salmon, stone crabs from the Florida Keys, white truffles, savory soups made from fresh veal, chicken and fish stocks, homemade sorbets, a paper-thin apple tart with a hazelnut crust. Taking her cues from the members, she added buffalo meat simply prepared and a selection of heart-healthy dishes.

In Mary Nell's kitchen, healthy didn't mean uninspired. She and her staff put their hearts into the taste, adding surprising ingredients like jalapeños or a touch of saffron to bring out the flavor of the food.

She also began training the kitchen staff to meet the highest standards – cultivating employees who had a potential for learning and an open mind. The motto for all the staff was, "At the Coronado Club there are no problems." To every request the response was, "We can do that. We can make that happen."

Then she turned her attention to the club's

interior, enlisting the board's help in the project. Rather than the expression herding cats, this was more like herding lions. Business executives who felt more at home with a balance sheet found themselves in committee meetings discussing the merits of china and club décor. Soon, the dark club interiors began to take on the warm and lustrous glow of beautiful furnishings, exquisite flower arrangements and thoughtful tending and care.

The Coronado Club's new glory found its fullest expression in the traditions Mary Nell established. The black-tie Wild Game Dinner, the Family Christmas buffet, the women's High Tea and the annual Member Christmas party became fast favorites, earning a prominent place on member's social calendars.

Culinary and wine organizations came to the Coronado Club, too, for their Bordeaux and Chevalier dinners. Wine merchants and international distributors began to seek out the club and Mary Nell's distinctive touch for product unveilings and special events.

"MARY NELL AND THE CORONADO CLUB FELL IN LOVE WITH EACH OTHER FROM THE BEGINNING...HER LEGACY IS OUR FUTURE."

A LONGTIME CORONADO CLUB MEMBER

Her influence was felt in other ways. When members were going through difficult times, they received a thoughtful note signed by all the employees. The employees became like members of her family. She organized classes so they could improve their English and helped them set up bank accounts and retirement plans, and even buy homes. A perfectionist, she believed in the perfectibility of people. She found satisfaction in helping to improve lives.

Mary Nell often spoke of her garden and how it had sustained her through life's trials. As she battled the breast cancer that would claim her life, she began to see her garden as a metaphor for patience, love, relationships and the power of dreams. A club member once pointed out that the Coronado Club became Mary Nell's own private garden – handsome, abundant, endlessly enjoyable. *The Flavors of Life* is a celebration of her joyful and generous spirit, and a loving tribute from the club members, staff, families and everyone who had the privilege of knowing her.

APPETIZERS

LAMB TOSTADAS

Recipe on page 17

GRILLED JALAPEÑO QUAIL BREAST WITH APPLE-SMOKED BACON

YIELDS 48 HORS D'OEUVRES

QUAIL

✳

The flavor of quail is delicate, with an underlying hint of cashews. Its texture plumps up to a full meaty texture after cooking.

The difference between the quail of Georgia and that of California is the size and quality of the bird. The California quail is a plumper bird with larger breasts and meatier legs. The deboning process is more precise and accurate with the California quail; the birds are packed dryer and more care seems to be taken with them.

Because of their size, quail are very elegant when stuffed. Best used to accentuate delicate sauces and marinades, they are superb accompaniments to risotto, polenta and other delicately flavored grain dishes.

MARINADE

1/2 cup lime juice

1 cup honey

1 cup virgin olive oil

2 tablespoons dried oregano leaves

1 cup chopped fresh cilantro

2 jalapeño peppers, seeded, deveined and chopped

2 tablespoons chopped garlic

1 teaspoon ground cumin

1 1/2 teaspoons cayenne

1 1/2 tablespoons salt

2 tablespoons freshly ground black pepper

QUAIL

12 boneless quail breasts

1 pound apple-smoked bacon, thinly sliced

2 whole jalapeño peppers, seeded and julienned

Metal skewers

Bamboo skewers

Combine all the ingredients for the marinade. Refrigerate in a covered plastic container.

Remove and discard the skin from the quail. Place quail in a glass container with 1 cup marinade and marinate for 1 hour. Cut into quarters. Wrap a half strip of bacon around each quarter of marinated quail breast and a julienned slice of jalapeño, and place on a long metal skewer. You will probably be able to get 5 or 6 on each skewer. Refrigerate until close to serving time.

Preheat the oven to 400 degrees. Place the skewers of prepared quail on a very hot grill. Brown on all sides. Place in the oven for 5 to 6 minutes or until the bacon is crisp. Transfer to individual bamboo skewers and serve immediately.

. . . .

THE MARINADE MAY ALSO BE USED FOR CHICKEN BREAST, FISH, AND SHRIMP.

QUAIL CAN BE BONED BY A BUTCHER.

USE PLASTIC GLOVES WHEN CUTTING AND SEEDING JALAPEÑOS.

SOAK BAMBOO SKEWERS IN WATER FOR 30 MINUTES TO HELP PREVENT THEIR FLAMING ON THE GRILL. IT IS BEST TO USE METAL SKEWERS WHEN GRILLING OVER A HOT FIRE.

. . . .

Quail Florentine

MARINADE

1 cup olive oil

2 1/2 tablespoons honey

2 teaspoons lemon juice

1/2 cup chopped cilantro

Salt and freshly ground
black pepper

QUAIL

1 1/2 pounds quail breast

1 pound spinach, cleaned
and chopped

1 tablespoon olive oil

3/4-1 cup heavy cream

Salt and freshly ground
black pepper

1/4 cup grated Parmesan cheese

32 tartlet shells (commercially
available or make your own)

Mix the oil, honey, lemon juice, cilantro, salt and pepper together. Add the quail and marinate for a minimum of 12 hours; 24 hours is preferred for the best taste.

Sauté the raw spinach in the olive oil over medium heat in a sauté pan. Add the heavy cream and reduce for about 3 to 5 minutes or until the cream is thickened. Add the Parmesan cheese and the salt and pepper to taste. Set aside.

Grill the quail breast until well marked. Cut into four pieces.

Preheat the oven to 350 degrees. Place the tartlet shells in the preheated oven for 2 minutes to refresh and warm. Spoon the spinach and cream mixture into the shell and top with the grilled quail. Serve immediately.

AMERICAN QUAIL

✳

American quail are known by various names depending on the region: bobwhite in the East, partridge in the South, quail in the North and blue quail in the Southwest. Most of the quail marketed today are raised on game bird farms. Fresh quail can be ordered through specialty butchers, which might also carry frozen quail.

SPICY PORK PIMENTON

YIELDS 50 HORS D'OEUVRES

1/4 cup virgin olive oil

1 tablespoon plus 1 teaspoon ground cumin

1 tablespoon ground coriander

1 1/2 teaspoons paprika

3/4 teaspoon cayenne

1/4 teaspoon turmeric

1 tablespoon chopped oregano

3/4 teaspoon salt

1/2 teaspoon freshly ground black pepper

1 tablespoon chopped garlic

2 tablespoons chopped parsley

2 tablespoons fresh lemon juice

1/2 pound pork loin, cut into 1-inch cubes

Metal skewers

Bamboo skewers

Place the olive oil, cumin, coriander, paprika, cayenne, turmeric, oregano, salt and pepper in a small saucepan and simmer gently over low heat for 4 minutes. Remove from the stove and place in a mixing bowl. Add the garlic, parsley and lemon juice to the warm marinade in the bowl. Taste and adjust the seasoning. Add the pork and gently toss to coat. Place the pork on metal skewers and grill to medium doneness. Transfer to individual bamboo skewers and serve hot as an appetizer.

. . . .

TUNA MAY BE SUBSTITUTED FOR PORK LOIN.

. . . .

CORONADO CLUB CREAM CHEESE SPREAD

YIELDS 3 CUPS

3 packages (8 ounces each) cream cheese, at room temperature

2 1/2 tablespoons butter, softened

2 tablespoons finely chopped capers

1/4 cup plain yogurt

1/2 teaspoon lobster base (found in gourmet markets)

1/4 teaspoon Worcestershire sauce

1 generous tablespoon finely chopped sun-dried tomatoes

1/4 teaspoon cayenne

1/2 teaspoon dried dill

1/2 teaspoon dried tarragon

1/2 teaspoon dried thyme leaves

1/2 teaspoon garlic powder

Combine all the ingredients in a mixer using the paddle attachment. Store in the refrigerator in covered plastic containers.

When ready to serve, spoon into 3-ounce ramekins. Serve with crackers as an appetizer. May be served cold or at room temperature.

. . . .

TO INCREASE THE HEART HEALTHINESS
OF THIS RECIPE, FAT-FREE CREAM CHEESE AND
NONFAT YOGURT MAY BE SUBSTITUTED.

. . . .

LAMB TOSTADAS

TOSTADAS

12 corn tortillas

Vegetable oil to fry the tortillas

1 14-ounce can black beans

1/4 cup bacon drippings or
vegetable oil

1/2 teaspoon cumin

1/2 teaspoon chili powder

Dash of salt and freshly
ground pepper

1/2 cup chopped rosemary

1/4 cup minced garlic

1 1/4 cups olive oil

1/2 tablespoon freshly ground
black pepper

1/2 teaspoon kosher salt

Rack of domestic lamb (8 bones)

17 ounces chèvre goat cheese or
equivalent goat cheese, cut into
1/2-inch squares

PICO DE GALLO

2 cups diced Roma tomatoes

1/2 cup diced red onions

1/2 cup chopped cilantro

1-2 jalapeños, seeded, deveined and
finely chopped

1 tablespoon lemon or lime juice

2 tablespoons olive oil

1/2 teaspoon salt

1/2 teaspoon freshly ground
black pepper

Cut the tortillas in quarters and fry in the vegetable oil until crisp. Drain well. Set aside.

Drain the black beans, reserving the liquid. Heat the bacon drippings or oil in a skillet. Add the beans and mash them up, adding the bean liquid if needed for consistency. This may take several minutes. Then add the cumin, chili powder, salt and pepper. Taste to correct the seasoning. Set aside.

Mix the rosemary, garlic, olive oil, black pepper and salt together and rub on the outside of the lamb. Let the lamb marinate for 1 to 2 hours.

Mix together all the ingredients for the pico de gallo. Taste and adjust the seasoning. Place in a covered container in the refrigerator.

Preheat the oven to 500 degrees. Grill the lamb until well marked or pan sear on high heat on the stovetop. Place on a baking sheet and cook in the preheated oven for 10 to 12 minutes or until medium rare. Remove from the bone and cut each chop into about six pieces.

Spread about 1 teaspoon of refried black beans on each tortilla. Place a piece of goat cheese on top of the black beans and put under the broiler to melt.

Once the cheese is warm and soft, remove from the oven and place one piece of lamb on each tortilla, then top with a small dollop of pico de gallo. Serve immediately.

TO MAKE LOW-FAT TORTILLA CHIPS

✳

Preheat the oven to 350 degrees.

Arrange the tortilla quarters in a single layer on a cookie sheet.

Bake for about 7 minutes, then rotate the pan and bake for another 8 minutes or until the chips are crisp, but not too brown.

ROASTED CORN QUESADILLAS

SERVES 6-8

QUESADILLAS

4 ears fresh corn

1 cup diced Roma tomatoes

1/2 cup diced red onion

1 avocado, sliced

*6 tablespoons coarsely chopped
cilantro leaves*

1-2 jalapeños, seeded and chopped

*1 1/2 cups grated Monterey
Jack cheese*

6 8-inch flour tortillas

1 1/2 tablespoons olive oil

GARNISH

Pico de gallo (see recipe on page 17)

Cilantro sprigs

Guacamole

Preheat the oven to 325 degrees.

Place the whole corn with its husks on a baking sheet in the preheated oven. Roast for 20 minutes or until aromatic. Remove from the oven. When cool enough to handle, remove and discard the husks and silks. Cut the kernels off the cob.

Divide the corn and all the remaining ingredients into thirds, layering them on three of the flour tortillas with the cheese last. Sprinkle the cheese to the edge of the tortilla. Place the remaining tortillas on top to form a sandwich.

Heat a griddle or large frying pan over moderate heat. Lightly drizzle the surface with olive oil (about 1/2 tablespoon). Carefully slide the quesadillas onto the griddle, turning to lightly brown both sides; this takes about 2 minutes. Remove from the heat.

To quickly reheat before serving, place the crisp quesadillas on a baking sheet and place in the preheated oven for 3 to 5 minutes. Cut into wedges, place on a warm platter and garnish with cilantro, pico de gallo and guacamole as desired. Serve immediately.

. . . .

THAWED AND DRAINED FROZEN CORN MAY BE USED IF
FRESH CORN IS NOT IN SEASON.

ADDING 2 CUPS OF SHREDDED ROASTED CHICKEN TO
THE QUESADILLA INGREDIENTS WILL CREATE A
HEARTY MEAL.

. . . .

QUESADILLAS

✳

Quesadillas, one of the mainstays of Mexico's street-side stands, are considered quintessentially Mexican. Quesadillas are hybrid creations, half indigenous and half Spanish, reflecting Mexican culture. The corn tortilla used for most quesadillas is native to the Americas; the cheese as well as the pork and/or beef that may accompany the cheese, is Spanish. Of possible garnishes, the hot sauce made with chili pepper is indigenous, but the shredded lettuce is Spanish.

SMOKED PHEASANT SPRING ROLLS
WITH SWEET AND SOUR SAUCE

YIELDS 30 HORS D'OEUVRES

MARINADE

1/4 cup red wine vinegar

1/4 cup soy sauce

2 tablespoons freshly ground
  black pepper

1 teaspoon salt

1 1/2 pounds pheasant breast meat

SWEET AND SOUR SAUCE

2 cups water

1/4 cup catsup

1/2 cup red wine vinegar

1/2 cup brown sugar

1/2 teaspoon cayenne

1 tablespoon grated fresh ginger

Salt and freshly ground white
  pepper to taste

2 tablespoons cornstarch mixed
  with 1/4 cup water

SPRING ROLLS

2 tablespoons olive oil

1/2 pound button mushrooms,
  chopped

1/4 pound wild mushrooms, chopped

1/2 pound carrots, peeled and cut in
  fine julienne

1/2 pound leeks, cleaned thoroughly
  and cut in fine julienne

1 large red bell pepper, finely diced

2 cloves garlic, minced

1/2 head Chinese cabbage, cut in
  fine julienne

1/2 cup chopped cilantro

1/4 cup finely diced ginger root

2 tablespoons seeded and finely
  chopped jalapeño pepper

Salt and freshly ground pepper
  to taste

30 spring roll pastry wrappers

1/2 cup flour mixed with
  2/3 cup water

Combine the marinade ingredients. Add the pheasant and marinate for at least 1 hour. Place the pheasant in a smoker for 20 to 30 minutes. A stovetop smoker is good for this; follow the manufacturer's instructions. Remove the pheasant when cooked and shred. Set aside.

Combine all the ingredients for the sweet and sour sauce except the cornstarch-water mixture in a saucepan. Bring to a boil. Taste and adjust the seasoning. Slowly add the cornstarch and water until the mixture thickens enough to coat a spoon.

Place the olive oil in a pan over medium heat and sauté the mushrooms. Remove and set aside. In the same pan, sauté the carrots, leeks, bell pepper and garlic using the same oil. Add the Chinese cabbage, then the mushrooms. Mix all the vegetables together with the cilantro, ginger and jalapeño. Season with salt and pepper. Gently add the shredded smoked pheasant.

Place a spring roll wrapper on the table with a corner facing you. Place a generous tablespoon of the filling on the wrapper. Roll the wrapper around the filling, tucking in the ends, until you have a package that looks like a sausage. Using a pastry brush, seal the spring roll with the flour paste. Fry the spring rolls in hot peanut oil until crisp and golden. Serve with the sweet and sour sauce.

. . . .

PHEASANT IS AVAILABLE IN
SPECIALTY SUPERMARKETS, BUT IT MAY
NEED TO BE ORDERED AHEAD.

. . . .

PHEASANT

✳

Pheasant meat is tender, moist yet firm. It possesses the tenderness of chicken and the firmness of venison. When pheasant is cooked correctly, this combination of qualities gives it a unique flavor.

GALANTINE OF PHEASANT

YIELDS 2 GALANTINES (32-40 SERVINGS)

GALANTINES

6 tablespoons chopped shallots

2 teaspoons butter

3 ounces shiitake mushrooms sliced

1/2 teaspoon chopped garlic

2 tablespoons cognac

1/2 cup white wine

SPICES

1/2 tablespoon whole black
    peppercorns

5 juniper berries

1/4 teaspoon whole cloves

1/4 teaspoon fennel seeds

1 teaspoon fresh thyme leaves

1/4 teaspoon nutmeg

1/4 teaspoon cinnamon

1/8 teaspoon cayenne pepper

PHEASANT

2 pounds pheasant breast, cut into
    1-inch pieces

1/2 pound dark pheasant meat from
    legs, cut into very small pieces

2 pounds ground pork

1 tablespoon salt

1 tablespoon cornstarch

1/2 cup pistachios

8 ounces thin sliced prosciutto
    (about 12 slices)

2 quarts rich chicken stock

1/2 bottle white wine

6 sprigs of thyme

6 bay leaves

CHERRY GINGER CHUTNEY

2 tablespoons butter

1 cup sliced red onion

1/2 cup sliced shallots

1 cup raisins

1 cup dried cherries

1 tablespoon chopped garlic

1/4 cup chopped ginger

3/4 cup brown sugar

1/2 cup granulated sugar

1/2 cup red wine vinegar

1/2 teaspoon salt

1 teaspoon mustard seed

1/2 tablespoon red pepper flakes

GALANTINE

✳

*Galantine is a classic
French dish that resembles
a meat-wrapped pâté.*

*The galantines may be
cut with an electric knife
to avoid tearing.*

Sauté the shallots in the butter. Add the mushrooms and garlic, and sauté over high heat until the mushrooms are brown and dry. Place in a mixing bowl. Add the cognac and wine to the pan, and boil to reduce by half. Add to the mushrooms.

Place the spices in a coffee grinder and grind to a fine powder. Add to the mushrooms in the mixing bowl.

Stir the pheasant and pork into the spiced mushroom mixture. Add the salt, cornstarch and pistachios. Mix very well with your hands. Sauté a small piece to taste and adjust the seasoning.

Lay the thin slices of prosciutto on a piece of cheesecloth. Place a 3-inch roll of the meat mixture on the prosciutto and wrap tightly with the cheesecloth. Tie with string. This makes two galantines. Place in the refrigerator overnight.

Combine the chicken stock with the wine and herbs, and bring to a boil. Place the galantines in a roasting pan and cover with the boiling stock. Simmer gently for about 2 hours, turning the galantines every 20 minutes. Do not let the liquid boil. Check the internal temperature with a meat thermometer to make sure the galantines reach 160 degrees. Remove from the heat and cool overnight, refrigerated, in the stock.

The next day, remove the galantines from the liquid. Remove the cheesecloth. Wrap with plastic wrap and chill until ready to serve.

To prepare the chutney, heat the butter and sauté the onions and shallots for 3 minutes or until half soft. Add the garlic and cook for 2 minutes more. Stir in all the remaining ingredients and bring to a boil. Cook for 20 minutes or until soft and thick. Taste and adjust the seasoning. If the chutney becomes too thick, add a little red wine or water. This makes 2 cups chutney.

To serve, cut the galantine into 1/2-inch thick slices. Place a mound of frisée on a chilled plate. Place a slice of galantine on the side of the salad. Serve with a mound of cherry ginger chutney and sesame flat bread. Alternatively, serve the galantine with good French bread or buttered toast rounds.

Galantine of Pheasant

CHICKEN SATE WITH PEANUT DIPPING SAUCE

YIELDS 50 HORS D'OEUVRES

CURRY POWDER

✳

Curry powder is a readily available blend of spices in a Western approximation of Indian spice blends. It typically contains turmeric, coriander, chilies, cumin, mustard, ginger, fenugreek, garlic, cloves and salt, among other spices.

The word "curry" in India simply means "sauce." Indian foods made with sauces are thus all curries.

SATE

✳

Sate is an Indonesian favorite consisting of small marinated cubes of meat, fish or poultry threaded on skewers and grilled or broiled. Sate is usually served with a spicy peanut sauce.

MARINADE

3/4 cup grated coconut

2 tablespoons chopped ginger

2 tablespoons curry powder

1/4 cup lime juice

1/4 cup soy sauce

1/4 cup olive oil

2 tablespoons minced garlic

1 teaspoon salt

1 teaspoon freshly ground
   white pepper

1 teaspoon crushed red pepper

SATE

3 whole chicken breasts

Bamboo skewers

DIPPING SAUCE

1 cup peanut butter

2 cloves garlic, minced

1/4 cup lime juice

1/4 cup soy sauce

2 teaspoons granulated sugar

1/2 teaspoon cayenne

1/2 cup water

Place all the marinade ingredients in a blender and process until smooth. Cut the chicken breasts into 1/2 x 2-inch strips and marinate for 3 hours. Soak the bamboo skewers in water so they do not burn while grilling.

Combine all the dipping sauce ingredients in a blender and process until smooth. Taste and adjust the seasoning as necessary. Set aside.

When ready to serve, thread the chicken onto the bamboo skewers and grill until well marked. You may also cook the skewered chicken under the broiler. Serve warm or at room temperature with the dipping sauce.

. . . .

PEANUT SAUCE IS NOW READILY AVAILABLE
IN MOST SUPERMARKETS.

ADD A LITTLE CAYENNE TO PROVIDE EXTRA SPICE.

. . . .

BELGIAN ENDIVE WITH SMOKED SALMON

SERVES 6-8

6 ounces cream cheese, softened

3 tablespoons heavy cream

2 tablespoons finely chopped chives

2 tablespoons finely chopped dill

1 teaspoon capers (optional)

1 tablespoon lemon juice

Salt and freshly ground
   white pepper

3 small heads Belgian endive

12 ounces smoked salmon

Sprigs of fresh dill

2-3 tablespoons fresh lemon juice

4-6 tablespoons extra virgin
   olive oil

GARNISH

Lemon slices

Greek olives

Roma tomato slices

Watercress sprigs

Pita triangles, toasted

Combine the cream cheese and cream in a small bowl with a whisk until smooth. Stir in the chives, dill, capers (optional), lemon juice, salt and white pepper. Separate the leaves of the Belgian endive. Place about a teaspoon of the cream cheese mixture at the base of each leaf, using a fork. Top with a rosette of smoked salmon, and place a sprig of fresh dill at the top of the cream cheese mound

Arrange on a serving plate with the garnishes. Sprinkle with lemon juice and drizzle with the olive oil.

. . . .

THIS RECIPE MAY ALSO BE SERVED AS A SALAD.

AFTER THE LEAVES OF THE ENDIVE ARE SEPARATED, THEY MAY BE PLACED IN A PLASTIC CONTAINER OF ICE WATER FOR AT LEAST 30 MINUTES TO CRISP THEM UP BEFORE PREPARING.

. . . .

ENDIVE

✳

Endive refers to a group of leafy vegetables falling under the general name of chicory. Some red types turn red only with the onset of cool weather.

The terms "chicory" and "endive" are frequently interchanged: Belgian endive or French endive are the forced products of witloof chicory. Another type of chicory, whose dried roots are used as a coffee substitute, is magdeburgh, or Italian dandelion. Chicory tops may also be used in cooking like spinach. Radicchio is often referred to as Italian chicory. Radichetta is asparagus chicory.

Endive's savory leaves spice salads, soups, stuffings and other dishes with a pleasantly bitter taste. When properly grown, endive has a delicious, piquant, full flavor.

There are two types of endive: curly and broadleaf. The curly types generally are called frisée (pronounced free-zay, it is French for "curly"). The broad-leaf, lettuce-like varieties are called escarole or sometimes scarole.

HOT AND CRUNCHY CRAWFISH (LOBSTER) WITH GINGER AIOLI AND MANGO CHOLULA® SAUCE

SERVES 10

CRAWFISH (LOBSTER)

2 pounds shelled crawfish or lobster tail meat

2 cups all-purpose flour, seasoned with salt and freshly ground white pepper

Egg wash: 3 eggs and 2/3 cup water

1 1/2 cups cornmeal

1/2 cup white sesame seeds

Oil for deep frying

GINGER AIOLI SAUCE

3 large egg yolks at room temperature

2 tablespoons lemon juice

2 tablespoons Dijon mustard

2 cloves garlic, finely minced

2 teaspoons finely chopped ginger

Pinch of cayenne

1/3 cup extra virgin olive oil

1/2 cup salad oil (safflower)

Salt and freshly ground white pepper to taste

1 tablespoon chopped chives

MANGO CHOLULA® SAUCE

1/2 cup Cholula® sauce (found in most grocery stores where hot sauces are located)

1 medium, ripe mango, peeled and seeded

1/2 medium habañero pepper, seeded

GARNISH

Cilantro sprigs

Lemon wedges

Chopped chives

Combine the cornmeal and sesame seeds. If using lobster, cut the meat into 1-1/2 inch pieces. Roll the crawfish or lobster in the seasoned flour. Shake and pat off the excess. Dip into the egg wash to lightly coat. Dredge in the cornmeal and sesame seeds to completely coat. Set aside and chill until ready to serve.

Drop a few pieces at a time into cooking oil heated to 360 degrees and deep fry until golden and crisp, about 2 minutes. Remove from the oil and drain. Serve with the two sauces below.

To prepare the ginger aioli sauce, place the egg yolks, lemon juice, Dijon mustard, garlic, ginger and cayenne in a medium mixing bowl. Whisk together to combine. Very gradually add the olive oil, then the vegetable oil, while whisking vigorously. The mixture will thicken as it emulsifies. Taste and season with salt and white pepper. Stir in the chives. Set aside. This sauce may also be made in a food processor.

To prepare the mango Cholula® sauce, place the ingredients in a blender and puree for a minute until smooth. Transfer to a small bowl for serving.

To serve the crisp crawfish or lobster as an hors d'oeuvre, place a mound on a platter with two small bowls of the sauces for dipping. To serve as a first course, place a serving of the crawfish or lobster on top of a bed of the ginger aioli sauce and dot the plate with the mango Cholula® sauce. Garnish with a sprig of fresh cilantro, a lemon wedge and a sprinkling of chopped chives.

. . . .

FOR A LESS SPICY DISH, OMIT THE HABAÑERO PEPPER AND SUBSTITUTE A SWEET ITALIAN PEPPER.

. . . .

SESAME SEEDS

❋

White sesame seeds taste measurably less earthy than their black counterparts. Black sesame seeds are jet black and are used whole to create a dramatic effect as a garnish in both Chinese and Japanese cooking.

Called "foreign hemp" by the Chinese, sesame is thought to be native to Africa, although some argue for Persia or even India, where it has been under heavy cultivation for millennia. The seed consists of about 50 percent oil. Sesame oil keeps well in tropical heat and is fine for cooking.

CHOLULA® SHRIMP

YIELDS 20-25 HORS D'OEUVRES

1 pound shrimp (21-25), peeled and deveined

1/2 cup Cholula® sauce (found in most grocery stores where hot sauces are located)

1 pound apple-smoked or other smoked bacon, thinly sliced

Metal skewers

Bamboo skewers

Preheat the oven to 375 degrees. Cut each slice of bacon in half crosswise.

Dip the shrimp in the Cholula® sauce, then wrap each one in a thin slice of the bacon. Thread the bacon-wrapped shrimp onto large metal skewers. You can probably get 5 or 6 of the shrimp on each skewer. Cook the skewered shrimp on the grill or in a sauté pan until the outside of the bacon is well browned and beginning to become crisp.

Remove the skewers from the grill or pan and place them on a baking sheet to finish in the oven. Bake for 8 to 10 minutes. Alternatively, the shrimp can be cooked completely on the grill or in the pan. If cooking on the grill, leave a small amount of space between each shrimp so that they are cooked evenly on all sides. Remove the shrimp from the large skewers and place on individual bamboo skewers to serve.

CRABMEAT GRUYÈRE TARTS

YIELDS 180 TARTLETS

180 tartlet shells

4 tablespoons butter

1 cup diced yellow onion

1/2 cup diced green bell peppers

3/4 cup diced red bell peppers

3/4 cup diced yellow bell peppers

1/2 cup diced jalapeño peppers

1 bunch of cilantro, diced

1 cup heavy cream

1 1/2 cups grated Gruyère cheese

1 pound fresh lump crabmeat

Dash of salt and freshly ground white pepper

Preheat oven to 375 degrees.

The tartlet shells may be either purchased or homemade. This recipe works well with frozen phyllo tartlet shells. Bake the shells before filling.

Heat the butter in a pan and sauté the yellow onions until tender. Add the green, red and yellow bell peppers, and jalapeño peppers. Continue to sauté for an additional 5 to 7 minutes. Remove from the heat and place in a bowl. Add the cilantro, Gruyère cheese and heavy cream. Combine smoothly and add the crabmeat. Place about a teaspoon in each tartlet shell.

Bake filled tartlets in the oven for about 7 minutes or until the cheese is thoroughly melted. Sprinkle with a dash of salt and pepper. This recipe freezes well. Before serving, remove from the freezer and bake for 13 to 15 minutes.

A BETTER WAY TO DEVEIN SHRIMP

❋

Hold the shrimp between your index finger and thumb, gently squeezing the head and tail together. The vein will become visible down the center of the shrimp. With a fork, carefully puncture the center of the back of the shrimp and loop the vein through the first tine of the fork. Gently pull up on the vein until it completely dislodges from the shrimp.

GRUYÈRE CHEESE

❋

Gruyère cheese is a yellow cheese made from cow's milk. Named after the village of Gruyères in Switzerland, it is hard, slightly salty and piquant. It contains numerous cells, and when fully aged (3 to 12 months), it tends to have small holes and cracks.

PHYLLOS

❋

Phyllos or filo is a delicately crisp, layered pastry originally used for Greek and Middle Eastern pastries. The paper-thin dough can be found in the freezer section of the supermarket.

CEVICHE

COCO LOPEZ®

✳

Coco Lopez® is a cream made from the tender meat of sun-ripened Caribbean coconuts that has been blended with natural cane sugar.

FISH

2 pounds fish (trout, redfish, salmon, snapper, tuna or swordfish, but not sole or flounder)

1 pound shrimp (36-42 pieces), peeled

3 cups fresh lime juice

1 1/2 cups Coco Lopez®

3/4 cup chopped scallions

3/4 cup chopped parsley

3 teaspoons dried oregano leaves

3 teaspoons finely diced jalapeño pepper

1 1/2 cups extra virgin olive oil

Dash of salt and freshly ground white pepper

GARNISH

2-3 ripe avocados, sliced

Pico de gallo (see the recipe on page 17)

Lime wedges

Parsley sprigs

Cut the fish into 1-inch pieces. Place in a large plastic container with the shrimp. Add the lime juice and Coco Lopez®. Cover and refrigerate overnight to "cook" the fish. It will become opaque and white.

Combine the marinated fish and shrimp with the scallions, parsley, oregano, jalapeño, olive oil, salt and white pepper. Divide the ceviche among 12 salad plates, placing the fish on the side of the plate. Place a mound of pico de gallo in the center and 3 avocado slices in a fan on the opposite side. Garnish with a twist or wedge of lime and a sprig of parsley.

. . . .

POMPANO MAY BE
SUBSTITUTED
FOR ANY OF THE FISH.

THE ACTION OF THE ACID IN
THE LIME JUICE "COOKS"
THE FISH, THEREBY FIRMING
THE FLESH AND TURNING
IT OPAQUE.

. . . .

BUYING
SHRIMP

✳

When buying fresh shrimp, select shrimp that smells of the sea with no hint of ammonia. If it smells strongly of iodine, it simply reflects the type of food on which the shrimp has fed.

WHOLE ARTICHOKE STUFFED WITH CRABMEAT

ARTICHOKES

6 medium artichokes

1 lemon, cut into wedges

2 tablespoons salt

4 celery tops

4 bay leaves

2 sprigs fresh thyme or 1 teaspoon
   dried thyme

2 cloves garlic

STUFFING

1 cup (2 sticks) unsalted butter

2 cups chopped yellow onions

4 cloves garlic, crushed
   and chopped

1 cup bread crumbs

2 cups freshly grated
   Parmesan cheese

1 cup chopped cilantro

1 tablespoon finely grated
   lemon peel

Dash of salt, freshly ground white
   pepper and cayenne

1 pound fresh lump crabmeat

Cut the stems from the artichokes so they stand. Snap off the lower leaves and trim the thorns from the leaf tips. With a sharp knife, cut off about 1 inch from the tops. Place the lemon, salt, celery, bay, thyme and garlic in a large pot of hot water and boil 10 minutes to develop the flavors. Drop in the artichokes. Cover with a plate so they are completely submerged. Boil for 20 to 25 minutes or until a leaf pulls out easily when tested for doneness.

Remove the artichokes from the water. Invert and drain. When cool enough to handle, scoop out the thistle with a grapefruit spoon. Set aside.

Melt the butter in a large frying pan. When hot, sauté the onions for 4 to 5 minutes or until soft. Stir in the garlic. Add the bread crumbs and cook, stirring, until golden brown. Remove from the heat and stir in the Parmesan cheese, cilantro, lemon peel, salt, white pepper, cayenne and lump crabmeat.

Spoon the mixture into the cavities and between the leaves of the artichokes. The artichokes may be prepared in advance to this point and refrigerated. When ready to serve, place on a rack in a pan of water. Cover and steam in the oven or on top of the stove for 15 minutes or until heated through. Serve immediately.

. . . .

SHARP KITCHEN SCISSORS MAY BE USED TO TRIM THE
ARTICHOKE LEAF TOPS.

PRE-GRATED PARMESAN IS AVAILABLE BUT DOES NOT
COMPARE WITH FRESHLY GRATED.

. . . .

ARTICHOKES

✳

The globe artichoke belongs to the thistle family. The "choke" in the center is actually an immature flower enclosed in leaf scales, which are the parts we eat.

Jerusalem artichokes are the tuberous roots of a member of the sunflower family and are sometimes called sunchokes. They are a source of insulin.

FOIE GRAS WITH CARAMELIZED PEAR AND COURVOISIER® SAUCE

SERVES 12 AS A FIRST COURSE

FOIE GRAS

✳

In antiquity, the Egyptians used to appreciate the meat of the wild geese that came to hibernate in the Nile delta. Were they also eating the geese's livers? The first real evidence of its presence on a table dates back to the first century B.C., when Apicius described raw liver that was sliced and macerated in "garum," a fish-based condiment, then grilled.

BREAD

12 slices French baguette
2 tablespoons olive oil

BROWN SAUCE

2 tablespoons butter
2 tablespoons all-purpose flour
1 1/2 cups beef stock
Dash of salt and freshly ground
    black pepper

COURVOISIER® SAUCE

1/2 cup heavy cream
2 tablespoons Courvoisier® cognac
Dash of salt and freshly ground
    black pepper

PEARS

3 ripe pears
3 tablespoons unsalted butter
4 tablespoons brown sugar
1 tablespoon lemon juice

FOIE GRAS

1 pound foie gras
Salt, freshly ground black pepper
    and granulated sugar to taste
3/4 cup Courvoisier® cognac
12 sprigs of fresh thyme

Preheat the oven to 325 degrees. Cut the bread into 2-inch rounds. Place on a baking sheet and drizzle with olive oil. Place in the oven and bake for 12 to 15 minutes or until the bread is crisp. Set aside until ready to use (this may be done earlier in the day).

Melt the butter and stir in the flour. Cook on medium-low heat until the flour has turned a nice golden brown, being careful not to burn the mixture. Add the beef stock, stirring with a whisk until the mixture is smooth and thickened. Season with salt and pepper. Set the brown sauce aside until ready to use (it may be prepared ahead of time and refrigerated).

Heat 1 cup of the brown sauce in a small saucepan. Add the cream and boil for 10 to 12 minutes to reduce. Season to taste with salt and pepper. Just before serving, add the Courvoisier™.

Slice the unpeeled pears about 1/2-inch thick from top to bottom (four slices per pear). Heat half the butter in a 12-inch frying pan. When the bubbling subsides, add half the sugar. Cook over moderately high heat until bubbles form on the surface and the sugar becomes aromatic. Place half of the pear slices in the pan and cook, shaking the pan, for about 1 minute or until golden on one side. Turn and cook the other side for about 30 seconds. Add half of the lemon juice. Set aside and keep warm while you repeat the above steps to caramelize the remaining pear slices.

Separate the two lobes of the foie gras. Slice into 3/8-inch thick medallions. When ready to serve, heat a frying pan over moderately high heat. Sprinkle the pan with salt, pepper and granulated sugar (no oil—the foie gras supplies its own!). Quickly sauté the foie gras medallions, shaking the pan. Turn once when light brown and add a splash of cognac to the pan. Shake and flame. Remove and keep warm while continuing to cook the remaining foie gras medallions. Do not cook the foie gras medallions any longer than 1 minute per side or you will end up with a lot of very expensive fat.

To assemble the dish, ladle the Courvoisier® sauce onto a warm plate. Place a toast round in the center of the sauce, place a caramelized pear slice to one side, and top the toast round with a foie gras medallion. Garnish the plate with a sprig of fresh thyme.

. . . .

THERE ARE MANY COMMERCIALLY MADE BEEF STOCKS AVAILABLE IN SPECIALTY STORES. FROZEN STOCKS ARE BEST, BUT SHELF STOCKS WITH MINIMAL PRESERVATIVES CAN ALSO BE USED.

SERVED SOLO, FOIE GRAS IS MUCH APPRECIATED COLD (BUT NOT FROZEN); IT MUST BE TAKEN OUT OF THE REFRIGERATOR 15 MINUTES BEFORE BEING SERVED. SERVE IT WITH A CÔTEAU DU LAYON, SAUTERNE, GEWÜRSTRAMINER, CHAMPAGNE OR LIGHT RED WINE.

. . . .

CAMPECHENA

CAMPECHENA

10 corn tortillas

Oil to use for frying

4 cups pico de gallo (see the recipe on page 17)

2 cups tomato catsup

1 tablespoon Cholula® sauce (found at most grocery stores in the hot sauce section)

1 teaspoon lime juice

1 whole avocado, diced

1 pound fresh lump crabmeat

2 limes, cut in 5 slices that are scored on one side to make a twist

Sprigs of cilantro

10 jumbo shrimp, boiled in seasoned water, peeled and deveined with the tails on

To make a tortilla basket, place a corn tortilla between two ladles, a larger one on the bottom and a smaller on the top, and lower into hot vegetable oil in a deep pan. Fry until crisp. Set aside.

Mix the pico de gallo, tomato catsup, Cholula® sauce, lime juice and avocado together. Add the crabmeat, being careful not to break up the pieces. Place about 1/2 cup of the mixture in each tortilla basket and serve on a bed of lettuce.

Garnish with the lime twist and a nice sprig of cilantro. Place a shrimp, tail standing up, on top of the campechana.

. . . .

TOMATO SAUCE MAY BE SUBSTITUTED FOR CATSUP IF YOU WANT TO OMIT THE SUGAR.

CHOLULA® HOT SAUCE HAS AN INCOMPARABLE FLAVOR AND AROMA THAT MAKES IT A GREAT COMPLEMENT TO A LARGE VARIETY OF FOODS.

. . . .

PASTIS, OUZO AND OJEN

✳

Pernod® is the brand name of a type of liqueur called pastis. Its relative in Greece is ouzo and in Spain ojen. Another French brand is Ricard. The leading characteristic of these drinks is their licorice flavor, which is produced either with licorice (the plant, not the candy) or anise. Its other interesting feature is that it clouds up with the addition of water.

OYSTERS FLORENTINE

SPINACH TOPPING

2 pounds fresh spinach

1/2 cup chopped shallots

2 tablespoons unsalted butter

2 tablespoons chopped garlic

1/4 cup dry vermouth

Salt and fresh white pepper to taste

Grating of fresh nutmeg

1 cup heavy cream

1/4 cup Pernod® liqueur

OYSTERS

36 raw oysters

1/2 cup grated Parmesan cheese

1/4 cup bread crumbs

1/4 cup melted butter

Rock salt for the pan

Blanch the spinach in a pot of rapidly boiling, salted water until wilted. Lift from the pot of water and transfer to a bowl of ice water. Drain, squeeze out the moisture, chop and set aside.

Sauté the shallots in a frying pan in the butter for 1 minute. Add the garlic, vermouth, salt, white pepper and nutmeg. Boil for 2 minutes. Add the cream and boil to thicken. When the cream is reduced and thick, stir in the blanched spinach and Pernod®. Taste and adjust the seasoning. Set aside.

Preheat the oven to 400 degrees. Place each raw oyster in an oyster shell on a baking sheet lined with rock salt. Cover with the spinach topping. Sprinkle with Parmesan cheese and bread crumbs. Drizzle lightly with melted butter. Bake 10 minutes or until hot and bubbly. Serve immediately.

OYSTERS

✳

Available already shucked, oysters can be kept refrigerated, covered by their liquor, in tightly covered containers for up to a week. You can also freeze shucked raw oysters in their liquor in airtight containers. They will keep for several months in a freezer set at 0°F or colder. Thaw oysters in the refrigerator, not at room temperature.

SESAME SEED FLAT BREAD

Recipe on page 36

BREAD & EGGS

JALAPEÑO BISCUITS

YIELDS 20 2-INCH BISCUITS

2 cups all-purpose flour

2 tablespoons granulated sugar

1/4 teaspoon salt

1/4 teaspoon freshly ground
    white pepper

1 tablespoon baking powder

Dash of cayenne

1/2 cup (1 stick) cold unsalted butter

1 tablespoon cored, seeded and
    finely chopped jalapeño peppers

1 1/4 cups heavy cream

Preheat the oven to 450 degrees.

Sift the dry ingredients into a mixing bowl. Cut the butter into 1/2-inch pieces. Using your fingertips, rub the butter and flour mixture together until it resembles a coarse meal. Add the jalapeños. Add the cream and stir with your hands. When barely combined, turn out onto a lightly floured board and knead just enough to bring the dough together.

Roll out to a 1-inch thickness. Cut with a floured 1 1/2 to 2-inch cutter. Arrange in a single layer on a parchment paper-lined baking sheet. Sprinkle with flour.

Bake in the center of the preheated oven for 10 minutes or until puffed and golden. Serve warm.

. . . .

THESE BISCUITS CAN ALSO BE MADE BY DELETING
THE JALAPEÑOS AND ADDING 2 TABLESPOONS
OF CHIVES. THEY ARE DELICIOUS MADE EITHER WAY.
THESE ARE A CORONADO CLUB FAVORITE.

. . . .

JALAPEÑO

❋

The official peppers of Texas are the jalapeño and the chiltepin, which are both used in its official dish, chili.

BISCUIT DOUGH

❋

Tossing or kneading biscuit dough lightly helps distribute leavening for even baking and rising.

WHOLE WHEAT BISCUITS

YIELDS 20 2-INCH BISCUITS

2 1/4 cups stone-ground whole
    wheat flour

1/4 teaspoon salt

1/4 teaspoon freshly ground
    white pepper

2 1/4 teaspoons baking powder

1/4 teaspoon cayenne

2 tablespoons seven-grain cereal meal

1/2 cup (1 stick) cold unsalted butter

1 1/4 cups heavy cream

Preheat the oven to 450 degrees.

Sift the dry ingredients into a mixer bowl. Stir in the seven-grain meal. Add the butter and beat on low speed until crumbly. Turn the mixer to the lowest setting and slowly add the cream while the beater is in motion. When barely combined, turn out on a floured board.

Divide the dough. Roll out half at a time to a thickness of 1 inch. Cut into 2-inch rounds with a floured cutter. Place on a parchment paper-lined baking sheet. Sprinkle lightly with flour.

Bake for 10 minutes or until puffed and golden.

WHOLE WHEAT

❋

Whole wheat is a nutritious grain containing more protein than rice and most other staple cereals.

JALAPEÑO BISCUITS

Rosemary Bread Sticks

ROSEMARY BREAD STICKS

SERVES 8

1 package dry or fresh yeast

1 tablespoon granulated sugar

3/4 cup warm water (100 degrees)

1/2 cup virgin olive oil

3/4 cup beer

2 tablespoons chopped fresh rosemary

1/2 teaspoon freshly ground
   white pepper

4 1/2 cups all-purpose flour

1 large egg

1 tablespoon water

1 1/2 teaspoons salt

Parmesan cheese for sprinkling

Place the yeast in a mixing bowl. Add the sugar, warm water, olive oil, beer, rosemary and white pepper. Stir until the yeast is dissolved. Gradually stir 3 1/2 cups of the unsifted flour into the yeast mixture. Stir with a wooden spoon until the dough becomes spongy in appearance. Turn out onto a lightly floured board to knead. The dough will be quite sticky at first until the remainder of the flour is incorporated.

Knead the dough with a fold, push, and turn motion, using the heel of your hand; add flour to keep the dough from sticking. When the dough is springy to the touch, after about 5 minutes, place in a lightly oiled bowl to rise. Be sure the dough is thoroughly coated with oil. Cover with a towel and set in a cold oven with a bowl of boiling water on a rack below it. Let stand for about an hour until double or triple in size.

After removing the dough, preheat the oven to 400 degrees. Push the dough down with your fist. Knead for a minute. Pinch off 2-inch balls of dough between your thumb and forefinger. (Do not attempt to pull the dough or you will have a mess on your hands.) Roll out the balls into 14-inch sticks with your hands on a lightly floured surface. Place the bread sticks on a parchment paper-lined baking sheet.

Beat the egg and water together in a small bowl. Lightly brush the egg wash on the surface of the bread sticks, being careful not to let it run down to the pan or it will burn. Sprinkle lightly with salt and Parmesan cheese.

Bake in the preheated oven for 12 to 15 minutes or until golden brown.

. . . .

THESE BREADSTICKS CAN ALSO BE MADE
USING 2 TABLESPOONS OF FENNEL SEEDS INSTEAD
OF THE ROSEMARY.

. . . .

ROSEMARY

✳

Rosemary's name is rooted in legend. The story goes that during her flight from Egypt, the Virgin Mary draped her blue cloak on a rosemary bush. She then laid a white flower on top of the cloak. That night, the flower turned blue and the bush was thereafter known as the "rose of Mary." Greeks, who wove rosemary wreaths into their hair, believed rosemary strengthened the brain and enhanced memory. It was also known as a symbol of fidelity.

In the Middle Ages, rosemary was used medicinally and as a condiment for salted meats. In Europe, wedding parties burned rosemary as incense. Judges burned it to protect against illness brought in to their courts by prisoners.

YEAST

✳

Yeast has been used in the preparation of food and drink for as long as there have been leavened bread and beer, but it was only in the 19th century, thanks to the work of Louis Pasteur, that its nature was understood.

Dried yeast, called "active dry (baking) yeast" in the United States, is in the form of dried granules and keeps for a year or more, all the better if refrigerated.

SESAME SEED FLAT BREAD

YIELDS ABOUT 50 PIECES

SESAME SEED

❋

History tells us that sesame seed is the first recorded seasoning, dating back to 3000 B.C. Assyria. The seed was brought to America by African slaves, who called it "benne seed." The seed is available packaged in supermarkets and can be found in bulk in Middle Eastern markets and health food stores. Sesame seeds turn rancid quickly. They can be stored airtight in a cool, dark place for up to 3 months, refrigerated for up to 6 months or frozen for up to a year.

3 cups all-purpose flour

1 1/2 teaspoons freshly ground black pepper

1/2 cup grated Parmesan cheese

Juice and grated zest of 2 lemons

1/2 cup (1 stick) cold unsalted butter

1/3 cup ice water

Cornmeal

Egg wash: 1 large egg mixed with 1/4 cup water

Coarse salt

Grated Parmesan cheese for top

Black and white sesame seeds (If black sesame seeds are unavailable, use all white sesame seeds instead.)

Preheat the oven to 400 degrees.

Place the flour, pepper, Parmesan cheese and lemon zest in a mixing bowl. Cut the butter into 1/2-inch pieces and place in the bowl. Mix together until crumbly and coarse in texture. While mixing at the lowest speed, add the lemon juice and ice water. Beat only enough to combine the ingredients. Adjust liquid as needed to hold the mixture together. Transfer the dough to a lightly floured board.

Roll out very thin. Line a half-sheet baking pan with parchment paper. Sprinkle with cornmeal. Lay the dough on the cornmeal. Brush with the egg wash and sprinkle with salt, Parmesan cheese and sesame seeds, as desired.

Bake in the preheated oven for 10 to 12 minutes or until crisp and golden. Break into 2 x 4-inch pieces.

JALAPEÑO CORNBREAD

YIELDS 16 PIECES

CORNBREAD

❋

Cornbread is a term that refers to breads based on maize. There are two corn bread traditions: the first is that of the Americas, where maize originated, while the second is that of Europe and Europeanized societies for whom maize was an ancillary rather than a staple good.

1 1/2 cups yellow cornmeal

1 1/2 cups all-purpose flour

3 teaspoons baking powder

1/2 teaspoon baking soda

1/2 teaspoon salt

3 tablespoons granulated sugar

1 cup buttermilk

3 large eggs

12 strips bacon

2/3 cup grated Cheddar cheese

1/3 cup finely chopped jalapeño peppers

3 scallions, chopped, including the green part

Preheat the oven to 425 degrees.

Place the cornmeal, flour, baking powder, baking soda, salt and sugar in a bowl. In a separate bowl, combine the buttermilk and eggs, beating with a fork until well mixed. Make a well in the center of the dry ingredients, pour in the liquid and gradually work it in with your hands.

Cut the bacon into 1-inch pieces and cook over moderate heat until crisp. Remove and drain; reserve the drippings. Add 6 tablespoons of the drippings to the cornbread batter. Stir in the bacon pieces, cheese, jalapeños and scallions.

Place 4 tablespoons of the drippings in a 10-inch iron skillet and heat very hot, until almost smoking. Pour the batter into the hot pan. Bake in the preheated oven for 20 to 25 minutes until puffed and golden. Cut into wedges and serve immediately with butter.

. . . .

MILDER CHILIES MAY BE SUBSTITUTED FOR THE FIERY, SPICY JALAPEÑO.

. . . .

EGGS HUSSARD

6 beef tenders (6 ounces each), split
   horizontally

6 English muffins, split, buttered
   and toasted

EGGS

12 large eggs, cold

1/4 cup vinegar

2 tablespoons salt

MARSALA HOLLANDAISE

2 cups dry Marsala wine

1/2 cup chopped shallots

1 sprig parsley

1 bay leaf

1/2 sprig fresh thyme

1 1/2 cups (3 sticks) unsalted butter

6 large egg yolks

2 tablespoons cold water

2 tablespoons lemon juice

1 teaspoon lemon zest

Salt and freshly ground white
   pepper to taste

GARNISH

Roasted new potatoes

Any green vegetable

Parsley sprigs

Season the meat with salt and pepper. Grill to order and set aside.

Prepare a bowl of ice water and bring 2 inches of water to a boil in a large shallow pan. Add the vinegar and salt. Quickly break the eggs into the boiling water, dropping them into the area of greatest turbulence. The cold eggs will lower the temperature to a simmer. Simmer the eggs about 3 minutes or until the white is set. Drop the eggs immediately into the bowl of ice water. Take each egg in one hand and trim away the ragged edges. Set aside.

Combine and boil the Marsala wine, shallots, parsley, bay leaf and thyme until reduced to 1/4 cup of liquid. Cool and strain. Set aside.

To clarify the butter, heat in a small saucepan until it boils, then set aside to separate and start to cool.

Place the egg yolks, cold water, lemon juice, lemon zest, salt and white pepper in a large mixing bowl. Beat vigorously with a whisk. Place the bowl over a pan of boiling water and continue whisking until the sauce is slightly thickened and fluffy. Quickly remove from the heat and gradually beat in the lukewarm clarified butter. When the sauce is thick, taste and adjust the seasonings. Add the Marsala reduction and correct the seasonings.

Before serving, return the eggs to boiling water for 20 seconds to reheat. Place a beef tender steak on a muffin half, put a poached egg on top and cover with the Marsala hollandaise. Serve with new potatoes, a green vegetable and parsley.

. . . .

IN MANY RECIPES, BEEF MAY BE SUBSTITUTED FOR
CANADIAN BACON OR HAM.

SOME NON-ALCOHOLIC SUBSTITUTIONS ARE:
RED WINE = RED GRAPE JUICE OR CRANBERRY JUICE
WHITE WINE = WHITE GRAPE JUICE OR APPLE JUICE

. . . .

**POACHED
EGGS**

✳

*Dropping poached eggs
into cold water after
cooking does several
things. It rinses off the
vinegar and salt, sets the
eggs and holds them in a
safe environment until
ready to serve.*

*Clarified butter is also
called drawn butter.
Simply defined, clarified
butter is unsalted butter
that has the milk solids
and water removed so all
that remains is pure
liquid golden-yellow
butterfat. The advantages
of this type of butter is its
long keeping quality
(several months refriger-
ated) and its high smoke
point (can be used in
frying without burning).
The disadvantage is that
it doesn't have that same
wonderful rich flavor of
regular unsalted butter
(since the milk solids have
been removed) but it does
have a more buttery taste
than other oils.*

*To make clarified butter
gently melt unsalted
butter over low heat until
the butter breaks down
and three layers form.
The top layer is a white
foam or froth (the whey
proteins) and should be
skimmed off with a
spoon. The milk solids
will drop to the bottom of
the saucepan and form a
milky layer of sediment.
What is left in the middle
is a pure golden-yellow
liquid called clarified
butter. When you have
skimmed all the white
foam from the surface of
the clarified butter, and it
has stopped bubbling,
remove the saucepan
from the heat. Let the
butter sit a few minutes
to allow the milk solids to
further settle to the
bottom, and then strain
the mixture through a
fine sieve or a cheese-
cloth-lined strainer. The
liquid collected is the
golden-yellow clarified
butter (butterfat) that
can be covered and
stored several months in
the refrigerator. Chilled
clarified butter does
become grainy.*

HOBO BREAKFAST

SERVES 6

HOBO HASH

2 pounds Italian sausage, crumbled

2 cups sliced yellow onions

*2 pounds new potatoes, cooked and
cubed*

*Dash of salt and freshly ground
black pepper*

EGGS

12 large eggs

*4 tablespoons (1/2 stick) clarified
butter*

*3/4 cup grated Monterey Jack
cheese*

*6 tablespoons pico de gallo (see the
recipe on page 17)*

Fry the sausage until brown. Remove from pan, leaving 1/4 cup
of drippings in the pan. Sauté the onions in the drippings.
When half cooked, add the potatoes and fry until brown.
Season with salt and pepper. Add the cooked sausage. Place the
hash in a warm gratin or large casserole dish.

Preheat the oven to broil. Fry the eggs in the clarified butter.
Place the eggs on top of the hash. Top with grated cheese and
melt under the broiler. Top with pico de gallo and serve.

EGGS IMPERIAL

SERVES 6

EGGS

3/4 cup sliced mushrooms

2 tablespoons clarified unsalted
butter

3/4 pound fresh lump crabmeat

Dash of salt and freshly ground
white pepper

6 tablespoons brandy liqueur

12 large eggs, cold

1/4 cup vinegar

2 tablespoons of salt

6 English muffins, split, buttered
and toasted

12 slices Roma tomatoes

12 ounces Swiss cheese, grated

GARNISH

Roasted new potatoes

Sauté the mushrooms in the clarified butter; add the crabmeat.
Season with salt and white pepper. Flame with a splash of brandy.

Prepare a bowl of ice water. In a large shallow pan, bring 2
inches of water to a boil. Add the vinegar and salt. Quickly
break the eggs into the boiling water, dropping them into the
area of greatest turbulence. The cold eggs will lower the
temperature to a simmer. Simmer the eggs about 3 minutes or
until the white is set. Drop the eggs immediately into the bowl
of ice water. Take each egg in one hand and trim away the
ragged edges.

Preheat the broiler. When ready to serve, plunge the eggs into
boiling water for 20 seconds to reheat. Place the crab mixture
on top of the toasted English muffin halves. Top with the
poached eggs. Place a tomato slice and grated Swiss cheese on
top of each egg and place under the broiler to melt the cheese.

Serve with new potatoes.

POACHED EGGS WITH SALMON

SERVES 6

EGGS

12 large eggs, cold

1/4 cup vinegar

2 tablespoons salt

CREAM SAUCE

4 tablespoons (1/2 stick) unsalted
butter

4 tablespoons all-purpose flour

2 cups milk, warmed

Dash of salt and freshly ground
white pepper

SALMON AND GARNISH

1 pound smoked salmon, thinly
sliced

2 tablespoons capers

Chopped dill

Roasted new potatoes

Lemon wedges

Parsley sprigs

Prepare a bowl of ice water and bring 2 inches of water to a boil
in a large shallow pan. Add the vinegar and salt. Quickly break
the eggs into the boiling water, dropping them into the area of
greatest turbulence. The cold eggs will lower the temperature to
a simmer. Simmer the eggs about 3 minutes or until the white is
set. Drop the eggs immediately into the bowl of ice water. Take
each egg in one hand and trim away the ragged edges. Set aside.

Melt the butter in a saucepan; add the flour. Mix until bubbly
and the flour cooks a bit. Do not brown. Add the heated milk
all at once, stirring with a whisk. Cook until thickened and
bubbly. Add the salt and white pepper.

When ready to serve, plunge the eggs into boiling water for 20
seconds. Place two poached eggs per serving on a hot plate.
Cover with the cream sauce. Lay the smoked salmon slices over
the eggs. Sprinkle with capers and fresh dill.

Serve with new potatoes and garnish with a lemon wedge and a
parsley sprig.

People have smoked food
since ancient times.
Smoking of food proba-
bly began after primitive
ancestors hung their
"kill" in the rafters of
timber or stone dwellings
to prevent animals from
eating it and discovered
that the food exposed to
smoke from the fire
remained in better
condition for longer. As
the idea developed,
smoking was then used
as a means of preserva-
tion to provide meat and
fish and other food for
the winter months.
Today, with the freezer
being used as our main
means of preservation,
fish is smoked to impart
a pleasant taste and
enhance natural flavors.

The smoking process
involves a number of
basic steps including
brining, air-drying,
smoking and finally
presentation. There are
two types of smoking,
cold and hot, and some
confusion exists as to the
difference. Cold smoking
is the "true" smoking
method by which the
food changes in color,
flavor and texture. It is
carried out in a temper-
ature range of 21-31
degrees, but ideally at
25 degrees. Hot smoking
takes place in a kiln at a
higher temperature of
70-80 degrees (and
sometimes higher), actu-
ally cooking the product
much like a conventional
oven. In both cases the
preparation (brining)
allows the smoke vapor
to enhance the flavor of
the resulting product.

EGGS FLORENTINE

FLORENTINE

✳

Catherine de' Medici,
daughter of Lorenzo,
Duke of Urbino, left
Florence in 1533 to
become Queen of France
and the mother of three
kings. But she was also
the mother of French
haute cuisine. She was so
fond of spinach that she
had it at every meal and
her royal cooks learned
to adapt it to all kinds of
dishes. Even today, any
dish employing spinach is
suffixed with "Florentine"
after Catherine.

SPINACH

2 pounds fresh spinach

1/2 cup chopped shallots

4 tablespoons (1/2 stick) unsalted
    butter

Salt and freshly ground black
    pepper to taste

1/4 teaspoon nutmeg

CROUTES

8 slices firm-textured white bread

Unsalted butter, softened

Chopped chives

EGGS

8 large eggs, cold

1/4 cup vinegar

2 tablespoons salt

HOLLANDAISE

3/4 cup (1 1/2 sticks) unsalted
    butter

3 large egg yolks

1 tablespoon cold water

1 tablespoon lemon juice

Dash of salt and freshly ground
    white pepper

2 teaspoons finely grated lemon peel

Carefully wash the spinach and remove the stems. In a 12-inch frying pan, melt the butter and sauté the shallots until they begin to brown. Let the butter brown as well. Add the spinach a little at a time, stirring until it wilts. Season the spinach with salt and pepper. Add the nutmeg. Set aside but keep warm.

Preheat the oven to 300 degrees. Cut the bread into 2 1/2-inch rounds. Brush lightly with soft butter and bake in the preheated oven for 8 to 10 minutes or until crisp and lightly golden. Set aside.

Prepare a bowl of ice water and bring 2 inches of water to a boil in a large shallow pan. Add the vinegar and salt. Quickly break the eggs into the boiling water, dropping them into the area of greatest turbulence. The eggs will lower the temperature to a simmer. Simmer the eggs about 3 minutes or until the white is set. Drop the eggs immediately into the bowl of ice water. Take each egg in one hand and trim away the ragged edges. Set aside.

To clarify the butter, heat in a small saucepan until it boils, then set aside to separate and start to cool.

Place the egg yolks, cold water, lemon juice, salt, white pepper and grated lemon peel in a large mixing bowl. Beat vigorously with a whisk. Place the bowl over a pan of boiling water and continue whisking until the sauce is slightly thickened and fluffy. Quickly remove from the heat and gradually add the lukewarm clarified butter. When the sauce is thick, taste and adjust the seasonings.

When ready to serve, plunge the eggs into boiling water for 20 seconds.

Place each croute on a warm plate and top with a mound of the sautéed spinach. Place a poached egg on the spinach and cover completely with hollandaise. Sprinkle with chopped chives. Serve immediately.

EGGS JUAREZ

ANCHO CHILI PUREE

1/2 pound ancho chilies

1/2 cup honey

1 teaspoon salt

*1 teaspoon freshly ground
    black pepper*

ANCHO CHILI HOLLANDAISE

4 large egg yolks

2 teaspoons lemon juice

1 teaspoon water

1/2 teaspoon salt

*1/2 teaspoon freshly ground
    white pepper*

*1 cup (2 sticks) unsalted butter,
    clarified*

1/4 cup ancho chili puree

SAUSAGE

1 pound ground pork

1 tablespoon paprika

1 teaspoon cayenne

*1 1/2 teaspoons freshly ground
    black pepper*

1 1/2 teaspoons salt

2 garlic cloves, finely chopped

PASTRY

2 pounds puff pastry dough

1 egg mixed with 2 tablespoons water

EGGS

8 large eggs, cold

1/2 cup vinegar

2 teaspoons salt

GARNISH

Sprigs of cilantro

Pour boiling water over the chilies and let them stand 1 hour until soft. Split the chilies, discarding the seeds and veins. Puree in a blender and season with the honey, salt and pepper. Set aside.

Place the egg yolks in a mixing bowl and add the lemon juice, water, salt and pepper. Beat until fluffy. Place the bowl over a pan of boiling water, beating vigorously until the yolks are the consistency of custard. Remove from the heat and gradually beat in the clarified butter until the sauce is thick and foamy. Add 1/4 cup of the ancho chili puree. Taste and adjust the seasoning. Set aside but keep warm.

Combine the pork, paprika, cayenne, pepper, salt and garlic. Chill the sausage for up to 3 days in advance. When ready to serve, form the sausage into 3-inch patties and grill until done. You may also pan fry the sausage over high heat. Set aside.

Preheat the oven to 400 degrees. Roll the puff pastry dough until it is about 1/8-inch thick. Cut into 4-inch squares and place two inches apart on a baking sheet. Place a 2-inch ramekin in the center of each square and brush the exposed pastry lightly with the egg wash. Be careful that the egg wash does not touch the ramekin or run down the pan. Bake 12 to 15 minutes until puffed and golden. Set aside.

Prepare a bowl of ice water and bring 2 inches of water to a boil in a frying pan. Add the vinegar and salt. Quickly break the eggs into the boiling water, dropping them into the area of greatest turbulence. The cold eggs will lower the water temperature to a simmer. Simmer the eggs for about 3 minutes or until the white is almost firm to the touch and the yolk is still soft. Plunge the eggs into the ice water. Set aside.

To assemble, reheat the pastry squares in the oven. Place on warm plates and top with the cooked sausage patties. Plunge the eggs into hot water for 10 to 15 seconds to reheat. Drain and carefully place on the sausage patties. Spoon the warm ancho chili hollandaise over the eggs. Garnish with 1/4 teaspoon of the ancho chili puree and sprigs of cilantro. Serve immediately.

. . . .

NOTE: ALL OF THE COMPONENTS OF THIS DISH MAY
BE PREPARED IN ADVANCE AND ASSEMBLED WHEN
READY TO SERVE.

. . . .

**ANCHO
CHILIES**

✳

The ancho chili is the dried form of the poblano chili. It rates between mild and medium hot and is considered in the "warm" class of chilies.

PAPRIKA

✳

Paprika, as a member of the capsicum family, is indigenous to the Western Hemisphere. The pepper is grown widely and takes on a slightly different flavor depending on local soil and climate conditions.

CHICKEN POMODORO SALAD

Recipe on page 46

Salads

SEDONA SALAD

SERVES 8

LEMON HONEY DRESSING

1/2 cup freshly squeezed
    lemon juice

1 teaspoon chopped lemon zest

1/4 cup mild honey

2 tablespoons Dijon mustard

1/2 cup extra virgin olive oil

1 cup safflower oil

Salt and freshly ground white
    pepper to taste

ROASTED WALNUTS

1 pound walnut halves

1/4 cup brown sugar

1/2 cup melted unsalted butter

2 tablespoons lemon juice

1/4 teaspoon cayenne

1/2 teaspoon salt

1/4 teaspoon freshly ground
    white pepper

SALAD

10 cups mixed salad greens, washed
    and dried

1 Granny Smith apple

4 ounces Stilton cheese, crumbled

Combine the lemon juice, zest, honey and mustard in a medium mixing bowl. Gradually whisk in the olive oil, then the safflower oil. Add salt and white pepper.

Preheat the oven to 300 degrees. Place the walnuts in a large mixing bowl. Add the remaining ingredients and toss to coat. Place on a baking sheet in the preheated oven and roast, stirring occasionally, for 12 to 15 minutes or until toasted and aromatic. Allow to cool to room temperature. Store in a tightly covered container.

When ready to serve, place the salad greens on 8 chilled salad plates. Cut the unpeeled apple into julienned strips. Place on top. Sprinkle with 1/2 cup roasted walnuts and the Stilton cheese. Drizzle the salads with the lemon honey dressing.

. . . .

APPLE STRIPS MAY BE PREPARED AN HOUR
BEFORE BY SQUEEZING A SMALL AMOUNT OF FRESH
LEMON JUICE OVER THE STRIPS TO KEEP THEM
FROM TURNING BROWN.

BLUE CHEESE MAY BE SUBSTITUTED
FOR STILTON CHEESE.

. . . .

CORONADO CLUB CHICKEN SALAD

SERVES 6

2 whole chickens, 3 1/2 pounds each

2 1/2 cups chopped celery

1/4 cup chopped scallions

3/4 cup finely chopped Italian parsley

2 tablespoons chopped fresh
    tarragon

1/2 cup capers

Dash of salt and freshly ground
    white pepper

1 1/2 cups mayonnaise

Preheat the oven to 350 degrees. Season the chicken and roast in the oven for 1 hour. Cool and pull all the meat from the bones. Discard the skin and chop the chicken into 2-inch pieces.

In a large mixing bowl, combine the chicken, celery, scallions, parsley, tarragon and capers. Add salt and white pepper to taste. Gently stir in the mayonnaise. Taste and adjust the seasoning as necessary.

. . . .

FOR A STRONGER FLAVOR, A WHITE ONION MAY BE
SUBSTITUTED FOR THE SCALLIONS.

. . . .

SOUTHWEST CHICKEN SALAD

SERVES 8

MARINATED CHICKEN

1/2 cup freshly squeezed lime juice

1 cup virgin olive oil

2 jalapeños, seeded and finely
   chopped

1/2 cup coarsely chopped cilantro

2 cloves garlic, peeled and crushed

1/4 cup honey

1/2 teaspoon whole cumin seed

Dash of salt and freshly ground
   black pepper

6 boneless, skinless whole chicken
   breasts

DRESSING

1/4 cup red wine vinegar

1/4 cup lime juice

2 tablespoons honey

2 cloves garlic

1 cup virgin olive oil

Generous pinch of cayenne

Salt and freshly ground black
   pepper to taste

SALAD

12 cups assorted salad greens
   (spinach, Boston, romaine, red leaf)

2 ripe avocados

4 Roma tomatoes

2 medium red bell peppers

1/4 cup toasted pumpkin seeds

Mix the marinade ingredients together in a bowl. Cut the chicken breasts in half and add to the marinade. Refrigerate at least 2 hours.

The marinated chicken may be grilled or sautéed. Have the grill or pan very hot so the juices are quickly sealed into the meat and you get a rich brown color on the surface. Cook the meat only 5 to 6 minutes or until it feels firm but not hard to the touch. Overcooking will cause the chicken to become tough and dry. Set aside.

Place the vinegar, lime juice, honey and garlic in a food processor or blender. Slowly add the olive oil while processing. The dressing will thicken as it emulsifies. Add the cayenne, salt and pepper. Refrigerate until ready to use.

Wash and dry the salad greens. Tear the leaves into 3-inch pieces, place in a bowl, cover with a damp towel and refrigerate until close to serving time. Peel and thinly slice the avocados and sprinkle lightly with a few drops of lime juice. Quarter the tomatoes. Cut the bell peppers crosswise into thin rings and remove the seeds and veins. Place these salad ingredients on a plate and refrigerate until ready to assemble.

When ready to serve, toss the salad greens in enough dressing to barely coat. Mound onto plates or in a large shallow bowl. Arrange the avocados, tomatoes and pepper rings around the perimeter of the salad. Thinly slice the chicken and arrange the slices in an overlapping circle on the salad greens. Drizzle a little additional dressing over the chicken and vegetables, and sprinkle with the toasted pumpkin seeds. Serve immediately.

. . . .

TO KEEP YOUR AVOCADO FROM BROWNING ONCE IT
HAS BEEN PEELED, CUT OR EVEN ADDED TO A RECIPE,
THROW THE PIT IN WITH THE AVOCADO AND THE
FLESH WILL MAINTAIN ITS BRILLIANT GREEN COLOR.

. . . .

CHICKEN POMODORO SALAD

SERVES 8

BASIL OIL DRESSING

1 cup extra virgin olive oil

*1/2 cup packed-down fresh basil
leaves, washed and dried*

1/2 teaspoon salt

1/4 cup freshly squeezed lime juice

CHICKEN SALAD

*6 boneless, skinless chicken breast
halves, grilled and sliced*

3 pounds Roma tomatoes, sliced

*12 marinated artichoke hearts, cut
into quarters*

*1 1/2 cups freshly grated
Parmesan cheese*

1/2 cup chopped fresh basil

1/2 cup sliced black olives

*1 tablespoon freshly ground
black pepper*

2 teaspoons salt

Lime juice

2 cups chopped romaine leaves

*1 red onion, thinly sliced
in rings*

6 basil leaves

Place the olive oil and basil leaves in a blender. Process until combined. Taste and add more basil as desired. Add salt. Place in a bottle and keep fresh at room temperature, reserving the lime juice, until ready to serve.

Place the chicken, tomato slices, artichoke hearts, Parmesan cheese, chopped basil, olives, black pepper and salt in a mixing bowl. Toss with 1 cup basil oil, adding more olive oil if desired. Sprinkle with the lime juice.

Place the romaine leaves on separate plates or in a large shallow bowl. Top with a tall mound of chicken salad. Place the onion rings on top and garnish with fresh basil leaves.

**BASIL OIL
VINAIGRETTE**

✻

*Basil oil vinaigrette may
also be brushed on fish
or poultry before grilling.*

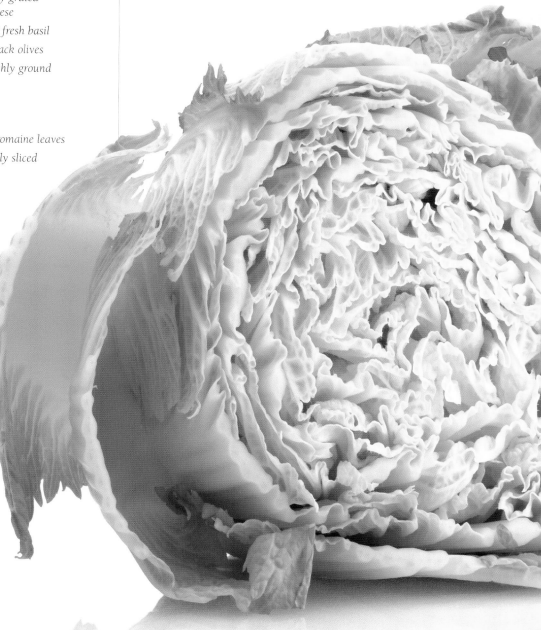

PASTA SALAD GENOVESE

RED WINE VINAIGRETTE

1/4 cup red wine vinegar

1 teaspoon Dijon mustard

1 teaspoon mayonnaise

1 shallot, minced

1 clove garlic, minced

1 teaspoon granulated sugar

3/4 cup olive oil

Dash of salt and freshly
  ground pepper

PASTA SALAD

1 pound dried shell pasta

5 tablespoons olive oil, divided

1 large yellow onion, chopped

1 cup pine nuts

2 tablespoons crushed garlic

1/2 pound Genoa salami, slivered

8 ounces fresh spinach, chopped

1 cup chopped parsley

2 cups chopped scallions

Dash of salt and freshly ground
  black pepper

1/2 teaspoon nutmeg

1 cup grated
  Parmesan cheese

LETTUCE AND GARNISH

Lettuce leaves

Parsley sprigs

Greek olives

Combine the vinegar, mustard, mayonnaise, shallot, garlic and sugar in a blender. Blend well. With the blender running, slowly add the olive oil in a thin stream to form an emulsified vinaigrette. Add salt and pepper.

Cook the pasta in boiling water with 1 tablespoon olive oil until al dente. Rinse well with cold water. Drain and set aside.

Sauté the onions in 4 tablespoons of olive oil. When half done, add the pine nuts and continue cooking until the pine nuts begin to brown. Add the garlic and salami, and cook 8 minutes more or until the salami begins to color and develop a rich aroma.

Transfer the sautéed mixture to a large mixing bowl along with the spinach, parsley, scallions, salt, pepper, nutmeg and Parmesan cheese. Toss in the cooked pasta. Add just enough vinaigrette to moisten and add flavor.

To serve, line each salad plate with lettuce leaves. Place a mound of pasta salad on the lettuce. Garnish with a parsley sprig and two Greek olives.

. . . .

PEPPERONI MAY BE SUBSTITUTED FOR THE SALAMI.

. . . .

GENOA SALAMI

✳

Genoa salami is a medium-spicy salami usually made from pork. It originated in the Genoa area of Italy.

TOMATO TOWER WITH LUMP CRABMEAT

SERVES 6

CRABMEAT SALAD

1/2 cup chopped Italian parsley
1/2 cup finely chopped celery
1 cup mayonnaise
1 teaspoon freshly ground white pepper
1 teaspoon salt
1/4 cup freshly squeezed lime juice
1 tablespoon Tabasco® sauce
1 pound fresh lump crabmeat

CHIPOTLE MAYONNAISE

20 chipotle chilies
1/2 cup chopped garlic
1/2 cup chopped shallots
1 teaspoon ground cumin
1 teaspoon freshly ground black pepper
Salt to taste
1/2 cup mayonnaise
1 teaspoon lemon juice

SALAD AND GARNISH

6 round beefsteak tomatoes, sliced and seasoned with freshly ground black pepper, salt and extra virgin olive oil
1 tablespoon basil oil (see the recipe on page 46)
Watercress leaves
Blanched green beans

Combine the parsley, celery, mayonnaise, pepper, salt, lime juice, and Tabasco® sauce. Mix well, then add the crabmeat, taking care not to break up the crabmeat as you fold it in.

Place the chilies in a pot. Pour boiling water over to cover. Boil 20 minutes. Strain, reserving the water. Puree in a blender the boiled chilies, garlic, shallots, cumin, pepper and salt. Add some of the reserved water a teaspoon at a time to get the desired consistency. It should not be thin in texture. Move the hot puree to a frying pan and pan sear for 8 to 10 minutes to reduce and develop the flavors. Cool. Add 2 tablespoons of the puree to the mayonnaise along with the lemon juice. Taste and adjust the seasoning.

Place one slice of beefsteak tomato on a plate, place some of the crabmeat mixture on the tomato slice, then layer another slice of tomato and more of the crabmeat mixture. For the top of the tower, use a slice from the edge of the tomato. Add salt and pepper to taste and sprinkle basil oil on top.

Surround the towers with watercress leaves tossed with lemon honey dressing (see the recipe on page 44) or arugula greens with a balsamic vinaigrette (see the recipe on page 56). Garnish with green beans around the plate and brush the beans with the chipotle mayonnaise.

· ·

USE ROMA TOMATOES FOR A SMALLER VERSION OF THIS DISH; USING ROMA TOMATOES WILL YIELD ABOUT 15 TOWERS.

· ·

Tomato Tower with Lump Crabmeat

CRABMEAT LOUIS

SERVES 8

LOUIS SAUCE

1 1/2 cups mayonnaise

1/4 cup tomato paste

2 tablespoons horseradish

2 tablespoons lemon juice

Dash of Tabasco® sauce

Salt and freshly ground white pepper

SALAD

6 tablespoons chopped scallions

4 tablespoons chopped parsley

2 tablespoons chopped fresh tarragon
    or 1 teaspoon dried tarragon

4 tablespoons chopped fresh basil or
    2 teaspoons dried basil

2 tablespoons capers

Pinch of cayenne

2 large eggs, hard-boiled and chopped

4 to 6 tablespoons mayonnaise

2 teaspoons lemon juice

Salt and freshly ground white pepper

1 pound fresh lump crabmeat

4 avocados, peeled and halved

Green leaf lettuce

GARNISH

Lemon wedges

Parsley sprigs

Combine the mayonnaise, tomato paste, horseradish, lemon juice, Tabasco® sauce, salt and pepper. Taste and adjust the seasoning. Cover and chill.

In a large mixing bowl, combine the scallions, parsley, tarragon, basil, capers, cayenne, chopped eggs, mayonnaise and lemon juice. Season with salt and white pepper. Gently toss in the crabmeat, lightly mixing until barely combined. Taste and adjust the seasoning.

Loosely stuff the crabmeat salad into the avocado halves. Serve chilled on lettuce leaves. Garnish with a lemon wedge and parsley sprig. Serve with the Louis sauce on the side.

. . . .

THIS SALAD MAY BE MADE WITH SHRIMP. THE LOUIS SAUCE IS GOOD ON ANY COLD SEAFOOD SALAD.

SAN FRANCISCO IS SAID TO BE THE ORIGIN OF THIS RECIPE. FROZEN CRAB MAY BE USED, BUT IT WILL NOT BE AS TASTY.

. . . .

SHRIMP SALAD WITH LIME ZEST AND DILL

SERVES 4-6

DRESSING

1/3 cup whipping cream

1 cup mayonnaise

3 tablespoons lime juice

1 tablespoon grated lime zest

1/2 cup chopped celery

1/4 cup chopped fresh dill

2 tablespoons chopped chives

Salt and freshly ground white
  pepper to taste

Dash of Tabasco® sauce

SALAD

1 1/2 pounds large shrimp, boiled,
  peeled and deveined

Lettuce

Blanched asparagus

Roasted red peppers

Yellow pear tomatoes

Red wine vinaigrette (see the recipe
  on page 47)

Sprigs of fresh dill

Lime wedges

Combine all the ingredients for the dressing.

Stir the boiled shrimp into the dressing. Place lettuce on each plate. Top with a mound of shrimp salad. Finish the plate with blanched asparagus, roasted red peppers and yellow pear tomatoes. Drizzle the vegetables with the red wine vinaigrette.

Garnish with a sprig of fresh dill and a lime wedge.

HERBS

❋

Dried herbs may be substituted for fresh herbs. One tablespoon of fresh herbs equals one teaspoon of dried herbs.

DILL

❋

Dill is relatively unique in that both its leaves and its seeds are used as seasonings. Dill's wispy green leaves have a soft, sweet taste. Its seeds are rather like caraway, aromatic and bittersweet.

Both the seeds and the aromatic, feathery leaves of dill weed are used. These are available in fresh and dried forms; however, the fresh forms of both provide the best flavor.

Fresh dill should be feathery, fernlike and deep green. Avoid leaves that are wet or wilted. For longer storage, chop the dill finely, mix with water and freeze in ice cube trays. Leaves may also be dried and stored in an airtight container in a cool, dark place. Dried dill has a shelf life of approximately 6 months.

Fresh dill adds elegance to fish dishes and green salads.

Heat diminishes the flavor of dill weed, so it is best to add it to a dish just before it is removed from the heat. On the other hand, heat brings out the flavor of dill seed.

Mixed Lettuces with Blackberry, Kiwi and Gorgonzola

SERVES 8

DRESSING

2 tablespoons honey

2 tablespoons Dijon mustard

2 teaspoons grated lemon zest

1/2 cup lemon juice

1/2 cup olive oil

2/3 cup vegetable oil

SALAD

4 cups spring mix

1 bunch watercress

1 cup arugula

2 heads Belgian endive, leaves separated and sliced in half crosswise

1/4 cup fresh tarragon leaves

6 ounces Gorgonzola cheese, crumbled

4 kiwi, peeled and sliced

1 pint fresh blackberries

1/2 cup toasted sliced almonds

Place the honey, Dijon mustard, lemon zest and lemon juice in a bowl. Whisk ingredients together to combine. Gradually add the olive oil, then the vegetable oil, while continuing to whisk. Place in a container and refrigerate until ready to use. This dressing lasts 6 weeks refrigerated.

Wash the lettuces in ice water. Drain and dry. Wrap in towels and place in a large bowl. Refrigerate until ready to serve.

To serve, toss the chilled lettuces, tarragon and Gorgonzola in just enough dressing to coat. Mound on chilled salad plates and arrange kiwi slices and blackberries over the salad. Sprinkle with toasted almonds.

GORGONZOLA

✳

Gorgonzola is one of Italy's great cheeses. It has an ivory-colored interior that may be lightly or thickly streaked with bluish-green veins. This cow's milk cheese is rich and creamy with a savory, slightly pungent flavor.

TEXAS CAESAR SALAD

SERVES 8

CAESAR DRESSING

3 large cloves garlic

8 anchovy filets

1/2 teaspoon Dijon mustard

1/2 teaspoon Worcestershire sauce

2 tablespoons lemon juice

2 tablespoons red wine vinegar

2 large egg yolks

1 cup olive oil

1 teaspoon freshly ground black
   pepper

1/2 cup grated Parmesan cheese

SALAD

16 cups cut romaine leaves, washed
   and dried

1 cup grated Parmesan cheese

1 cup toasted croutons

3 pounds New York strip steak,
   grilled medium rare and cut into
   thin slices

1/2 pound corn, grilled and cut off
   the cob

1/4 cup diced red bell peppers

1/4 cup crisp-fried julienned tortilla
   strips

Sprinkling of grated Parmesan
   cheese

Combine the garlic, anchovy, Dijon mustard, Worcestershire sauce, lemon juice, vinegar and egg yolks in a blender. Puree the mixture. With the blender running, drizzle in the olive oil. The mixture should emulsify to form a thick dressing. Pour the dressing into a bowl and stir in the black pepper and Parmesan. Taste and correct the seasoning. Set aside or refrigerate until ready to use.

Run a sink of iced water. Remove the outer and bruised leaves from the romaine. Cut the remaining leaves into 2-inch pieces and wash thoroughly in the water. Drain and refrigerate.

Place the romaine leaves in a large mixing bowl. Add 2 cups Caesar dressing, the Parmesan cheese and croutons. Gently toss the salad with tongs until uniformly coated. Pile high on a chilled dinner plate. Arrange strips of grilled steak on top. Sprinkle with roasted corn and diced red bell pepper. Place the tortilla strips on top in a mound. Sprinkle the salad and plate with Parmesan cheese. Serve immediately.

. . . .

LETTUCE KNIVES THAT WILL NOT BRUISE THE
LETTUCE MAY BE PURCHASED IN SPECIALTY STORES.

. . . .

CAVIAR SALAD WITH BELGIAN ENDIVE

CAVIAR

✳

If removing the caviar
from its original
container before serving,
use a mother-of-pearl
caviar spoon or a gold-
plated utensil. Do not use
a silver spoon as it affects
the taste of the product.

The world's most expen-
sive caviar is called
Almas (Russian for
"diamond"). This beluga
caviar is white in
appearance. The caviar
comes from fish that are
over 100 years old. As a
general rule, the lighter
the color of beluga
caviar, the older the fish,
and the more elegant
and exquisite the flavor.
Almas is extremely rare
and extremely expen-
sive. Caviar House
Almas Iranian caviar is
packed in a 24-carat
gold tin and is sold for
an amazing price of
14,705 British pounds
(about $23,308) per
kilogram (35 ounces).

For the frugal gourmet,
sevruga caviar has an
amazing semblance in
taste to beluga cavier.
The eggs, though far
smaller in size, have a
lustrous gray to dark
gray color.

6 ounces soft cream cheese

3 tablespoons heavy cream

2 tablespoons finely chopped chives

2 tablespoons finely chopped fresh dill

1 tablespoon lemon juice

Salt and freshly ground white pepper

3 small heads Belgian endive

4 ounces fresh caviar

Sprigs of fresh dill

4 bunches watercress, washed
    and dried

2 to 3 tablespoons freshly squeezed
    lemon juice

4 to 5 tablespoons extra virgin
    olive oil

Combine the cream cheese and cream in a small bowl with a fork until smooth. Stir in the chives, dill, lemon juice, salt and white pepper to taste. Separate the leaves of the Belgian endive. Using a fork, place about a teaspoon of the cream cheese mixture at the base of each leaf. Top with 1/2 teaspoon of caviar and place a sprig of fresh dill above the cream cheese mound.

Place three or four of the stuffed endive leaves on each chilled salad plate. Remove the stems from the watercress and place half a bunch on each plate. Sprinkle the lemon juice over the watercress and endive, then drizzle with the olive oil. Serve immediately.

. . . .

THIS RECIPE MAY ALSO BE USED
AS AN HORS D'OEUVRE.

. . . .

Caviar Salad with Belgian Endive

SPINACH AND ENDIVE SALAD WITH BLUEBERRY TARRAGON VINAIGRETTE

SERVES 8

TARRAGON

✳

Tarragon has a warm, aromatic taste and a slightly numbing aftereffect on the tongue. Strip the tips and leaves from the mature stems. When finely chopped, fresh tarragon enhances the flavor of poultry, mayonnaise, vegetables (especially green beans), cream and butter sauces, and salad dressings. It is ideal for flavored vinegars and oils. Use it sparingly in butter and cottage cheese. To freeze, chop the leaves and add to a little water in an ice cube tray. Tarragon does not dry well.

Tarragon is a perennial aromatic herb known for its distinctive aniselike flavor. Tarragon is widely used in classic French cooking for a variety of dishes including chicken, fish and vegetables, as well as in many sauces, the best-known being béarnaise.

Tarragon was widely used in ancient times to ward off dragons, and judging from the relative absence of dragons in the world, it must have worked!

SALAD

4 cups baby spinach leaves, washed and dried

2 heads Belgian endive

1/4 cup toasted pine nuts

4 ounces Asiago cheese, grated

DRESSING

1/4 cup raspberry vinegar

1/4 cup lime juice

1/2 cup safflower oil

1/2 cup extra virgin olive oil

1/2 teaspoon granulated sugar

1/2 cup coarsely chopped blueberries

1/2 cup whole blueberries

Salt and freshly ground white pepper

1/4 cup coarsely chopped fresh tarragon leaves

Place the spinach leaves in a salad bowl. Trim the stem from the Belgian endive and separate as many large leaves as possible. Set aside in a separate bowl in the refrigerator. Chop the remaining smaller endive leaves into 1/2-inch pieces and place in the bowl with the spinach. Refrigerate until ready to serve.

Combine the raspberry vinegar, lime juice, safflower oil, olive oil and sugar in a small mixing bowl. Stir to combine. Add the chopped and whole blueberries, and salt and white pepper to taste. Set aside until ready to use. Just before serving, add the tarragon. Makes almost 2 cups of dressing.

Arrange the whole endive leaves on chilled salad plates to form a starlike pattern, with the bases of the endive touching. Make sure the leaves do not extend beyond the rim of the salad plate. Mound the baby spinach leaves and the chopped endive in the center over the base of the endive leaves. Drizzle with the vinaigrette. Sprinkle with the toasted pine nuts and Asiago shavings.

. . . .

YOU CAN REFRIGERATE THE DRESSING WITHOUT THE TARRAGON FOR UP TO 2 WEEKS.

THIS VINAIGRETTE IS DELICIOUS SERVED OVER GRILLED BREAST OF CHICKEN.

. . . .

BALSAMIC VINAIGRETTE

YIELDS 3 CUPS

1 cup balsamic vinegar

2 cups virgin olive oil

1/4 teaspoon freshly ground black pepper

Dash of salt

Slowly whisk the olive oil into the vinegar. Add pepper and salt. Alternatively, place the vinegar and black pepper in a blender. While running the blender, slowly add the olive oil to make an emulsified mixture. Taste and adjust the seasoning as necessary. Store in a covered container in the refrigerator.

SESAME GINGER VINAIGRETTE DRESSING

YIELDS 3 CUPS

3/4 cup red wine vinegar

3 tablespoons Dijon mustard

1 1/2 tablespoons honey

6 tablespoons soy sauce

6 tablespoons sesame oil

1 1/2 cups vegetable oil

3/8 teaspoon cayenne

*Salt and freshly ground pepper
   to taste*

Combine the vinegar, mustard, honey and soy sauce. Whisk in the oils. Season with cayenne, salt and pepper to taste. Store in the refrigerator.

RED ROQUEFORT VINAIGRETTE

YIELDS 2 CUPS

1/2 cup red wine vinegar

2 teaspoons Dijon mustard

2 teaspoons mayonnaise

2 shallots, minced

2 garlic cloves, chopped

2 teaspoons granulated sugar

1 1/2 cup olive oil

*Salt and freshly ground pepper
   to taste*

1/4 cup lemon juice

1 tablespoon tomato paste

1/4 cup granulated sugar

1 tablespoon paprika

1 1/2 teaspoon cayenne

*3/8 teaspoon freshly ground
   white pepper*

4 ounces Roquefort cheese, crumbled

Combine the vinegar, mustard, mayonnaise, shallots, garlic and sugar in a blender. Blend well. With the blender running, slowly add the olive oil in a thin stream to form an emulsified vinaigrette. Season to taste with salt and pepper.

Whisk 2 cups of the vinaigrette dressing with the lemon juice, tomato paste, sugar, paprika, cayenne and white pepper. Stir in the crumbled Roquefort cheese. Pour into covered plastic jars and refrigerate

SESAME OIL

✳

Sesame oil is a cold-pressed oil made from untoasted sesame seeds. Asian sesame oil, from China and Japan, is made from roasted seeds and has an amber color and a full, rich flavor, but its low smoking temperature makes it unsuitable for use alone for cooking, so it is used almost exclusively as a seasoning.

The rich, almost odorless oil expressed from untoasted seeds is popular as a cooking oil in India and China. It is also highly nutritious, rich in vitamins A, B and E as well as in iron, calcium, magnesium, copper, silicic acid and phosphorus.

The sesame plant (Sesamum indicum) is an annual shrub with white bell-shaped flowers tinged with a hint of blue, red or yellow. It is grown particularly in India, China, South America and Africa. It was cultivated for over 4,000 years in Mesopotamia, and evidence of the plant was found in Tutankhamen's tomb.

CITRUS VINAIGRETTE

YIELDS 2 CUPS

1/4 cup freshly squeezed lemon juice

1/4 cup rice wine vinegar

2 tablespoons honey

3 tablespoons mayonnaise

1 shallot, minced

3/4 cup lemon oil

3/4 cup canola or light olive oil

Dash of salt and freshly ground
    black pepper

Mix the lemon juice, vinegar, honey, mayonnaise and shallot in a bowl and whisk until combined. Continue to whisk constantly while slowly drizzling in the two kinds of oil. Add salt and pepper.

THIS DRESSING MAY ALSO BE MADE IN THE BLENDER BY PUREEING THE FIRST FIVE INGREDIENTS, THEN DRIZZLING THE OIL IN WHILE THE BLENDER IS RUNNING.

VINAIGRETTE

❋

One of the five "mother sauces," vinaigrette is a basic oil-and-vinegar combination, generally used to dress salad greens and other cold vegetable, meat or fish dishes. In its simplest form, vinaigrette consists of oil, vinegar (usually 3 parts oil to 1 part vinegar), salt and pepper.

THOUSAND ISLAND DRESSING

YIELDS 5 CUPS

2 cups chili sauce

2 1/2 tablespoons red wine vinegar

2 1/2 cups mayonnaise

1/2 cup sweet relish

1 3/4 teaspoons Worcestershire sauce

1 3/4 teaspoons dry mustard

2 dashes Tabasco® sauce

2 large eggs, hard-boiled and chopped

Combine all ingredients, mix well,
    and store in a covered container
    in the refrigerator.

Slowly whisk the olive oil into the vinegar. Add pepper and salt. Alternatively, place the vinegar and black pepper in a blender. While running the blender, slowly add the olive oil to make an emulsified mixture. Taste and adjust the seasoning as necessary. Store in a covered container in the refrigerator.

THOUSAND ISLAND DRESSING

❋

Thousand Island dressing was named for the Thousand Island region of upstate New York, where the dressing originated. The key ingredients in the dressing are mayonnaise and chili sauce, which is made of peppers and tomatoes. The tiny chunks in the dressing are finely chopped pickles, onions, olives and hard-cooked egg.

BLUE CHEESE DRESSING

YIELDS 3 CUPS

1 cup sour cream

1 cup mayonnaise

1 cup buttermilk

1/2 teaspoon lemon juice

3/8 teaspoon salt

Dash of freshly ground white pepper

5 ounces blue cheese, crumbled

In a large mixing bowl, combine the sour cream, mayonnaise, buttermilk, lemon juice, salt and white pepper. Stir well until completely combined. Gently stir the blue cheese into the cream mixture. Stir only enough to combine; if it is overbeaten, the dressing will turn gray. Taste and adjust the seasoning. Must be stored in the refrigerator until ready to serve.

CANOLA OIL

✳

Canola oil is derived from a genetically engineered version of rapeseed, a wild mustard. It has less saturated fat than any other oil. Its taste is bland and the oil is used for both cooking and salads.

BLUE CHEESE

✳

Blue cheese is a general classification of cow's milk and/or goat's milk cheeses with a blue or blue-green mold.

Roquefort cheese is a particular blue cheese that is made in the south of France. Some other blue cheeses are Stilton (England), Gorgonzola (Italy), Danablu (Denmark), and the U.S. entry, Maytag Blue Cheese. There are many more blue cheeses.

The blue mold in these cheeses is produced by mold spores from Penicillium roqueforti or Penicillium glaucum, etc. Originally each of these cheeses was produced in a cave in its respective area where the mold was naturally present. The unique nutrients feeding the mold in the caves then affected the flavor, texture and blue-green color of the mold that developed in each of these cheeses.

Pasta & Soup

SMOKED SALMON FETTUCCINE

Recipe on page 63

FETTUCCINE WITH MUSSELS

Mussels are one of my favorites not only because of their delicious taste, but also because of the flavorful broth they produce. They are outstanding served hot in their own liquids as well as cold with a simple sauce. The subtle flavor of mussels is enhanced by almost any sauce.

— *Mary Nell Reck*

SERVES 8-10

MUSSELS

1 teaspoon dried thyme leaves

1 teaspoon black peppercorns

2 bay leaves

1 sprig of parsley

1 teaspoon salt

2-3 slices lemon

2 cups white wine

2 cups water

36-40 fresh mussels

FETTUCCINE

1 tablespoon salt

1 tablespoon vegetable oil

1/2 pound green fettuccine

1/2 pound white fettuccine

8 ripe Roma tomatoes

1 1/2 cups heavy cream

Salt and freshly ground white pepper

1 cup coarsely chopped fresh
    basil leaves

3/4 cup freshly grated
    Parmesan cheese

In a large pot, place the herbs, spices, lemon, wine and water for steaming the mussels. Boil for 10 minutes to develop the flavors. Thoroughly scrub the mussels and remove the fibrous beards. Drop the mussels into the pot. Cover and steam for 3 to 5 minutes or until the shells pop open. Do not overcook or they will become tough and rubbery.

Remove the cooked mussels. Strain the liquid and reserve for use in the sauce. Place a large quantity of water in the pot with the salt and oil, and bring to a rolling boil. Drop in the pasta and boil for 1 to 1 1/2 minutes. Cook until "al dente." If you are using dried pasta, cook for 10 to 12 minutes or according to the package directions. Set aside.

Meanwhile, remove the stems from the tomatoes. Coarsely chop into 1-inch pieces.

In a 10-inch frying pan, combine 1/2 cup of the mussel liquid with the cream and bring to a boil. Reduce over high heat until thick enough to coat a wooden spoon. Add a dash of salt and white pepper.

When the sauce is thick, add the chopped tomatoes and basil. Boil for 2 minutes, then add the mussels. Shake the pan, coating the mussels in the sauce. Cook together for about 2 minutes or until heated through.

Add the cooked pasta and toss with two wooden spoons until the sauce is evenly distributed. Shaking the pan, cook for 2 to 3 minutes more or until the pasta is reheated. Remove from the heat and toss in the Parmesan cheese. Serve immediately.

SMOKED SALMON FETTUCCINE

SERVES 8

SAUCE

4 tablespoons all-purpose flour

4 tablespoons (1/2 stick) butter

2 cups milk, heated

Salt and freshly ground white
  pepper to taste

FETTUCCINE

3 ounces clarified butter

6 tablespoons chopped shallots

3/4 pound fresh spinach

Salt and freshly ground white
  pepper to taste

1/2 teaspoon nutmeg

3/4 cup toasted pine nuts

1 tablespoon chopped fresh dill

1 1/2 pounds cooked green and
  white fettuccine

GARNISH

12 ounces smoked salmon, sliced

Sprinkling of freshly grated
  Parmesan cheese

3 ounces caviar

Mix the flour and butter in a saucepan over medium heat until the butter melts and the mixture is well combined. Cook for several minutes but do not let the mixture brown. Add the heated milk all at once, stirring with a whisk. The sauce will thicken as it reaches the boiling point. Add salt and white pepper. Set aside.

Heat the clarified butter until very hot. Sauté the shallots for 30 seconds. Add the spinach, salt, white pepper and nutmeg, and sauté for 30 seconds or until the spinach wilts and looks half-cooked. Add the toasted pine nuts, dill, cooked pasta and 1 1/2 cups of the cream sauce. Toss to heat through.

To serve, heap the pasta on heated plates. Place the smoked salmon slices on top of the pasta or to the side. Sprinkle with Parmesan cheese. Place a mound of caviar on top. Serve immediately.

FETTUCCINE WITH
SHRIMP AND MUSHROOMS

SERVES 8

CREAM SAUCE

4 tablespoons plus 1 teaspoon butter

4 tablespoons plus 1 teaspoon all-purpose flour

2 1/4 cups milk, heated

Dash of salt and freshly ground white pepper

FETTUCCINE

2 red bell peppers, julienned

4 tablespoons (1/2 stick) butter

48 medium size shrimp, peeled with tail left on

1 pound mushrooms, sliced

1 bunch asparagus, blanched and cut into 2-inch pieces

3 tablespoons chopped basil leaves

Dash of salt and freshly ground white pepper to taste

2 pounds cooked fettuccine, green and white

GARNISH

Freshly grated Parmesan cheese

Melt the butter in a saucepan. Add the flour and cook on medium low heat until well mixed and cooked a bit. Do not brown. Add the heated milk all at once, stirring with a whisk until thickened and bubbly. Add salt and white pepper.

Sauté the red pepper in the butter for 2 minutes. Add the shrimp and sauté for 1 minute. Add the mushrooms, asparagus and basil leaves. Add salt and white pepper to taste.

In another pan combine the cooked fettuccine with 2 1/4 cups of the cream sauce and cook until heated through. Put the pasta on a heated plate. Sprinkle with Parmesan cheese. Top with the shrimp mixture and serve.

BLANCHING

✳

To blanch a vegetable or fruit, plunge the food into boiling water briefly, then into cold water to stop the cooking process.

Lobster Quenelles with Crawfish Sauce

SERVES 6

PASTA

2 pounds spinach

1 1/2 pounds fresh ricotta

5 large eggs

Dash of nutmeg

1 teaspoon salt

1/4 teaspoon freshly ground white pepper

2 cups chopped lobster meat

3 1/2 cups sifted all-purpose flour

SAUCE

2 pounds fresh crawfish

1 large onion, diced

2 carrots, diced

1 leek, diced

2 tablespoons vegetable oil

3 tablespoons tomato paste

2 tablespoons cognac

1/2 cup dry white wine

2 cups cream

Dash of salt and pepper

Cook the spinach in boiling water. Squeeze out the water and finely chop. Set aside.

Place the ricotta and eggs in a mixing bowl. Mix well. Add the spinach and lobster. Season with the nutmeg, salt and white pepper. Sift in the flour and stir. Taste and adjust the seasoning. Chill. When cold, remove from the refrigerator and roll into long tubes 1-inch wide. Return to the refrigerator. When you are ready to cook, cut the quenelles into 1 1/2-inch pieces. Drop into rapidly boiling salted water and cook until they rise to the surface. Remove and drain.

Preheat the oven to 375 degrees. Cook the crawfish in a pot of rapidly boiling salted water. Peel the crawfish, reserving the shells and heads. Put the tail meat aside to combine with the sauce when it is finished.

Toss the crawfish shells and heads, onions, carrots and leeks in the oil. Place the mixture on a sheet pan and roast in the preheated oven until lightly browned. Transfer the roasted shells and vegetables to a saucepot.

Add the tomato paste and stir over medium heat until the paste is evenly distributed. Add the cognac and cook until almost dry. Add the white wine and cook until the liquid has reduced by one-half. Add the cream and simmer for 5 to 10 minutes or until the sauce coats the back of a spoon. Strain. Season with salt and pepper. Return the reserved crawfish to the sauce.

To serve, place the quenelles on plates and spoon the sauce over them.

QUENELLES

✳

A quenelle (kuh-NEHL) is a light and delicate dumpling made of seasoned minced or ground fish, meat or vegetables bound with cream, fat, eggs or a thick paste. This mixture is formed into small ovals and gently poached in stock or boiling water. Quenelles are usually served with a rich sauce and can be used as a first course, main course or garnish.

CRAWFISH

✳

Crawfish, also called crayfish, crawdads, and mudbugs, are delicious crustaceans that resemble small lobsters and, in fact, are closely related. Louisiana crawfish season is usually January through June, depending on the weather. A good rule about crawfish, as with most crustaceans, is not to overcook them.

BASIL LINGUINE WITH SALMON

Italy graciously provided the world with pasta—three kinds, to be exact: red, green and white.
America innovatively flavored it in every manner imaginable. It is no longer unusual to find red pepper
pasta, lemon thyme linguine, garlic and parsley fettuccine, cilantro or jalapeño fettuccine and, yes,
chocolate lemon spaghetti. This recipe uses basil linguine. Flavoring the pasta itself not only produces interesting
colors but fully integrates the taste of the dish rather than confining flavor to the sauce.

— Mary Nell Reck

SERVES 6 AS ENTREE, 8-10 AS A FIRST COURSE

CRIMINI OR ITALIAN BROWN MUSHROOMS

✳

Crimini mushrooms are darker in color and thave a richer flavor and a denser texture than the common button mushroom. Criminis, once imported, are now grown domestically.

PASTA

12 ounces fresh basil linguine

1 tablespoon salt

1 tablespoon olive oil

SALMON

1 medium red bell pepper, seeded and deveined

2 large crimini mushrooms or 1/2 pound assorted wild mushrooms

1/4 cup fresh basil leaves

1 1/2-pound salmon fillet

2 tablespoons virgin olive oil, divided

SAUCE

1 cup heavy cream

1/2 cup fish fumet or chicken stock

1/2 cup dry white wine

Dash of salt and freshly ground white pepper

2 tablespoons capers

GARNISH

10-12 chives, chopped

Freshly grated Parmesan cheese

Bring a large pot of water to a rolling boil. Separate the pasta. Add the salt and olive oil to the water. Cook the pasta, uncovered, over high heat for about 2 minutes or until al dente. The actual cooking time will vary slightly depending on the freshness and thickness of the pasta. Drain. Rinse under hot water. Drizzle with a tablespoon of olive oil to prevent the linguine from sticking together and set aside.

Cut the red pepper into 2-inch julienne strips. Quickly rinse the mushrooms under cool water. (Crimini mushrooms tend to be dirty, but do not wash or soak them so much you allow them to absorb water.) Remove the large stem. Thinly slice the caps. Coarsely chop the basil leaves. Set aside.

Run your fingertips along the inside of the salmon fillet to feel for tiny bones. Using a strawberry huller or needle-nosed pliers, pull out the bones. Place the fillet, skin side down, on a cutting board. With a long, thin-bladed knife, remove the skin by cutting through the flesh to the skin at the tail end: firmly grasp the skin with one hand, jiggling it from side to side while pushing the knife forward, then lift the flesh from the skin in one piece.

Heat 1 tablespoon of the olive oil over high heat in a 12-inch frying pan. When hot, add the peppers and sauté for about 1 minute. Add the mushrooms and sauté for another minute or until moist and darkened in appearance. Transfer to a plate and return the frying pan to moderately high heat. Heat the other tablespoon of olive oil and swirl around the pan.

Sauté the salmon, shaking the pan to prevent sticking. Sprinkle with salt and freshly ground white pepper to taste. When one side has a golden appearance, turn and cook until tender to the touch. The total cooking time will be about 6 minutes, depending on the thickness of the fish. Transfer to a plate and return the pan to high heat.

Combine the cream, stock and wine in the pan, and boil until slightly thickened. Add salt and white pepper. Cook for 4 to 5 minutes or until the sauce is bubbly and coats a wooden spoon. Add the cooked pasta to the sauce.

Add the sautéed pepper and mushrooms, along with the basil. Break the salmon into large chunky pieces, about 1 by 2 inches. Gently toss the salmon and capers with the linguine. Transfer to a warm serving platter. Garnish with chopped chives. Sprinkle with freshly grated Parmesan cheese and pass more at the table. Serve immediately.

LINGUINE PRIMAVERA

*Leafing trees, magenta azaleas and yellow daffodils are reminders of spring. I also associate
the warming of the weather with the bountiful array of fresh fruits and vegetables newly available in the markets.
Linguine primavera was created in celebration of the season. The vegetables will vary according to
availability but should be selected to convey a spirit of springtime.*

— *Mary Nell Reck*

SERVES 8

ROASTED TOMATOES

*2 pounds Roma tomatoes, stems
removed and quartered*

1 tablespoon chopped garlic

*2 tablespoons finely chopped
rosemary*

*Dash of salt and freshly ground
black pepper*

2 tablespoons virgin olive oil

PASTA

1 1/2 pounds linguine

1 tablespoon salt

1 tablespoon olive oil

SAUCE

1 cup heavy cream

1/4 cup white wine

Salt and freshly ground white pepper

*24 marinated artichoke heart
halves, grilled*

1 cup fresh basil leaves

*1/2 pound fresh asparagus spears,
blanched*

Freshly grated Parmesan cheese

Preheat the oven to 400 degrees. Combine the tomatoes, garlic, rosemary, salt, pepper and oil in a large mixing bowl. Gently toss with your hands to evenly distribute. Taste and adjust the seasoning. Place in a shallow pan and roast in the preheated oven for 25 to 30 minutes or until brown on the surface and slightly dehydrated looking.

Drop the pasta into a large pot of boiling water with the salt and oil. Boil rapidly, uncovered, for about 6 minutes or until tender but al dente. Drain, rinse and drizzle with additional olive oil to lightly coat. Set aside until close to serving time.

Heat the cream and wine in a 12-inch frying pan. Season with salt and white pepper. Add the pasta and toss to coat. Add the grilled artichoke hearts, roasted tomatoes and basil. Using tongs, lightly toss until heated through. Taste and adjust the seasoning. Quickly reheat the asparagus by dropping into boiling water for 5 seconds.

To serve, mound the pasta onto heated plates and place two or three blanched asparagus spears on top. Sprinkle with freshly grated Parmesan cheese.

PRIMAVERA

✳

*Primavera is an Italian
word meaning "in the
spring style." In cooking
it refers to a dish served
with assorted fresh or
barely cooked vegetables.*

TOMATO BASIL SAUCE

SERVES 4

1 1/2 cups chopped red onions

4 tablespoons virgin olive oil

2 cloves garlic, peeled, crushed and chopped

3 tablespoons tomato paste

4 cups chopped Roma tomatoes

1/4 cup chopped fresh basil leaves

2 tablespoons fresh thyme leaves

1 bay leaf

Dash of salt and freshly ground black pepper

In a large frying pan, sauté the onions in the hot oil over moderately high heat for 4 to 5 minutes or until soft. Add the garlic, tomato paste, chopped tomatoes, basil, thyme, bay leaf, salt and freshly ground black pepper. Bring to a boil over high heat.

Reduce the heat, cover and simmer for 20 minutes or until the tomatoes render their liquid but continue to hold their shape somewhat. If more liquid is needed, add tomato juice.

Use as a sauce for pasta—penne or fettuccine would be good. Sprinkle with Parmesan cheese and serve.

THYME

❈

Thyme, one of the best known and most widely used culinary herbs, is sometimes considered a nearly perfect herb. If a cook has any doubt about which herb to use, a general rule is that this mint perennial will work.

It is an essential ingredient in the classic bouquet garni—a combination that also includes fresh parsley sprigs and bay leaves—which gives greater flavor to salads, vegetables, meats, soups, stews and sauces, and even desserts. There are over 100 varieties of thyme, all of them fragrant. Thyme is easy to grow in the home garden, and no kitchen should be without it. Store fresh thyme in a plastic bag in the refrigerator. Strip fresh or dried thyme leaves from the stem before using. As with most dried leafy herbs, be sure to crush the leaves between your hands before adding them to your recipe.

RED PEPPER RAGU

YIELDS 3-4 CUPS

1 cup chopped shallots

2 tablespoons olive oil

2 teaspoons chopped garlic

4 sprigs of fresh thyme

4 sprigs of fresh oregano

4 bay leaves

2 cups finely chopped red bell pepper

2 cups finely chopped yellow bell pepper

1 cup diced Roma tomatoes

Salt and freshly ground black pepper to taste

1/4 cup chopped basil

Sauté the shallots in the olive oil for 1 minute. Add the garlic, thyme, oregano and bay leaves. Sauté for 2 minutes more. Add the red and yellow peppers and sauté for 5 minutes or until half tender. Add the Roma tomatoes and sauté for 30 seconds more. Season to taste with salt and black pepper. Remove from the heat. When ready to serve, add the basil. Serve over pasta.

FRESH PASTA

SERVES 6-8

3 1/2-4 cups all-purpose flour, divided
4 large eggs
4 teaspoons olive oil
1/2 teaspoon salt

Using a food processor, pulse together all the ingredients except 1/2 cup of the flour until the mixture just begins to form a ball. Knead the dough on a work surface, incorporating additional flour as necessary, for about 8 minutes or until smooth and elastic. Divide the dough into 4 pieces and keep each wrapped in plastic wrap until ready to roll out.

Set the smooth rollers of a pasta machine at the widest setting. Flatten 1 piece of dough into a rectangle and feed through the rollers. Fold in half and feed through the rollers again. Do this 8 or 9 more times to continue kneading, dusting with flour as necessary to prevent sticking.

Turn the pasta machine dial to the next narrower setting and feed the dough through the rollers without folding. Select the next narrower setting and feed the dough through. Continue until the narrowest setting is reached. Halve the resulting sheet crosswise and arrange on a dry kitchen towel, letting the pasta hang over the edge of the work surface. Roll out the remaining dough in the same manner.

Attach the 1/8-inch-wide pasta cutter to the pasta machine. Line a tray with a dry kitchen towel. Feed the first slightly dry pasta sheet through the cutter. Toss the cut pasta with some flour, form loosely into a nest and arrange on the towel-lined tray. Make more cut pasta with the remaining dough. Cover with plastic wrap until ready to use.

Cook in rapidly boiling salted water for 1 to 2 minutes.

HOMEMADE PASTA

✳

Homemade pasta is a divinely delicious treat. Pasta ingredients are inexpensive, quickly put together (if you have a pasta machine) and not difficult to manage after a little practice. Your guests are sure to be impressed with the fresh taste.

GAZPACHO WITH CRABMEAT

GAZPACHO WITH CRABMEAT

A chilled soup is an appropriate beginning for dinner on a balmy day. Gazpacho, a classic from Spain,
is fresh and invigorating. While its flavors aggressively jump out at you, it is surprisingly light and non-filling.
There are many versions and many interpretations of gazpacho; this recipe is my favorite. The crabmeat
is an untraditional variation but adds a touch of elegance and succulence to the dish.

— Mary Nell Reck

SERVES 8-10

5 large ripe tomatoes

2 medium cucumbers, peeled
    and seeded

1 small red onion, peeled

1 green bell pepper, halved
    and seeded

1 red bell pepper, halved and seeded

1 clove garlic, peeled and crushed

2 cups chicken stock

1 1/2 cups V-8 juice or tomato juice

1/4 cup virgin olive oil

1/4 cup red wine vinegar

Dash of salt, freshly ground black
    pepper and cayenne

1/2 pound fresh lump crabmeat

2 tablespoons chopped chives

Cut the tomatoes, cucumbers, onion and bell peppers into large pieces. Place in a food processor along with the garlic, chicken stock, V-8 juice, olive oil and vinegar. Process for 10 to 12 seconds or until chopped but chunky. Season with salt, black pepper and cayenne.

Chill several hours. To serve, ladle into chilled bowls and top with a mound of fresh crabmeat and a sprinkling of fresh chives.

COLD SOUPS

❋

In hot countries, cold soups are very popular. Creative cooks in fruit-producing countries have developed cold soup recipes to take advantage of seasonal fruits. A creamy cherry soup or a refreshing strawberry soup on a hot day can make a delightful repast.

As far back as antiquity, cold soups have played an important role in the hot summers of Mediterranean countries. Soups rehydrate the body, and the garlic and wine vinegar in many soups provide important salts and antiseptics.

Boulanger, a famous Parisian restaurateur, was the first to specialize in restorative broths in 1765, thus the term restaurant emerged to describe a place where one restores spent energy.

The most well-known cold soup in Spain is gazpacho, whose main ingredient is tomato. Tomatoes are ideal for cold soups; they contain water, acidity and a hint of sweetness.

POBLANO SOUP

SERVES 4

2 large poblano peppers

1/2 jalapeño pepper, optional

Olive oil for coating

1/2 onion, diced

1/4 cup (1/2 stick) butter

6 tablespoons all-purpose flour

4 cups cold chicken stock

1 cup heavy cream

Salt and freshly ground black
    pepper to taste

GARNISH

4 ounces fresh lump crabmeat

Diced scallions

Roast the poblano peppers by coating them lightly with oil and placing them on a hot grill until they are blackened and blistered. Place the blackened peppers in a small bowl, cover with plastic wrap and allow to steam from their own heat until cool enough to handle. When they are cool, rub the skins off, split the peppers and remove the ribs and seeds. Roughly chop the roasted flesh of the peppers. If the peppers are very mild, you may choose to include a roasted jalapeño pepper for extra spice.

Sauté the onions in the butter until translucent. Sprinkle the flour over the butter and onions, and stir to make a roux. Add the cold chicken stock and whisk until smooth. Add the peppers and allow the soup to simmer gently for 20 minutes, stirring occasionally. Puree the hot soup in a blender until perfectly smooth, then stir in the cream and season with salt and pepper to taste. (You may adjust the consistency with a little chicken stock if the soup is thicker than desired.)

Garnish each bowl of soup with a spoonful of lump crabmeat and diced scallions.

CRABMEAT BISQUE

*"Bisque is a cream soup containing shellfish. Although delicate, bisque has a certain richness of flavor.
The primary liquid used is fish fumet, which is enriched at the end with heavy cream. A well-seasoned, homemade
fish stock, of course, results in the best flavor. You may substitute an equal amount of shrimp, lobster,
clams or oysters for the crab. Bisque establishes an elegant beginning for a meal when served as a first course.
It is also ideal as a main course for a luncheon or light supper."*

— *Mary Nell Reck*

SERVES 8

BISQUE

1/2 cup chopped onion

1/2 cup chopped celery

1/4 cup (1/2 stick) unsalted butter

2 tablespoons all-purpose flour

1 quart fish stock (homemade or from a gourmet market)

2 bay leaves

1 sprig of fresh thyme or 1/2 teaspoon dried thyme

Dash of salt and freshly ground white pepper

CRABMEAT AND GARNISH

4 cups heavy cream

1 pound fresh lump crabmeat

Dash Tabasco® sauce

2 tablespoons chopped dill

In a large heavy soup pot, sauté the onion and celery in the hot butter for about 4 to 5 minutes or until soft. Sprinkle the flour over the vegetables and cook for another 2 minutes without browning. Add the fish stock, bay leaves, thyme, salt and white pepper. Bring to a boil. Reduce the heat and simmer gently for 15 to 20 minutes to develop the flavors.

The soup may be made in advance and refrigerated for two to three days at this point. Close to serving time, add the cream and bring to a boil. Gently stir in the crabmeat. Season with Tabasco™. Taste and adjust the seasoning. Barely heat through.

To serve, pour the bisque into warm bowls and sprinkle with chopped dill. Serve hot.

. . . .

AVOID EXCESSIVE STIRRING AFTER
THE CRAB IS ADDED, AS IT TENDS TO BREAK UP
AND BECOME STRINGY.

AFTER ADDING THE CREAM, DO NOT
ALLOW THE BISQUE TO RETURN TO A BOIL,
WHICH CAUSES IT TO SEPARATE.

IF STORING THE BISQUE IN A REFRIGERATOR
OVERNIGHT, USE A GLASS OR PORCELAIN BOWL
RATHER THAN METAL.

. . . .

ROASTED CORN CHOWDER

The sprigs of fresh cilantro serve as more than just a splash of color. They provide the perfume that gently lightens an otherwise rich-tasting dish, contrasting with the natural sweetness of all the other ingredients. With the increasing respect for all-American dishes, this recipe stands near the top of the list with its fine blend of natural flavors of the Southwest. The appearance and taste of Roasted Corn Chowder nurtures the soul with its earthy simplicity. With each bite, one can almost visualize a Southwest sunset.

— Mary Nell Reck

SERVES 12

CHOWDER

6 ears corn with husks

3 tablespoons olive oil

1 large yellow onion, chopped

2 stalks celery, chopped

6 tablespoons all-purpose flour

3 quarts veal or chicken stock

Dash of salt, freshly ground white pepper and cayenne

2 cups whipping cream

ANCHO CHILI SAUCE

6 ancho chilies

3 shallots, sliced

2 tablespoons olive oil

1/2 cup raspberry preserves

2 tablespoons honey

Salt and freshly ground black pepper

CRABMEAT

1/2 pound fresh lump crabmeat

2 tablespoons butter

2 tablespoons chopped chives or scallions

Salt and freshly ground pepper

2 tablespoons brandy

GARNISH

Sprigs of cilantro

Grill the whole corn on a rack 3 to 4 inches from the heat. Remove the husk only in one area about 2 inches wide. These kernels will blacken while the remainder steam. Grill for several minutes or until the corn is well marked.

Remove the corn from the grill. When cool enough to handle, remove the husks and silks. Cut the kernels from the cob and scrape the cob with the knife's edge to extract the sweet, juicy pulp. Set aside.

Heat the olive oil in a soup pot. Add the onions and celery and sauté for 6 to 8 minutes or until soft. Stir in the corn. Sprinkle the contents of the pan with the flour. Cook and stir for 2 minutes more. Add the stock and stir to combine. Bring to a boil, reduce the heat and summer for 30 to 40 minutes or until the corn is tender. Season with salt, pepper and cayenne. Stir in the cream and keep warm until ready to serve.

Split the ancho chilies and remove the seeds and veins. Pour boiling water over them to soften. When soft, puree in a blender. Sauté the shallots in the olive oil. Stir in the ancho chili puree, raspberry preserves, honey, salt and pepper. Cook for 4 to 5 minutes or until thick. If it becomes too thick, add a little stock.

Sauté the crabmeat in the butter. Add the chives, salt, and pepper. Add the brandy and ignite.

To serve, ladle the chowder into warm bowls. Drizzle about 2 teaspoons of the ancho chili sauce over the surface. Top with a tablespoon of lump crabmeat mixture and garnish with a sprig or two of cilantro.

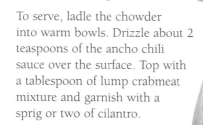

CORN

✳

Corn, also called maize, is a plant whose food value and wide variety of uses make it one of the most important crops grown in the United States. Corn was first used for food about 10,000 years ago by the native peoples living in what is now Mexico. Corn is used as food for people and livestock and has industrial uses as well. Alcohol made from corn is mixed with gasoline to make gasohol. Corn is also used to make ethanol and butyl alcohol.

Corn is very nutritious with a high protein and carbohydrate content. It is a good source of vitamin C.

TEXAS SEAFOOD STEW

2 cups chopped red onions

2 cups chopped celery with leaves

4 tablespoons (1/2 stick) butter

1 cup chopped green bell peppers

1 cup chopped red bell peppers

1 cup chopped yellow bell peppers

2 cloves fresh garlic, minced

4 bay leaves

4 sprigs of thyme

6 tablespoons all-purpose flour

3 quarts fish stock or water

Dash of cayenne

Dash of Tabasco® sauce

1/2 teaspoon allspice

Salt and freshly ground white
   pepper to taste

3 cups diced Roma tomatoes

3 pounds fish and shellfish: choose
   from shrimp, crawfish, crabmeat,
   scallops, lobster, mussels, oysters,
   clams, or snapper

GARNISH

Crisp tortilla confetti

Chopped cilantro

In a large soup pot, sauté the onions and celery in the butter. Cook for 2 minutes, then stir in the bell peppers, garlic, bay leaves and thyme. Sauté for another 4 to 5 minutes or until half-cooked. Stir in the flour and cook for 2 more minutes.

Add the fish stock. Stir and season with the cayenne, Tabasco™, allspice, salt and pepper. Bring to a boil. Reduce the heat and simmer for 20 to 30 minutes to develop the flavors. Add the diced tomatoes and cook for 5 minutes more.

When you are ready to serve, bring the stew to a boil. Sauté, steam or poach the fish and shellfish, as you prefer. Distribute the seafood equally in hot bowls and ladle the boiling stew on top. Garnish with crisp tortilla confetti and chopped cilantro.

. . . .

FOR A NICE PRESENTATION THIS STEW CAN BE
SERVED IN A HOLLOWED OUT ROUND BREAD LOAF.

. . . .

MUSSELS

✳

The best fresh mussels smell clean as the ocean, and the shells of live mussels are tightly closed. If the mussel is slightly open, tap the shell. The healthy mussel will close in less than half a minute. Discard any that do not try to stay closed after you tap their shells or ones that have broken shells or an "off" odor. Also discard any mussels that do not open after cooking.

Rinse the mussels under clean, running water and refrigerate them in a bowl covered with a damp cloth or paper towel. Never store mussels covered in water or in an airtight container—either method will kill them.

Texas Seafood Stew

HOMEMADE BEEF STOCK

When a recipe calls for beef stock, it is referring to the rich, natural essence that comes from cooking the bones for many hours with herbs and aromatic vegetables. Canned beef stock tends to be oversalted and lacking in flavor. The stock you make yourself has a richness no commercial product can duplicate. You may substitute veal or lamb bones for beef or use them in combination with the beef bones. The most flavorful bones are round bones containing marrow. As you work with meat, reserve the bones, keeping them in your freezer until you have enough for stock. If beef stock is always on hand, you are in a good position to create a hearty soup or an impressive sauce on a moment's notice.

— Mary Nell Reck

YIELDS 5 QUARTS

STOCK

✳

One of the first lessons of any cooking course is how to make stocks. Stocks form the basis of most sauces and soups. A stock is the liquid derived from simmering bones and/or meat with vegetables, herbs and seasonings. Types of stock include beef, veal, chicken, fish and vegetable.

MIREPOIX

✳

A mirepoix is a mixture of diced vegetables, carrots, onions and celery sautéed in butter. Sometimes ham or bacon is added to the mixture.It is said to have been created in the 18th century by the chef of the Duc de Levis-Mirepoix in France. Mirepoix is used to season sauces, stews, soups, stocks, etc. as well as for a bed on which to braise meat or fish.

10 pounds round beef
    marrowbones, cut into 2-inch
    pieces (have the butcher do this)
4 tablespoons all-purpose flour
4 carrots
4 yellow onions
4 stalks celery
2 tablespoons salt
1 tablespoon black peppercorns
4 sprigs of parsley
3 bay leaves
2 teaspoons thyme
2 cups water or wine

Preheat the oven to 450 degrees. Place the bones in a large roasting pan and sprinkle with the flour. Roast in the oven for 1 hour or until richly browned. As the bones begin to brown, turn them occasionally. Coarsely chop the unpeeled vegetables. Stir them into the browned bones. Return to the oven for an additional 45 minutes or until the vegetables begin to brown.

Place the vegetables and bones in a large stockpot. Add the herbs and seasonings, and cover with water. Bring to a boil over high heat. Meanwhile, pour off the excess grease in the roasting pan. Place the pan over a high flame, add the 2 cups of water or wine and bring to a boil.

As the liquid boils, deglaze the pan by scraping away the crust that has adhered to the bottom. Continue boiling until the liquid has reduced by one-half. Add the reduced liquid to the stockpot. When the water reaches a full, rolling boil, reduce the stock to a simmer. Simmer partially covered for 6 to 9 hours. Do not allow the liquid to boil or the fat will emulsify into the stock. This will make it greasy and cloudy.

Strain the stock into jars or freezer containers. Skim off the fat, which rises to the surface. The stock may be refrigerated for about a week or frozen indefinitely.

BROWN VEAL STOCK AND DEMI-GLACE

YIELDS 3 QUARTS

20 pounds veal bones
4 tablespoons tomato paste
1/2 bottle red wine
1 pound carrots, coarsely chopped
2 pounds onions, coarsely chopped
1 pound leeks, coarsely chopped
1 pound celery, coarsely chopped
3 bay leaves
1/2 tablespoon black peppercorns
1 1/2 bunches parsley, stems only
3 sprigs of thyme
Water

Preheat the oven to 375 degrees. Place the veal bones in a single layer on sheet pans and oil lightly. Roast in the oven for 1 1/2 to 2 hours, turning occasionally, until mahogany brown and aromatic. Check often: if the bones get black, they will be ruined and the stock will be bitter. When the bones are almost as brown as you want them, brush with the tomato paste. Return to the oven and roast for 5 to 7 minutes or until the tomato paste is beginning to brown lightly. Again, you must watch—do not rely on time as a guide. If the paste gets black and burned, you cannot use the bones.

Transfer the browned bones to a large stockpot. Fill the pot up two-thirds of the way with bones and the rest of the way with cold water. Deglaze the roasting pans with the red wine, then transfer this liquid to the stockpot.

Bring to a simmer, being careful not to let the stock boil. Simmer gently for about 12 hours, periodically skimming the impurities off the top of the stock.

Meanwhile, roast the carrots, onions, leeks and celery until golden brown at the edges.

After the bones have simmered for 12 hours, add the carrots, onions, leeks and celery to the stockpot. Add the bay leaves, peppercorns, parsley stems and thyme (either tied in cheesecloth or loose). Simmer for 3 to 4 more hours. Strain the stock and immediately place in an ice bath.

To make a modern demi-glace, reduce the brown veal stock by approximately two-thirds or until it will coat the back of a spoon. The natural gelatin from the bones is the only thickening agent needed for this style of demi-glace.

DEMI-GLACE

❋

Demi-glace (DEHM-ee-glahs) is a French sauce that most chefs today consider essential in classical cuisine and a staple in the fine home cook's repertoire. Restaurant goers often marvel at the professional chefs' velvety rich brown sauces and wonder how they do it. The answer is a good demi-glace. Patience and time are required for the preparation, but the seductive meaty-flavored glaze adds levels of concentrated flavor that will have your guests pleading for the recipe. Demi-glace can be frozen in an ice cube tray and stored in a tight container in the freezer for future use.

PARSLEY

❋

There are about 30 varieties of parsley, but flatleaf, or Italian, parsley and curly leaf parsley are the two most commonly used. Italian parsley can be easily confused with cilantro. The way to tell the difference is that cilantro leaves have rounded tips instead of the pointed tips that Italian parsley has.

BASIC CHICKEN STOCK

CHICKEN
STOCK

✳

The more you reduce
chicken stock, the more
intense its final flavor
will be. To eliminate fat
from the stock, refriger-
ate it first no matter
what your intended use
is—most of the fat will
have congealed on the
surface the next day,
making for easy
removal. A good way to
load up on good chicken
pieces for stock is to buy
whole chickens, cut them
up yourself, and save the
parts you do not use in a
freezer container until
you have enough.

For a brown chicken
stock, chop the chicken
bones and pieces with a
heavy knife. Sprinkle
with olive oil, and put in
a roasting pan in a
preheated 400 degree
oven for about 30
minutes or until brown.
Add the vegetables for
another 10 minutes, then
transfer to the water in
the stockpot, picking up
the recipe above.

Pour chicken stock into
ice cube trays and freeze,
then save the cubes in
plastic bags in the freezer
for future use.

1 pound carrots

1 pound onions

1/2 pound celery

1/4 pound leeks

Olive oil

5 bay leaves

5 sprigs of thyme

3 sprigs of parsley

1 tablespoon white peppercorns

1 tablespoon salt

4 cloves garlic

Bony chicken parts (necks, backs
    and wings)

One whole chicken, cut into pieces

5-6 quarts water

Coarsely chop the vegetables and place in a large stockpot containing a light coating of hot olive oil. Stir and add the herbs, spices and garlic. Stir in the chicken bones. Stir over a high flame until the bones begin to color and the aroma begins to develop. Add the whole chicken.

Add water to cover. Bring to a boil over a high flame. Skim off the textured foam that rises to the surface during the first 15 minutes of cooking. Reduce the heat and simmer gently for 4 hours. Strain. Cool the stock and freeze or refrigerate until ready to use. Do not put hot stock directly into the refrigerator.

FISH FUMET (BASIC FISH STOCK)

2 tablespoons olive oil

1 pound carrots

1 pound yellow onions

1/2 pound celery

1/4 pound leeks

5 bay leaves

5 sprigs of thyme

3 sprigs of parsley

1 tablespoon white peppercorns

1 tablespoon salt

2 lemons, sliced

Fish bones

Shrimp shells

Lobster shells

4 quarts water or more

1 bottle dry white wine

Coarsely chop the vegetables and place in a large stockpot containing a light coating of hot olive oil. Stir. Add the herbs, spices and lemons. Stir in the fish bones and shells. Stir over high heat until the shells begin to color and the aroma begins to develop.

Add water and white wine to cover. Bring to a boil over high heat. Reduce to a gentle simmer for 1 hour. Strain. Cool the stock and freeze or refrigerate until ready to use. Do not put the hot stock directly into the refrigerator.

CHARRO BEAN SOUP

SERVES 8

3/4 pound chopped bacon

1 large yellow onion, chopped

1 fresh poblano pepper, seeded and
    chopped

1 1/2 bay leaves

1 sprig of fresh thyme

2 pounds pinto beans

2 tablespoons chopped garlic

1 tablespoon freshly ground
    black pepper

2 tablespoons chicken base
    (found in the soup section of the
    grocery store)

3 quarts chicken stock

1 large green bell pepper, chopped

1 jalapeño pepper, seeded and
    finely chopped

1 cup diced fresh Roma tomatoes

1/4 cup chopped cilantro

Dash of salt and freshly ground
    black pepper

Cook the bacon in a large stockpot until half brown. Add the onions and sauté until soft. Add the chopped poblano pepper and continue cooking until the bacon is brown. Total cooking time will be about 20 minutes. Reserve 4 tablespoons of the bacon drippings. Add the bay leaves, thyme, pinto beans, garlic, black pepper, chicken base and chicken stock. Bring to a boil. Reduce the heat and simmer gently, uncovered, for 1 hour or until the beans are tender.

In a frying pan, sauté the bell pepper and jalapeño in the 4 tablespoons reserved bacon drippings for 6 to 8 minutes or until half tender. Just before serving the soup, stir in the sautéed peppers, diced tomatoes and cilantro. Add salt and pepper. Taste and adjust the seasoning. Add more stock as need to maintain the desired consistency.

POBLANO
PEPPERS

✳

The poblano pepper in
its fresh form is used
most commonly as a
relleno shell. It is
medium to hot and has
something of a bell
pepper flavor. About 4
inches long, the fresh
poblano has a medium
thick flesh and is dark
green..It ripens to a dark
red or brown. The name
poblano comes from the
town of Pueblo, Mexico,
where it is the favorite
chili. In its dried form, it
is called an ancho
pepper (which turns
brick red after soaking).

CHICKEN NOODLE SOUP

SERVES 8

4 tablespoons (1/2 stick) butter

2 cups chopped yellow onions

1 cup chopped celery with leaves

1 1/2 cups chopped carrots

2 sprigs of thyme

1 sprig of parsley

2 whole bay leaves

10 cups homemade rich chicken stock

Salt and freshly ground pepper
    to taste

3 chicken breast halves, poached
    and diced

1 1/2 tablespoons chopped fresh dill

4 ounces cooked pasta in
    4-inch pieces

1 tablespoon lemon juice

Melt the butter in a soup pot and add the onions, celery, carrots, thyme, parsley and bay leaves. Sauté for about 10 minutes or until half done.

Add the chicken stock and simmer for 20 minutes or until the vegetables are tender. Add salt and white pepper.

Add the chicken, dill, pasta and lemon juice to the pot. Heat through and serve.

. . . .

IT IS ESSENTIAL THAT THIS SOUP BE MADE WITH
HOMEMADE STOCK.

. . . .

CHARROS

✳

Charros are skilled
Mexican horsemen noted
for their traditional,
elaborate costumes. The
charros have long
symbolized the brave,
self-reliant and proud
Mexican cowboy. Charro
beans found on Mexican
and Tex-Mex menus
often use pinto beans.

CHICKEN
NOODLE SOUP

✳

Chicken noodle soup,
often called the quintes-
sential comfort food, is
the most popular soup in
the United States, particularly during the cold
and flu season. All soups
are improved immeasur-
ably when a good, rich
homemade stock is used
to prepare them.

LEMON CHICKEN
Recipe on page 88

POULTRY

COQ AU VIN

COQ AU VIN

*

Coq au vin (coke-oh-VANH), or chicken with wine, is a classic dish that has stood the test of time and never goes out of style. This chicken stew with the fancy French name was made wildly popular by Julia Child's 1960s television program. The long, slow cooking time of the chicken, red wine, mushrooms and bacon results in a dish that will thrill and delight for either a special occasion or a family dinner. It is often served with wide, flat noodles and a simple salad with a light garlic dressing. The sumptuous sauce begs for a good bread for "sopping." Cooking can also be done by simmering on the stove instead of baking in the oven.

MARINADE

4 carrots, coarsely chopped

2 yellow onions, coarsely chopped

2-3 celery tops, coarsely chopped

3 cloves of garlic, chopped

4 bay leaves

4 sprigs of thyme

2 sprigs of parsley

2 teaspoons salt

2 teaspoons black peppercorns

1 bottle dry red wine

CHICKEN

2 frying chickens (3 pounds each), cut in quarters

All-purpose flour seasoned with salt and freshly ground pepper

12 slices bacon

1 pound button mushrooms, ends trimmed and sliced

Beurre-manie: 3 tablespoons flour mixed with 3 tablespoons butter

Salt and freshly ground black pepper

Combine all the marinade ingredients. Place the chicken pieces in the marinade. Cover with plastic wrap and refrigerate for 12 hours or overnight.

Preheat the oven to 500 degrees. Close to serving time, remove the chicken from the marinade. Reserve the marinade. Coat the chicken pieces with the seasoned flour, dusting off the excess. Set aside. Cut the bacon into 1-inch pieces and cook in an ovenproof frying pan until crisp and richly browned. Remove, drain and set aside. Pour off all but 4 tablespoons of the pan drippings, reserving the excess, and over moderately high heat brown both sides of the chicken pieces. Add more drippings if needed. When the chicken is rich in color, place the pan in the preheated oven for 15 minutes until the chicken is fully done.

While the chicken is baking, trim the ends of the mushrooms and slice. Set aside. Strain the marinade into a saucepan, discarding the vegetables. Bring to a boil and continue boiling, uncovered, for 8 to10 minutes to reduce. Thicken to a sauce consistency by whisking in the beurre-manie a little at a time. Season with salt and black pepper. Add the cooked bacon and the mushrooms. Cook the sauce for 1 minute more and pour over the cooked chicken.

Pechuga à la Parilla

Pechuga a la Parilla means 'chicken from the grill.' Represented in this recipe is my personal interpretation of a classic Mexican dish. This variation is abundant in the rich flavors of the Southwest. The same marinade may be used for shrimp, pork, chops, even quail. One aspect of the dish that I love is the fact that the marinade becomes the sauce. Another is that it results in a meal which is sure to keep one lean and looking good. Each component in the dish is fresh, alive and abundant in nutritional value.

— Mary Nell Reck

SERVES 6

MARINATED CHICKEN

1 tablespoon cumin

1 cup fresh lime juice

2 teaspoons cayenne

3 tablespoons salt

2 cups honey

4 tablespoons dried oregano leaves

1/2 cup chopped cilantro

4 jalapeños, seeded, deveined and finely chopped

2 cups olive oil

4 tablespoons minced garlic

1 tablespoon freshly ground black pepper

6 boneless, skinless chicken breasts (6 ounces each)

BLACK BEANS

1 pound dried black beans, washed

2 tablespoons salt

1 large yellow onion, quartered

4 bay leaves

2 teaspoons thyme leaves

1/2 teaspoon ground cumin

1 teaspoon freshly ground black pepper

2 cups finely diced carrots

2 cups finely diced yellow onions

2 cups finely diced celery with leaves

3 tablespoons olive oil

Salt and freshly ground black pepper

GARNISH

6 slices each red, yellow and green bell peppers, cut crosswise 3/4-inch thick

Parsley sprigs

Combine the ingredients for the marinade. Reserve 1/2 cup of the marinade. Place the rest in a plastic container with the chicken breasts and marinate for 2 hours or overnight.

Place the beans in a large soup pot. Cover with water. Add the salt, onion, bay leaves, thyme, cumin and black pepper. Bring to a boil and simmer gently for about 1 to 1 1/2 hours or until tender. Add additional water as needed to keep beans covered. Meanwhile sauté the diced carrots, onions and celery in a large frying pan with the olive oil. When bright in color and half tender, remove from the heat.

Remove and discard the onions and bay leaves from the beans when they are almost tender. Stir the sautéed vegetables into the pot of beans for the last 15 minutes of cooking. When tender, remove from the heat. Add salt and black pepper to taste. Set aside.

Grill the sliced peppers until marked and hot. Grill the marinated chicken breasts until done. Do not overcook. Place on a warm plate. Spoon 1 tablespoon of the reserved marinade over the top. Garnish each grilled chicken breast with 3 grilled pepper rings and a sprig of parsley. Serve immediately with the black beans and a fresh vegetable.

SAFE HANDLING OF RAW CHICKEN

✳

Always check the date on the chicken package or ask the butcher. Just before you check out at the market, pick the freshest chicken and put it in a plastic bag (to keep the juices from leaking), or ask the butcher to put it on ice. Use the chicken within one or two days, or freeze it at 0 degrees.

Wash your hands and utensils frequently when preparing raw chicken in order not to cross-contaminate. Prepare raw chicken on a plastic cutting board, or clean a wooden board before you use it with a water/bleach solution.

Always marinate chicken in the refrigerator and do not reuse raw poultry marinades. Put the cooked meat on a separate clean dish; do not put it back on the platter used for the raw meat. Cook poultry thoroughly until the juice runs clear.

CHICKEN MONTEREY

*This dish combines the vibrancy of the great Southwest with the mellow touch of California cooking.
A breast of chicken is grilled over a flavorful wood such hickory or pecan. It is then topped with fresh avocado
slices, grilled shrimp, melted Monterey Jack and fresh salsa. While the salsa may be made several hours in
advance and refrigerated, the remainder of the dish is grilled and assembled just before serving. The result is
an entree that is light yet flavorful, with a refined character and a real sense of visual drama.*

— *Mary Nell Reck*

SERVES 6-8

MONTEREY JACK CHEESE

✳

*Monterey Jack cheese is
one of several cheeses
said to originate in the
United States, in this
case in Monterey,
California. It is a semi-
soft skim or whole milk
cooked cheese. It resem-
bles Cheddar when aged
or dry, and its flavor is
similar to Muenster
when soft and unaged. A
soft version with
jalapeño peppers called
Pepper Jack or Jalapeno
Jack is widely available
in the United States.*

CHICKEN AND SHRIMP

*4 whole boneless, skinless
     chicken breasts*

16 large shrimp, peeled

Salt and freshly ground white pepper

4 tablespoons lime juice

4 tablespoons virgin olive oil

SALSA

*1/2 medium red onion, peeled and
     finely chopped*

6 ripe Roma tomatoes, finely diced

1 cup chopped cilantro

*2 jalapeños, seeded, deveined and
     finely diced*

*Salt and freshly ground black
     pepper to taste*

TOPPING

2 avocados, halved and seeded

*6-8 ounces Monterey Jack cheese,
     grated*

Sprigs of cilantro

Halve the chicken breasts and arrange side-by-side on a platter. Thread the shrimp on skewers. Sprinkle the chicken and shrimp with salt and freshly ground white pepper. Drizzle with the lime juice and olive oil. Refrigerate until ready to grill.

To make the fresh salsa, toss the chopped vegetables together in a mixing bowl and season to taste with salt and freshly ground black pepper. Refrigerate.

Slice the avocado halves lengthwise about 1/2-inch thick. Remove the skin. Place the slices on a small plate, sprinkle with a few drops of lime juice and set aside.

Close to serving time, grill the chicken and shrimp about 3 inches from the heat for about 5 minutes, or until well marked and firm to the touch. Remove the chicken from the grill and place on a baking sheet. Top with the grilled shrimp and avocado slices, and a mound of grated Monterey Jack. Place under an oven broiler for a minute or two to melt the cheese.

Transfer the chicken breasts to a warm serving platter and top each piece with a mound of fresh salsa. Allow some of the salsa to fall onto the platter. Garnish with sprigs of fresh cilantro. Place the remaining salsa in a small bowl and pass at the table. Serve immediately.

Chicken Monterey

SOUTHWEST GRILLED CHICKEN

*This grilled chicken dish blends the tastes of Mexico and Texas to create an intriguing light meal
that is rich in character and robust in flavor. This recipe evolved over time and has become a popular backyard
favorite for friends and family. It is easy (most of the work is done ahead) and looks really colorful
on the plate, especially when served with a helping of black beans. The chicken is delicious served warm or
at room temperature. Leftovers can be cut into strips and tossed into a salad.*

— *Mary Nell Reck*

SERVES 8

MARINADE

1/4 cup fresh lime juice

1/2 cup honey

1/2 cup virgin olive oil

1/2 teaspoon ground cumin

1/2 teaspoon cayenne

1 tablespoon dried oregano leaves

2 tablespoons chopped cilantro leaves

1 jalapeño, seeded and chopped

1 tablespoon chopped garlic

1 teaspoon freshly ground
   black pepper

2 teaspoons salt

CHICKEN

8 boneless, skinless chicken breasts

2 medium red bell peppers

2 medium green bell peppers

Cilantro sprigs

Combine all the marinade ingredients in a glass or plastic container large enough to hold 8 chicken breasts. Reserve 1/2 cup of the marinade for the sauce. Place the chicken breasts in the marinade. Cover and refrigerate for at least 2 hours or overnight. Cut the red and green bell peppers into 1/2-inch thick rings. Remove and discard the seeds and veins.

Close to serving time, grill the chicken on a rack about 4 inches from the heat. Dip the red and green pepper rings in the marinade and place on the grill. Place the reserved marinade in a small pan and heat over the grill. Cook the chicken and pepper rings for 6 to 8 minutes or until well marked.

Place the grilled chicken on a warm serving platter. Top each chicken breast with red and green pepper rings. Spoon a little of the warm marinade over each. Garnish the platter with sprigs of cilantro. Serve warm.

GRILLED CHICKEN WITH BASIL AND GARLIC

SERVES 8

STUFFED CHICKEN

1 cup (2 sticks) butter, softened

2 cups chopped fresh basil leaves

2 tablespoons chopped garlic

1/2 tablespoon salt

1 tablespoon freshly ground
    black pepper

8 boneless chicken breasts with
    the skin on

MARINADE

1 cup dry white wine

1/2 cup olive oil

1 teaspoon salt

1 teaspoon freshly ground
    black pepper

2 tablespoons chopped garlic

SAUCE

1 cup chopped shallots

2 tablespoons butter

2 cups chicken stock

1/4 cup whipping cream

Marinade from the chicken

Salt and freshly ground black
    pepper to taste

GARNISH

Chopped basil

Parsley sprigs

Combine the ingredients for the stuffing mixture and slide
under the skin of the chicken breasts. Curl under the edges of
the breasts so they form a rounded shape. Mix the marinade
ingredients together and place in a plastic container. Add the
stuffed chicken and marinate 2 hours or overnight.

Sauté the shallots in the butter until soft. Add the chicken stock
and whipping cream, and boil for 10 minutes to reduce.
Remove the chicken from the marinade and add the marinade
to the sauce. Boil for 10 minutes more. Taste and season with
salt and pepper.

Grill the chicken breasts. Place on a hot plate, skin side up.
Ladle 4 tablespoons of the warm sauce over the top and sprin-
kle with chopped basil. Serve with rice and two vegetables.
Garnish with parsley sprigs.

BASIL

✳

Basil (BAY-zihl or BAH-
zihl) is a remarkable
herb. It belongs to the
mint family and is truly
the king of the herbs.
There are over 40
known varieties of this
annual herb. Sweet basil
is the most widely grown
and used. Other flavors
include lemon, anise,
cinnamon and lime. It
has a mildly peppery
and spicy flavor with
something of a mint
trace. Basil is easily
perishable and darkens
quickly after cutting, but
can be preserved by
freezing in ice cubes or
putting fresh leaves in oil
or vinegar. It is a
primary ingredient in
classic pesto.

LEMON CHICKEN

SERVES 8

LEMONS

✳

One medium lemon produces about 3 table-spoons of juice and 3 tablespoons of grated peel.

The best lemons are firm and fine textured with a bright yellow color; they seem heavy for their size. Thin-skinned lemons are likely to have more juice, whereas lemons with a greenish cast are likely to be more acidic. Lemons can be stored at room tempera-ture for several weeks. They will stay good for about six weeks in a plastic bag in the refrig-erator. Lemons should be used soon after cutting. Fresh lemon juice can be frozen in ice trays for easy later use.

LEMON CHICKEN

2 extra large egg whites

1/4 cup cornstarch

1/4 cup julienned fresh ginger

2 tablespoons chopped lemon peel

1/2 tablespoon salt

1 teaspoon freshly ground white pepper

2 tablespoons dried lemon grass

2 1/2 pounds chicken breast, cut into 1 1/2-inch pieces

HONEY SAUCE

2 tablespoons lemon juice

1/2 cup honey

1 cup chicken stock

1 tablespoon soy sauce

1 tablespoon sesame seed oil

Dash of salt and freshly ground black pepper

2 tablespoons cornstarch

1/2 cup dry sherry

VEGETABLES

1/2 cup clarified butter

2 cups julienned red bell pepper

2 cups blanched snow peas

1 1/2 cups quartered mushrooms

2 cups toasted cashews

4 tablespoons diced jalapeño peppers

Place the egg whites, cornstarch, ginger, lemon peel, salt, white pepper and lemon grass in a large mixing bowl. Beat with a whisk to combine. Add the chicken pieces and stir to completely coat. Cover and refrigerate to marinate and tender-ize until ready to serve.

Place the lemon juice, honey, chicken stock, soy sauce, sesame oil, salt and pepper in a saucepan. Bring to a boil. Mix the corn-starch and sherry together in a bowl and slowly add to the boil-ing sauce while stirring with a whisk. The sauce will quickly thicken and become clear. Taste and adjust the seasoning. Keep in a warm place during until ready to serve.

Stir-fry the chicken in the clarified butter in a very hot sauté pan. After 1 minute, or when almost done, add the bell pepper, snow peas, mushrooms, cashews and jalapeños. Stir-fry for 1 minute more. Add 2 cups of the honey sauce. Stir to coat.

Transfer to a warm plate. Serve with rice and a yellow vegetable.

CHICKEN VESTITO

LEMON BUTTER SAUCE

3/4 cup fish stock (found frozen
at gourmet markets or use
homemade)

2 tablespoons cornstarch

1/4 cup lemon juice

1/2 cup (1 stick) unsalted butter,
softened

Dash of salt and freshly ground
white pepper

Dash of Worcestershire sauce and
Tabasco® sauce

VESTITO SAUCE

3 tablespoons chopped shallots

1/2 cup (1 stick) butter

3/4 cup diced tomatoes

1 cup sliced mushrooms

24 artichoke heart halves, rinsed
and drained

Salt and freshly ground white
pepper to taste

3/4 cup white wine

3/4 cup lemon butter sauce

2 tablespoons capers (optional)

CHICKEN AND GARNISH

6 chicken breasts

Olive oil

Dash of salt and freshly ground
white pepper

Parsley sprigs

Using a whisk, combine the fish stock and cornstarch in a
saucepan. Bring to a boil over high heat. Reduce by half. Stir in
the lemon juice and return to a boil. Keep boiling and add half the
butter, piece by piece, while beating with a whisk. Remove from
the heat and whisk in the remaining butter until the sauce is thick
and creamy. Add salt, pepper, Worcestershire and Tabasco® to
taste. Do not keep too warm or the sauce will break.

Sauté the shallots in the butter for 1 minute. Add the tomatoes
and sauté for 1 minute more. Add the mushrooms, artichoke
hearts, salt and white pepper. Add the wine and evaporate the
alcohol. Remove from the heat and add 3/4 cup of the lemon
butter sauce and the capers (optional). Keep warm and set aside.

Brush the chicken breasts with olive oil. Place on a hot grill and
sprinkle with salt and white pepper. Grill until well marked on
both sides. Place on warm plates and spoon the vestito sauce
over the top. Serve with rice and two vegetables. Garnish with
parsley sprigs.

. . . .

THIS SAUCE IS BEST IF MADE WITH A LIGHT FISH
STOCK, SO DILUTE YOUR FISH STOCK BASE A BIT
MORE THAN DIRECTED.

. . . .

BRINING CHICKEN

✳

*Brining chicken makes it
more moist and tender,
and brings out the flavor.
It is a simple process and
requires only a little
preplanning. Take the
chicken out of its market
wrapping and rinse it
well, inside and out,
under the kitchen faucet.
For a moderate brining
solution, mix 1/2 cup
table or kosher salt with
2 tablespoons sugar in 1
gallon water. Place the
chicken in the solution
and put in the refrigera-
tor for at least 1 hour,
preferably overnight. For
easy cleanup, put the
chicken and brining solu-
tion in a gallon freezer
bag, then in a bowl.
Rinse the chicken well
after removing it from
the brining solution.*

GRILLED TENDERLOIN OF BUFFALO WITH CABERNET SAUCE

Recipe on page 107

GAME

GRILLED BREAST OF QUAIL ON ROSEMARY CAPELLINI WITH ROMA TOMATO SAUCE

SERVES 8

MARINATED QUAIL

1/4 cup fresh lemon juice

1/2 cup honey

1/2 cup olive oil

3 tablespoons chopped rosemary

1 tablespoon chopped thyme

2 tablespoons crushed and chopped garlic

1/2 teaspoon salt

1/2 teaspoon freshly ground black pepper

1/2 teaspoon cayenne

8 whole quail breasts

CAPELLINI

1 pound dried capellini

Boiling water with 1 tablespoon salt and 1 tablespoon olive oil

4 tablespoons extra virgin olive oil, plus extra for drizzling

2 tablespoons crushed and chopped garlic

3 tablespoons whole rosemary leaves

1 tablespoon crushed coriander seeds

Salt and freshly ground black pepper

ROMA TOMATO SAUCE

2 tablespoons extra virgin olive oil

1 cup chopped red onion

1/2 cup chopped shallots

1 tablespoon crushed and chopped garlic

2 cups diced Roma tomatoes

Salt and freshly ground black pepper

1/2 cup chopped fresh basil leaves

GARNISH

Parmesan cheese

Rosemary sprigs

Combine the marinade ingredients in a glass bowl and stir to combine. Taste and adjust the seasoning. Place the quail breasts in the marinade. Cover with plastic wrap and chill for about 1 hour or until close to serving time.

Drop the pasta into a large pot of boiling water with the salt and oil. Cook until al dente. Drain, rinse and drizzle with olive oil. Set aside.

Place the olive oil in a large, hot frying pan. Add the garlic, rosemary, coriander, salt and pepper, and allow to sizzle while the flavors develop. Add the pasta and toss to reheat and coat with the herbs. Taste and adjust the seasoning.

Heat the olive oil in a 12-inch frying pan. Sauté the onions for 4 minutes or until soft. Add the shallots and garlic, and continue cooking over moderately high heat for about 1 minute or until aromatic and soft. Stir in the diced tomatoes; shake the pan and cook over high heat for about 2 minutes or until just heated through and half soft. Add salt and black pepper. Remove from the heat and stir in the fresh basil.

When ready to serve, grill the quail breast until well marked. The quail breast can also be pan seared for about 4 minutes or until golden on both sides. Place a mound of pasta in the center of each warm plate. Spoon a ribbon of sauce around the pasta. Sprinkle with Parmesan cheese. Place the grilled breast of quail on the pasta. Garnish with a sprig of fresh rosemary. Serve immediately.

GRILLED BREAST OF QUAIL EN CROUTE WITH TWO SAUCES

In today's markets all over the country, we now have available fresh game birds raised with tenderness and high-quality diets. One nice thing about serving quail is that even though it is such an elegant little bird, you must pick up the legs with your fingers. This will relax even the tensest guest!

— Mary Nell Reck

SERVES 8

MARINATED QUAIL

1 jalapeño, finely chopped

4 tablespoons honey

2 tablespoons fresh lime juice

1/2 cup virgin olive oil

4 tablespoons cognac

Salt and freshly ground black pepper

8 quail breasts

PASTRY

1 pound commercial puff
  pastry dough

All-purpose flour

Egg wash: 1 large egg mixed with
  1/4 cup water

PESTO CREAM SAUCE

3 cloves garlic, crushed and chopped

1/4 teaspoon salt

1/2 teaspoon freshly ground
  black pepper

2 cups firmly packed basil leaves

1/2 cup parsley

1/3 cup raw pine nuts

1/2 cup freshly grated
  Parmesan cheese

1/4-1/2 cup virgin olive oil

1 1/2 cups heavy cream

Salt and freshly ground white pepper

RED PEPPER CREAM SAUCE

3 sweet red bell peppers

1 1/2 cups heavy cream

Salt and freshly ground white pepper

Combine the ingredients for the marinade. Taste and adjust the seasoning. Reserve one half of the marinade. Place the quail breasts with the other half of the marinade in a plastic bag for at least 30 minutes. Chill. When ready to serve, grill the quail over hot coals until firm to the touch and lightly marked.

Preheat the oven to 350 degrees. Roll the pastry dough to a thickness of 3/16 inch. Cut into 16 ovals 2 1/2 inches wide. Brush 8 ovals with the egg wash. Cut a 2-inch center out of the remaining ovals and save for another use. Matching the shapes, place the oval pastry rings on the pieces coated with egg wash. Place them on a baking sheet lined with parchment paper. Lightly brush with the egg wash. Bake in the preheated oven for 10 to 12 minutes or until puffed and golden. Remove from the oven and set aside. They should resemble oval-shaped pastry shells.

Place the garlic, salt, pepper, basil leaves, parsley, pine nuts and Parmesan cheese in a food processor. Process until the mixture is thoroughly ground. Gradually add the olive oil while continuing to process. Taste and adjust the seasoning. Tightly covered, the pesto may be refrigerated for 2 weeks.

Reduce the cream in a 10-inch frying pan. When thick enough to coat a spoon, remove from the heat. Season with salt and white pepper. Just before serving, stir 1/2 cup of the pesto into the cream.

Roast the peppers on a hot grill until blackened and blistered on all sides. When cool enough to handle, peel the skin. Remove the seeds and veins. Puree the peppers in a blender. Place the puree in a hot frying pan to evaporate the excess moisture. Transfer to a bowl. Return the same frying pan to high heat and add the cream, reducing until thick enough to coat a spoon. Season with salt and white pepper. Stir in the reduced red pepper puree.

To serve, spoon the two sauces side by side on an 8-inch plate. Arrange the pastry in the center. Place a grilled quail breast inside each pastry shell and spoon a little of the reserved marinade over the top. Serve immediately.

QUAIL

❋

Quail is the smallest of the European game birds. Although not eaten in classical times, today they are savored despite their small size. In Europe they are raised commercially for both their eggs and meat.

In Pakistan quail is prepared in curry-type dishes, and it also appears further east in countries like Laos as a popular food.

Grilled Quail with Raspberry Vinaigrette

GRILLED QUAIL WITH
RASPBERRY VINAIGRETTE

This exquisite dish is rich in the flavors of the Southwest and carries an amazing impact despite its delicate appearance.

— *Mary Nell Reck*

SERVES 6

MARINATED QUAIL

1 cup virgin olive oil

1/4 cup lime juice

*1 jalapeño pepper, seeded and
 finely chopped*

*2 cloves garlic, peeled, crushed and
 finely chopped*

*3 tablespoons fresh thyme leaves or
 1 teaspoon dried thyme*

1/4 cup mild honey

*Salt and freshly ground black
 pepper to taste*

1/4 teaspoon ground cumin

6 boneless quail, split

VINAIGRETTE

1/4 cup chopped shallots

2 tablespoons virgin olive oil

*2 cloves garlic, peeled, crushed and
 finely chopped*

1/2 cup raspberry vinegar

1 cup chicken stock

1 tablespoon Dijon mustard

2 tablespoons cognac

*Salt and freshly ground black
 pepper to taste*

1/2 cup fresh raspberries

GARNISH

*4 cups packed fresh spinach leaves,
 prepared as a chiffonade*

Fresh raspberries

Place the olive oil, lime juice, jalapeño, garlic, thyme, honey, salt, black pepper and cumin in a large mixing bowl. Stir until thoroughly combined. Taste and adjust the seasoning. Toss the quail in the marinade. Cover with plastic wrap and refrigerate for 1 hour or overnight.

Sauté the shallots in a 10-inch frying pan in the olive oil. Add the garlic, vinegar and stock, and boil for 5 minutes. Whisk in the mustard and cognac. Season to taste with salt and freshly ground black pepper. Remove the quail from the marinade and set aside. Add the remaining marinade to a small frying pan and simmer for a few minutes. Remove from the heat and stir in the cognac/mustard mixture and the raspberries. Set aside but keep warm.

Grill the marinated quail on both sides for about 5 to 6 minutes or until well marked. Arrange the spinach chiffonade on a platter. Place the grilled quail halves on top. Spoon two or three tablespoons of the warm raspberry vinaigrette over the quail and spinach leaves. Garnish with fresh raspberries. Serve immediately.

CHIFFONADE

✳

Literally translated, this French phrase means "made of rags." It refers to thin strips or shreds of vegetables (such as spinach, sorrel and lettuce). To make a chiffonade, you stack the leaves one on top of the other and roll them tightly into a cylinder. The cylinders of leaves are then sliced crosswise into thin strips and either lightly sautéed or used raw to garnish soups.

GRILLED BREAST OF QUAIL AND BLACK
BEANS WITH ROASTED RED PEPPER SAUCE

SERVES 8 AS A FIRST COURSE

MARINATED QUAIL

1/4 cup fresh lemon juice

1/2 cup honey

1/2 cup olive oil

1/2 cup chopped cilantro

1 tablespoon chopped thyme

1 tablespoon chopped oregano

1 jalapeño, seeded and chopped

2 tablespoons chopped and
   crushed garlic

1/2 teaspoon cayenne

1/2 teaspoon ground cumin

1/2 teaspoon salt

1/2 teaspoon freshly ground
   black pepper

16 boneless quail breasts

BLACK BEANS

4 tablespoons extra virgin olive oil

1 cup chopped red onions

1 teaspoon coriander seeds, crushed

2 tablespoons crushed and
   chopped garlic

4 1/2 cups cooked black beans

Dash of salt and cracked
   black pepper

2 cups diced Roma tomatoes

3 tablespoons chopped cilantro

ROASTED RED PEPPER SAUCE

6 large red bell peppers

2 cups chicken stock

Dash of salt and freshly ground
   white pepper

GARNISH

Chopped chives

Cilantro sprigs

Corn tortillas, julienned and fried

Combine the marinade ingredients in a glass bowl and stir to
combine. Taste and adjust the seasoning. Place the quail breasts
in the marinade. Cover with plastic wrap and chill for about 1
hour or until close to serving time. Cook the quail on a hot grill
until well marked or pan sear in a hot sauté pan for about 4
minutes or until golden on both sides. Keep warm.

Heat the olive oil in a large, hot frying pan. Add the onions and
coriander seeds, and sauté for 4 minutes or until half tender.
Add the garlic and cooked beans; stir to combine. Season with
salt and black pepper. When heated through, stir in the tomatoes and cilantro. Keep warm.

Split the peppers and remove the seeds and veins. Grill for
about 6 minutes or until blackened and blistered. Place in a
bowl and cover with plastic wrap for 10 minutes to soften. Peel
by scraping the blistered skin with a small sharp knife. Place in
a blender and puree with enough chicken stock to form a sauce
of desired consistency. Season to taste with salt and white
pepper. Keep warm until ready to serve.

Place about 3 tablespoons of the red pepper sauce on each
warm plate. Place a mound of black beans in the center. Put
two grilled quail breasts on top of the beans. Sprinkle with
chopped chives. Garnish with a sprig of cilantro and a sprinkling of crisp tortilla strips.

GRILLED BREAST OF QUAIL WITH SOUR CHERRY COUSCOUS AND CASSIS SAUCE

SERVES 12

MARINATED QUAIL

1/4 cup lime juice

1/2 cup honey

1/4 cup virgin olive oil

1/2 teaspoon ground cumin

1/4 teaspoon cayenne

2 tablespoons chopped oregano leaves

3 tablespoons chopped cilantro leaves

1 jalapeño, seeded and chopped

1 tablespoon chopped garlic

1 teaspoon freshly ground
   black pepper

2 teaspoons salt

12 boneless breasts of quail

COUSCOUS

3/4 cup couscous

3 cups boiling chicken stock

1/2 cup chopped shallots

1 tablespoon extra virgin olive oil

1 tablespoon crushed and
   chopped garlic

2 tablespoons thyme leaves

2 bay leaves

2 tablespoons finely chopped
   orange zest

1 cup sun-dried cherries

1/2 cup toasted pine nuts

Salt and freshly ground white pepper

CASSIS SAUCE

1/2 cup chopped shallots

1 tablespoon virgin olive oil

1 tablespoon all-purpose flour

2 bay leaves

2 sprigs thyme

2 tablespoons brown sugar

1 tablespoon balsamic vinegar

1/2 cup orange juice

1 tablespoon orange zest

3 cups chicken stock

1 cup white wine

1/4 cup cassis liqueur

Place all the marinade ingredients in a glass or plastic container. Stir to combine. Taste and adjust the seasoning. Add the quail and marinate for 1 hour or overnight.

Place the couscous in a medium bowl. Pour the boiling stock into the bowl and tightly cover with aluminum foil. Let stand for 5 to 6 minutes or until soft.

Heat a 10-inch frying pan over moderately high heat. Sauté the shallots in the olive oil for 3 minutes or until slightly tender. Add the garlic, thyme, bay leaves, orange zest and cherries. Sauté for another 2 minutes to develop the flavors. Add the couscous and pine nuts to the sautéed mixture. Add salt and white pepper to taste. Adjust the seasoning. Keep warm or reheat close to serving time.

Sauté the shallots for the sauce in the olive oil over moderately high heat. After about 4 minutes or when the shallots are tender, sprinkle with flour. Stir to coat. Add the bay leaves, thyme, brown sugar, vinegar, orange juice, zest and chicken stock. Bring to a boil. Boil for 10 minutes to develop the flavors and reduce. Add the white wine and continue simmering for 10 minutes more. Strain the sauce. Add the cassis. Taste and adjust the seasoning.

When ready to serve, grill the marinated quail breasts on a hot grill until well marked on both sides. Set aside to rest in a warm place for about 5 minutes. Place on a bed of couscous and surround with the sauce.

COUSCOUS

✳

Couscous is a dish that originated in North Africa. According to Larousse Gastronomique, the French first discovered couscous, a hard wheat semolina, during the conquest of Algeria in the reign of Charles X. Today, couscous is a mainstay in France's Algerian, Moroccan and Tunisian restaurants. You can garnish it with stewed meat, vegetables or chickpeas.

The origin of the word "couscous" is debated. Some say it comes from the Arabic word kousk-ous and the Berberian word k'seksu. Some think that it is an onomatopoeic reference to the rattling of the semolina grains when they are being hand rolled. Others believe it could come from the Arabic word kaskasah that means grinding or crushing.

CASSIS

✳

Cassis is a blood-red, sweet, black currant-flavored liqueur. It dates back to the 16th century, first produced by monks in France as a cure for snakebite, jaundice and wretchedness.

QUAIL WITH FOIE GRAS AND COURVOISIER® SAUCE

SERVES 8

MARINATED QUAIL

1/2 cup fresh lemon juice

1/4 cup honey

1 cup olive oil

3 tablespoons chopped rosemary

1 tablespoon chopped thyme

2 tablespoons crushed and chopped garlic

1/2 teaspoon salt

1/2 teaspoon freshly ground black pepper

8 whole quail

Olive oil, salt and pepper

FOIE GRAS

1 pound fresh foie gras

Salt, freshly ground black pepper and granulated sugar to taste

1/2-3/4 cup Courvoisier® cognac

COURVOISIER® SAUCE

1 cup chopped shallots

1 tablespoon olive oil

2 bay leaves

2 sprigs thyme

1 tablespoon chopped garlic

1 cup red wine

4 cups brown veal or beef stock

Salt and freshly ground black pepper

2 tablespoons butter, softened

2 tablespoons all-purpose flour

2 to 3 tablespoons Courvoisier® cognac liqueur

Combine the marinade ingredients in a glass bowl and stir to combine. Taste and adjust the seasoning. Place the whole quails in the marinade. Cover with plastic wrap and chill for about 2 hours, turning the quail over after the first hour so that the other side can marinate.

Separate the two lobes of foie gras and trim the sinew. Place in a container of ice and refrigerate for 2 to 3 days. Remove from the refrigerator and slice into 2-ounce medallions. Heat a frying pan over moderately high heat and sprinkle with salt, pepper and a dusting of sugar. Quickly sauté two or three of the foie gras medallions, shaking the pan. Turn once when light brown and add a splash of cognac to the pan. Shake and flame. Remove from the heat and keep warm while cooking the remaining foie gras.

Place a foie gras medallion inside each marinated quail and tightly truss the little birds. Preheat the oven to 350 degrees. In a frying pan over moderately high heat, pan sear the outside of the birds in olive oil, salt and pepper. After searing, place the quail in a roasting pan and finish in the oven for about 7 minutes.

Sauté the shallots in the olive oil in a heavy saucepan. Add the bay leaves and thyme, and continue cooking, stirring until brown. Add the garlic and cook for 1 minute. Add the wine and reduce by half. Add the beef stock and boil for 20 to 30 minutes or until reduced and flavorful.

Strain the sauce into a clean saucepan, pressing the essence from the shallots. Bring to a boil and reduce by one-fourth. Taste and adjust the seasoning with salt and black pepper. Make a paste of the soft butter and flour, and whisk into the sauce to thicken slightly. Add the cognac to taste just before serving.

FOIE GRAS: GOOSE OR DUCK?

✳

Duck liver is more rustic, with a stronger taste.

Goose liver is softer, more delicate and more creamlike.

Expert opinion classifies the different kinds of foie gras as follows: Whole liver is considered the purest, containing one or more whole lobes of foie gras; foie gras has pieces of various lobes put together; block with pieces is reconstituted liver with at least 30% pieces (the Bizac standard is 50%); and block is reconstituted emulsified liver.

CHICKEN FRIED QUAIL WITH BLACK PEPPER GRAVY

SERVES 24 AS AN APPETIZER OR 8 AS AN ENTREE

QUAIL

24 skinless quail breasts

4 tablespoons olive oil

2 cloves garlic, finely minced

Salt and freshly ground white pepper

2 cups all-purpose flour

Egg wash: 4 large eggs mixed with
*   1/2 cup buttermilk*

Canola oil for frying

GRAVY

1/4 cup all-purpose flour

4 cups whole milk

1/2 cup heavy cream

Salt and freshly ground black pepper

Rub the outside of the quail breasts with the olive oil, garlic, salt and white pepper. Marinate for 1 hour.

Dredge the quail breasts in the flour, then the egg wash, then the flour again. Fry in canola oil until golden and crisp, being careful not to overcook the quail as it dries out quickly. Remove from the pan and drain, but reserve the drippings.

Stir together 4 tablespoons of the drippings with 1/4 cup of flour to make a roux. Stirring constantly, cook for no more than 3 to 4 minutes, making sure not to let the flour brown. While the roux is hot, whisk in the cold milk and bring the gravy to a simmer. Allow to simmer until thickened, then add the cream. Season to taste with salt and black pepper.

How much and what kind of pepper to use is primarily a personal taste choice. Both the white peppercorn and the black peppercorn come from the same plant; the difference lies in how ripe they are and when they are picked. A black peppercorn is picked when still green and is sun-dried until it turns black. White peppercorns ripen completely on the vine before they are picked. To many people, the black peppercorn has a somewhat hotter aroma and more robust taste. Many cooks use white pepper in recipes with lighter colored food for aesthetic reasons. White pepper is more commonly used in Europe.

Whole pink peppercorns are a different plant seed that has many of the characteristics of black peppercorns. Pink peppercorns are used in anything from fish to vegetables. Green peppercorns come from the same Indian vines as black Tellicherry peppercorns, but they are harvested before they mature, yielding a fresh, clean flavor. Green peppercorns are thought to be well suited for poultry, vegetables and seafood.

As is the case with any spice, there will be more flavor if you do not grind the peppercorns until right before you use them. Any spice that is exposed to heat or light, or that has been on the shelf for many months, will lose its flavor. To maintain maximum spice taste, check your pantry once a year and dispose of those that have passed their prime.

PHEASANT ENCHILADAS

ANCHO CHILI SAUCE

2 ancho chilies

1 tablespoon chopped shallots

2 teaspoons chopped fresh garlic

2 tablespoons butter

1/4 cinnamon stick

1 tablespoon brown sugar

2 tablespoons chicken stock

Dash of salt and freshly ground
   black pepper

PAPAYA SALSA

2/3 cup diced papaya

2 tablespoons diced red onion

1 teaspoon finely chopped jalapeño
   without seeds

1 tablespoon chopped cilantro

1 1/2 teaspoons lime juice

Dash of salt

CREAM SAUCE

3 tablespoons butter

3 tablespoons all-purpose flour

1 cup chicken stock

1 cup half and half or milk

1/2 teaspoon salt

Dash of freshly ground white pepper

ENCHILADAS

1/3 cup chopped yellow onion

1 teaspoon butter

2 tablespoons each diced red, green
   and yellow peppers

2 teaspoons chopped garlic

1/3 pound cooked pheasant meat
   (approximately 1/2 pheasant),
   chopped

1/3 pound cooked chicken meat (1
   large chicken breast), chopped

2 tablespoons chopped,
   seeded jalapeños

2 tablespoons chopped cilantro

2 cups grated Monterey Jack cheese,
   divided

1/2 teaspoon ground cumin

1/4 teaspoon salt

1/4 teaspoon freshly ground
   black pepper

12 corn tortillas, softened

PHEASANT

✳

*There are three kinds
of pheasant. The common
pheasant, the golden
pheasant, and silver
pheasant.*

*Originally from the
Caspian Sea region of
Europe, the common
pheasant was quite easily
domesticated and is now
farmed with good results.*

Place the ancho chilies in a large bowl and cover with boiling water. Let stand for 10 minutes to soften. Remove and discard the seeds and stems. Puree the soft chilies in a food processor with about 3 tablespoons of water or more as needed. Set aside.

Sauté the shallots and garlic in the butter. When soft, add the cinnamon stick, brown sugar and ancho chili puree. Gradually stir in the stock and simmer gently for 10 minutes. Taste and adjust the seasoning with salt and black pepper. Set aside until ready to use (the chili sauce will keep in the refrigerator or may be frozen).

Combine the ingredients for the papaya salsa and lightly toss together. Taste and adjust the seasoning. Place in a covered container. It will hold in the refrigerator up to 3 days.

Melt the butter for the cream sauce in a saucepan, then stir the flour in, being careful not to let it brown. Gradually add all the liquid, stirring constantly to avoid lumping. Cook gently, stirring with a whisk, until thickened and smooth. Season with salt and pepper. Set aside.

Sauté the onions in the butter in a large sauté pan for five minutes. Add the mixed bell peppers and garlic, and cook for five minutes more or until tender. Remove from the heat and transfer to a large mixing bowl. Add the chicken and pheasant meat, cilantro, jalapeño, 1/2 cup of the cheese, cumin, salt and pepper to the sautéed mixture in the bowl. Gently combine, then taste and adjust the seasoning.

Preheat the oven to 350 degrees. Place 2 tablespoons of the enchilada mixture in the center of each tortilla and roll up. Place in a parchment paper-lined rectangular baking pan with the seam side down. Ladle the cream sauce over the enchiladas to cover completely. Sprinkle with the remaining 1 1/2 cups of cheese. Bake in the oven for 15 minutes or until the cheese is melted and the enchiladas are heated through.

Place two enchiladas on each plate. Top with a ribbon of ancho chili sauce and a small mound of papaya salsa.

. . . .

THE ANCHO CHILI SAUCE AND PAPAYA SALSA
CAN BE PREPARED WELL AHEAD.
THE CHILI SAUCE MAY EVEN BE FROZEN.

ALTHOUGH THIS RECIPE IS VERY HANDY FOR USING
PHEASANT THAT HUNTERS HAVE IN THE FREEZER,
PHEASANT IS QUITE EXPENSIVE TO PURCHASE.

IF YOU DO NOT HAVE PHEASANT ON HAND, ANY TYPE
OF POULTRY WILL SUBSTITUTE; THE QUICKEST AND
EASIEST ROUTE IS TO PURCHASE A ROTISSERIE
CHICKEN—ONE WHOLE CHICKEN WILL FURNISH THE
RIGHT AMOUNT OF MEAT FOR THE RECIPE.

. . . .

Pheasant Enchiladas

PHEASANT STOCK AND COOKED PHEASANT

YIELDS 6 QUARTS STOCK AND 5 CUPS MEAT

*3 carrots, unpeeled and
   coarsely chopped*

*1 large yellow onion, unpeeled and
   coarsely chopped*

*2 stalks celery with leaves,
   coarsely chopped*

5 bay leaves

5 sprigs fresh thyme

2 sprigs parsley

2 whole cloves garlic

1/2 teaspoon salt

1 1/2 teaspoons black peppercorns

*5 pounds pheasant legs, bones
   and backs*

1 pound boneless pheasant breasts

Place all the ingredients except the pheasant breasts into a large stockpot. Cover with water and bring to a boil. Reduce to a simmer and cook gently for 2 hours or until the meat is tender.

Strain and save the stock for soups and sauces. Discard the vegetables. Remove the pheasant meat from the bones and set aside. Place 2 inches of the stock in a sauté pan and bring to a boil. Place the pheasant breasts in the boiling stock and immediately reduce to a gentle simmer. Simmer for 4 minutes or until almost done. Remove from the stock. Cut up the meat for stew, enchiladas, cannelloni, etc. Reserve the stock in the refrigerator or freeze it for later use.

PHEASANT

✳

Although smaller, pheasant hens are likely to prove more plump and tender than cocks. Older and tougher birds are best braised or cooked in stews, while very old birds make a delicious pheasant soup.

The pheasant is possibly the most important game bird in the world, and great efforts have been made to maintain artificially large populations in those parts of Europe where natural conditions are favorable to the species.

PHEASANT STEW

SERVES 8

4 tablespoons unsalted butter

*2 cups coarsely chopped
   yellow onions*

2 cups peeled and diced carrots

2 cups coarsely chopped celery

3 cloves garlic, crushed and chopped

4 sprigs fresh thyme

4 bay leaves

1/2 cup all-purpose flour

1 cup white wine

*12 cups pheasant stock (see the
   recipe above)*

4 cups cooked pheasant meat

*Dash of salt and freshly ground
   white pepper*

Cayenne to taste

1 cup frozen English peas

4 cups cooked rice (optional)

Heat a large flat-bottomed soup pot or sauté pan over moderately high heat. Melt the butter. When the bubbling subsides, sauté the onions for 4 minutes, stirring. Add the carrots, celery, garlic, thyme and bay leaves. Sauté, stirring, until the onions are soft and the carrots and celery are half soft.

Sprinkle the sautéed vegetables with the flour. Stir and cook for 2 minutes or until all the flour is absorbed. Stir in the wine and stock; bring to a boil. Lower the heat and simmer gently for 10 to 12 minutes or until the carrots are tender but not too soft. Add the cooked pheasant meat. Taste and adjust the seasoning by adding salt, white pepper and cayenne. Just before serving, stir in the English peas.

Serve hot with the cooked rice, if desired. A green salad and crusty French bread served with the stew make a great hearty meal.

GRILLED BREAST OF PHEASANT
AND SUN-DRIED CHERRY COUSCOUS
WITH SAUTERNES SAUCE

*One important thing to remember about game birds is that fat is virtually absent. Therefore, they dry
out quickly and overcooking results in toughness. For this reason they should be barely cooked to the point of
"just doneness." Juices should run light amber-pink and clear when the thigh is pierced.*

— Mary Nell Reck

SERVES 8

PHEASANT

Salt and freshly ground white pepper

*1 tablespoon crushed and
chopped garlic*

3 tablespoons finely chopped oregano

2 tablespoons finely chopped rosemary

1 tablespoon finely chopped thyme

3 tablespoons extra virgin olive oil

8 boneless pheasant breast halves

SUN-DRIED CHERRY COUSCOUS

3/4 cup couscous

3 cups boiling chicken stock

1/2 cup chopped shallots

1 tablespoon extra virgin olive oil

*1 tablespoon crushed and
chopped garlic*

2 tablespoons thyme leaves

2 bay leaves

*2 tablespoons finely chopped
orange zest*

1 cup sun-dried cherries

Salt and freshly ground white pepper

SAUTERNES SAUCE

1/2 cup chopped shallots

1 tablespoon virgin olive oil

1 tablespoon all-purpose flour

2 bay leaves

2 sprigs thyme

2 tablespoons brown sugar

1 tablespoon balsamic vinegar

1/2 cup orange juice

1 tablespoon orange zest

3 cups chicken stock

*1 cup sauternes or late harvest
sweet white wine*

2 tablespoons Grand Marnier® liqueur

GARNISH

Sprigs of thyme

Combine all the seasonings with the olive oil. Rub evenly on both
sides of each pheasant breast. Chill until close to serving time.

Place the couscous in a medium bowl. Pour the boiling stock
into the bowl and tightly cover with aluminum foil. Let stand
for 5 to 6 minutes or until soft.

Heat a 10-inch frying pan over moderately high heat. Sauté the
shallots in the olive oil for 3 minutes or until half tender. Add
the garlic, thyme, bay leaves, orange zest and cherries. Sauté for
another 2 minutes to develop the flavors. Add the couscous to
the sautéed mixture. Add salt and white pepper to taste. Adjust
the seasoning. Keep warm or reheat close to serving time.

Sauté the shallots for the sauternes sauce in the olive oil over
medium heat for about 4 minutes or until tender. Sprinkle with
the flour. Stir to coat. Add the bay leaves, thyme, brown sugar,
vinegar, orange juice, zest and chicken stock. Bring to a boil
and continue boiling for 10 minutes to develop the flavors and
reduce. Add the sauternes and continue simmering for 10
minutes more.

Strain the sauce. Add the Grand Marnier®; taste and adjust
the seasoning.

Preheat the oven to 300 degrees. Grill the pheasant until well
marked on both sides. Transfer to the warm oven and cook for
4 to 6 minutes or until firm to the touch. (The birds will hold
longer in the oven at a lower temperature.)

Ladle the sauternes sauce onto each warm plate. Place a mound
of couscous in the center. Slice the pheasant breast horizontally
and place on one side of the plate. Garnish the plate with a
sprig of fresh thyme. Serve immediately.

SWEET WHITE
WINES

✳

*The great sauternes of
France and the
Beerenauslesen of
Germany are the classic
sweet white wines. And
the older they get, the
more intense their
flavors become—flavors
of honey and apricot.
These wines are in a
class by themselves.*

*Late harvest wines are
unique. They're sweet
but not syrupy sweet.
They are harvested a lot
later than others, a few
even after the first frosts.
Because they are labor
intensive, these are
expensive wines.*

*Under the right condi-
tions, a mold called
Botrytis infects the
grapes. Known as the
"noble rot," it evapo-
rates the water in the
grape. Less water
means more concen-
trated juice. Instead of
picking the grapes when
they're ripe, vintners
must plan the picking to
make sure the grapes
are at just the right
stage of overripeness.*

DUCK WITH ROSEMARY

This dish represents a refreshing departure from the sweet sauces we so often see served with duck.

— *Mary Nell Reck*

SERVES 8

TO MAKE DUCK STOCK

❊

Roughly chop the bones of 1 duck and sauté with 2 chopped carrots, 1 chopped onion, 1 stalk celery, 2 cloves garlic, 1 bay leaf, 1/4 cup tomato paste and 1 teaspoon black peppercorns. Add enough water to cover the ingredients. Bring to a boil, skimming off the fat occasionally. Lower the heat to simmer until the volume is reduced to half.

DUCK BREAST

2 lemons

2 cloves garlic, finely chopped

4 tablespoons chopped fresh rosemary leaves

1/2 cup virgin olive oil

1 teaspoon salt

1 teaspoon freshly ground black pepper

8 boneless duck breasts

TOMATOES

2 pounds Roma tomatoes

2 tablespoons fresh rosemary leaves

1/2 cup chopped fresh mint leaves

1/4 cup virgin olive oil

1 1/2 teaspoons salt

3/4 teaspoon freshly ground black pepper

SPINACH

2 pounds fresh spinach

4 tablespoons butter

Salt and freshly ground black pepper to taste

Pinch of nutmeg

1/2 cup pine nuts, toasted

SAUCE

Pan drippings from roasted duck

1 cup chicken or duck stock

1/2 cup white wine

Dash of salt and freshly ground black pepper

Using a sharp knife or a vegetable peeler, peel the thin outer skin from the two lemons. Cut into strips and finely dice. Combine the lemon zest, garlic and rosemary with the olive oil, salt and pepper. Pat the herb marinade on both sides of the duck breast and refrigerate for at least 1 hour.

Remove the stems from the tomatoes and cut into wedges, dividing each into 6 to 8 pieces. Place in a bowl with the rosemary, mint, olive oil, salt and pepper. Set aside in a baking pan.

Preheat the oven to 425 degrees. Place the marinated duck breast in a roasting pan on the top rack of the oven to brown and crisp the skin. Place the pan with the tomatoes on a lower rack. After 15 minutes, remove the duck from the oven and allow to rest.

Lower the oven temperature to 300 degrees and continue baking the tomatoes for an additional 15 minutes.

While the duck and tomatoes are roasting, wash, trim and dry the spinach leaves. Heat a frying pan until very hot. Add the butter and allow it to brown, but not burn. Add the spinach in handfuls with the salt, pepper and nutmeg. Toss and continue adding the rest of the spinach until it wilts. Stir in the toasted pine nuts. Adjust the seasonings. Set aside.

Pour off and discard the grease from the roasting pan with the duck. Place the pan over high heat and add the stock and wine. Boil to reduce while scraping the pan with a spatula.

To serve, arrange the spinach on a warm serving platter. Quickly slice the duck into horizontal strips and place on the spinach. Place the roasted tomatoes at either end of the platter. Drizzle the duck with the sauce and serve the remainder at the table.

DUCK RAVIOLI
WITH GINGER CREAM SAUCE

SERVES 12-15 AS AN APPETIZER OR 8 AS A MAIN COURSE

DUCK

1 medium yellow onion,
 coarsely chopped

1/2 cup chopped flat leaf parsley

1 tablespoon chopped thyme leaves

8 cloves garlic, halved

2 bay leaves

1 large celery rib, sliced

Herbes de provence

Salt and freshly ground black pepper

1 duck (5 1/2 pounds), quartered

RAVIOLI

2 tablespoons clarified butter

1 1/2 cups chopped yellow onion

1 tablespoon chopped garlic

1 tablespoon chopped thyme leaves

3 bay leaves

1/2-1 cup chopped orange slices,
 sautéed in a bit of olive oil

1/2 cup dried sour cherries, plumped
 in hot water and chopped

Salt and freshly ground black pepper

1/3 cup chopped basil leaves

120 wonton wrappers,
 preferably round

1/3 cup all-purpose flour

1/2 cup water

GINGER CREAM SAUCE

2 tablespoons clarified butter

1/2 cup chopped ginger

2 tablespoons chopped garlic

1/4 cup lemon zest

1 cup chicken stock

2 quarts heavy cream

1/4 cup lemon juice

1/2 cup whole tarragon leaves

Salt and freshly ground white pepper

RED PEPPER CREAM SAUCE

3 sweet red bell peppers

1 1/2 cups heavy cream

Salt and freshly ground white pepper

GARNISH

Grated Parmesan cheese

Preheat oven to 475 degrees.

In a small roasting pan, spread the onion, parsley, thyme, garlic, bay and celery. Prick the duck skin all over with a fork and rub the duck with salt, pepper and herbes de provence. Set the duck quarters on the vegetables and herbs, cut side down, and roast for 10 minutes. Prick the duck skin again, cover the pan with foil and turn the oven down to 275 degrees. Roast the duck for 3 hours or more or until the meat is very tender and most of the fat is rendered. Cool. Remove the meat from the bones and chop.

Heat the butter and sauté the onions, garlic, thyme and bay leaves until the onions are soft. Stir in the duck meat. Simmer for 5 to 10 minutes or until dry. Stir in the orange slices and cherries. Season with salt and black pepper. Remove the bay leaves, and stir in the basil leaves. Set aside.

Remove the wonton wrappers from their package and cover with a damp towel. Mix the flour and water together until they form a smooth paste. Place one wonton wrapper on the counter. Put 1 to 2 tablespoons of the stuffing in the middle of the wrapper. Using a pastry brush, brush some of the flour paste around the outside edge of the wrapper. Put another wrapper on top and press the edges together to seal. Set aside, covered with a damp towel. Continue in this fashion until all of the wrappers or stuffing is used. At this point, the ravioli may be frozen.

To make the ginger cream sauce, melt the butter over low heat and sauté the ginger, garlic and lemon zest for 2 minutes or until aromatic. Add the chicken stock, cream and lemon juice, and boil until reduced. Stir in the tarragon. Season to taste with salt and white pepper.

To make the red pepper cream sauce, roast the peppers in a hot oven or on the grill until blackened and blistered on all sides. When cool enough to handle, peel. Remove the seeds and veins. Puree in a blender. Place in a frying pan to evaporate the excess moisture, then transfer to a bowl. Return the same frying pan to high heat, add the cream and reduce until thick enough to coat a spoon. Season with salt and white pepper. Stir in the reduced red pepper puree.

Cook the ravioli in boiling water for 2 to 3 minutes or until al dente. If frozen, cook for 4 to 5 minutes. Place the ginger cream sauce in a small sauté pan over low heat. Add the ravioli, shake the pan to coat and heat through. Place on a warm plate and sprinkle lightly with grated Parmesan cheese, then drizzle with the red pepper cream sauce.

- -

AFTER DEBONING THE DUCK, USE THE CARCASS FOR
DUCK STOCK. EITHER FREEZE THE CARCASS TIGHTLY
IN DOUBLE FREEZER BAGS OR PREPARE THE STOCK AND
FREEZE IT IN AIR-TIGHT CONTAINERS FOR LATER USE.

- -

HERBES DE PROVENCE

✳

Herbes de provence is a dried herb blend typical of the Provence region of south-central France. It may include rosemary, thyme, savory, oregano, basil, sage, marjoram, fennel, mint and lavender blossoms. Crush the dried herbs in the palm of the hand to release their flavor.

BRAISED DUCK WITH PORT AND THYME

BRAISED DUCK

2 whole ducklings

1 liter port wine

2 cups chicken stock

1/2 cup honey

5 sprigs thyme

5 bay leaves

5 sprigs parsley

1 1/2 oranges, sliced

10 whole cloves

10 slices fresh ginger

1 1/2 teaspoons black peppercorns

1 1/2 teaspoons salt

5 cloves garlic

GLAZE

1/2 cup honey

1/2 cup Dijon mustard

1 tablespoon soy sauce

1/2 tablespoon chopped rosemary

1/2 tablespoon lemon juice

PEKIN DUCK

✳

The Pekin duck comes from Long Island. The breasts and legs are medium size, with enough fat on the duck to render. The breasts have a fair amount of fat and need to be scored before cooking; they shrink considerably during the cooking process. When raw, the Pekin duck has about equal amounts of fat and meat.

This is the most lightly flavored of the three types of duck. The taste is stronger than quail, but not as pronounced as squab. The firm meat is tender to eat. If the skin is scored, it crisps during the cooking process, plumping up the meat and making it moist and juicy. The legs are excellent for making a soft confit. Pekin duck is used in the classic Chinese dish.

Braise the ducks one day in advance. Preheat the oven to 350 degrees. Brown the ducks in a large heavy frying or braising pan. Combine the ingredients for the braising liquid. Place the ducks, breast side up, in a roasting pan and pour the liquid over them. The liquid should cover at least two-thirds of the ducks; if more liquid is needed, add chicken broth. Cover with aluminum foil and place in the preheated oven. Reduce the temperature to 300 degrees and braise for 2 hours. Remove the foil, turn the ducks over and return to the oven for 1 hour or until tender. When done, the flesh will have pulled away from the leg bones and the meat will be extremely tender.

Remove from the oven and let stand at room temperature until cooled slightly. Cover and refrigerate in the braising liquid overnight.

The next day, mix the honey, mustard, soy sauce, rosemary and lemon juice together. Set aside.

Preheat the oven to 400 degrees. Remove the ducks from the refrigerator. Discard all the duck fat that has risen to the surface. Remove the ducks from the pan and cut into serving portions. Arrange on a parchment-lined baking sheet. Coat the skin side with the honey mustard glaze. Shortly before serving, place in the preheated oven to heat through and brown the surface. If necessary, place under the broiler until golden.

Place the roasting pan with all its liquids over moderately high heat to warm the juices. Strain into a saucepan. Taste, adjust the seasoning and boil until reduced to the desired consistency, then serve with the duck.

. . . .

THE PORT WINE MAY BE SUBSTITUTED WITH
SWEET SHERRY OR A FRUIT-FLAVORED LIQUEUR.
A NON-ALCOHOLIC ALTERNATIVE WOULD BE
ORANGE JUICE OR APPLE JUICE.
(SUBSTITUTE AN EQUAL AMOUNT OF LIQUID.)

. . . .

GRILLED TENDERLOIN OF BUFFALO
WITH CABERNET SAUCE

SERVES 12

BUFFALO

1/4 cup chopped, crushed garlic

1/2 cup chopped rosemary

1/4 cup freshly ground black pepper

2 tablespoons salt

12 6-ounce fillets of buffalo
  tenderloin

Olive oil

CABERNET SAUCE

2 tablespoons virgin olive oil

1 cup sliced shallots

2 tablespoons chopped, crushed garlic

1/2 cup chopped dried prunes

2 bay leaves

2 sprigs thyme

2 slices orange with rind

Juices from grilled meat

4 cups beef or veal stock

2 cups cabernet wine

Salt and freshly ground black pepper

1 tablespoon grated lemon zest

Combine the garlic, rosemary, pepper and salt. Arrange the meat in a layer on a baking sheet. Press the herb mixture into the steaks, coating both sides. Chill until ready to grill.

Just before serving, lightly drizzle the meat with olive oil. Place on a very hot grill for 3 to 4 minutes per side, turning only once. The meat should be medium rare and well marked on both sides. Transfer to a warm oven and allow to rest for at least 5 minutes. Save the juices.

Heat the olive oil in a large saucepan. Sauté the shallots, garlic and chopped prunes with the bay leaves and thyme for 3 to 4 minutes or until the shallots are tender and beginning to brown. Add the orange slices, juices from the grilled meat, stock and cabernet. Boil rapidly for 10 minutes or longer to reduce to a sauce consistency and develop the flavors. Add salt and black pepper to taste.

Strain the sauce through a sieve, forcing the pulp through with a spoon. Return to low heat. Add the lemon zest. Serve with the grilled buffalo.

. . . .

AS A VARIATION BEEF TENDERLOIN MAY BE
SUBSTITUTED FOR THE BUFFALO.

. . . .

BUFFALO

✳

Buffalo meat is known for its tenderness; it has a sweet, juicy flavor with a mild but hearty taste. It has been described as "sweeter and cleaner than beef." Because buffalo meat is extra-lean and dense, it will not shrink down after cooking.

Buffalo is the lowest fat meat, even lower than white meat chicken. Because the buffalo is a strong, highly disease-resistant animal, its meat is hormone-free, antibiotic-free and pesticide-free.

Buffalo ranchers treat these animals with respect, raising them on grassy rangeland where they can socialize in herds and not in over-crowded feedlots.

GRILLED BACK STRAP OF VENISON WITH BURGUNDY SAUCE AND ROASTED GARLIC

SERVES 12

VENISON

4 pounds venison back strap

1/4 cup chopped fresh
   rosemary leaves

2 tablespoons chopped thyme leaves

2 tablespoons granulated sugar

1 tablespoon finely chopped
   lemon zest

4 tablespoons crushed and
   chopped garlic

1/4 cup freshly ground black pepper

Salt to taste

1/4 cup olive oil

BURGUNDY SAUCE

1 cup sliced shallots

1 tablespoon olive oil

2 tablespoons crushed and
   chopped garlic

4 sprigs fresh thyme

4 bay leaves

2 sprigs fresh rosemary

1 teaspoon coarsely chopped
   juniper berries

1 tablespoon Worcestershire sauce

4 cups veal stock

2 bottles burgundy wine

Salt and black pepper

ROASTED GARLIC

4 whole pods fresh garlic

2 tablespoons olive oil

VENISON

✳

The back strap or loin of a deer is very much like filet mignon. The best of this cut comes from a two- to three-year-old deer, preferably a doe. With meat this fantastic, it takes little effort to create a gourmet entree. Some cooks like to wrap the slices of loin in bacon, just like a filet mignon. If prepared properly, venison is one of the heart-healthiest meats available.

Trim the back strap of all sinew and connective tissue. Combine the remaining ingredients into a paste and rub over the meat, firmly pressing into the surface. Refrigerate until ready to grill.

Preheat the oven to 200 degrees. Close to serving time, cook the seasoned back strap on a very hot grill until well marked on all sides. Place in the preheated oven to finish cooking for about 8 to 10 minutes.

Sauté the shallots in hot olive oil for about 2 minutes. Add the garlic, thyme, bay leaves, rosemary and juniper berries, and sauté for 1 or 2 minutes more. Stir in the Worcestershire sauce, veal stock and wine, and bring to a boil. Boil rapidly for 15 to 20 minutes or until reduced and flavorful. Season with salt and black pepper. Strain the sauce and set aside until ready to serve.

Preheat the oven to 400 degrees. Place the garlic in a shallow pan and coat with the olive oil. Roast uncovered for 20 to 30 minutes or until light brown. Remove from the oven. When cool enough to handle, peel and separate the cloves.

When ready to serve, slice the venison into 1/4-inch thick medallions and arrange on individual plates with 2 cloves of roasted garlic and the burgundy sauce.

. . . .

SAUCE VARIATIONS

TO THE BASIC BURGUNDY SAUCE, ADD:
1/2 CUP REDUCED CREAM
1/4 CUP POMMERY (OLD FASHIONED GRAINY) MUSTARD

OR

1 CUP DICED ROMA TOMATOES
1 TABLESPOON FINELY CHOPPED LEMON ZEST

OR

1/2 CUP REDUCED CREAM
2 TABLESPOONS COGNAC

OR

2 CUPS SAUTÉED MUSHROOMS

. . . .

VENISON LINGUINE

SERVES 6-8

1 pound venison sausage

1 medium red onion, chopped

2 cloves garlic, minced

3 ripe tomatoes, chopped in
3/4-inch pieces

1/2 pound button mushrooms, sliced

2 tablespoons fresh oregano

Salt and freshly ground black pepper

4 quarts water with 1 tablespoon
each salt and olive oil

1 pound fresh linguine

3/4 cup grated Parmesan cheese

Slice the venison sausage into 1/2-inch slices. Cook in a frying pan over moderately high heat to render the fat. Allow the sausage to brown on both sides. Remove and drain. Pour off all but 3 tablespoons of fat. Sauté the onion in the pan drippings for 4 to 5 minutes. Add the garlic and tomatoes, and cook for 5 minutes. Add the mushrooms and oregano, and season to taste with salt and black pepper. Cook for 1 minute longer. Set aside.

Bring the water to a boil and drop in the linguine. Boil for 1 to 2 minutes or until al dente. Drain and toss with the sautéed vegetable mixture and the sausage. Add the cheese slowly. Transfer to a warm platter and sprinkle with additional cheese.

VENISON SAUSAGE

✳

Homemade venison sausages are economical, taste better and can be seasoned to individual preferences. To make sausages, use meat cut from filets or odd cuts and trimmings.

Retail sausage kits are available that contain all the equipment needed to make sausage, along with instructions.

VENISON TAMALES

TAMALES

❋

The tamale is recorded as early as 5000 B.C., and possibly 7000 B.C., in Pre-Columbian history. Initially, women went along in battle as army cooks to make the masa for the tortillas and the meats, stews, drinks, etc. As the warring tribes of the Aztec, Mayan and Incan cultures grew, the task of readying the nixtamal (corn) itself became so overwhelming that the armies sought a more portable foodstuff. Hence the tamale was born.

Tamales could be made ahead and packed, to be warmed later as needed. They were steamed, grilled on the comal (grill) over the fire or put directly on top of the coals to warm. They were also eaten cold. There is no record of which culture actually created the tamale, but it's believed that one started and the others soon followed.

VENISON FILLING

3 pounds venison meat, cut from the leg or loin

1 tablespoon vegetable oil

1 medium onion, chopped

1 cup red wine

1 1/2 cups reduced brown veal stock

Salt to taste

TAMALES

24 fresh green or dried corn husks

1 cup shortening or lard

4 cups masa harina (found in the Mexican section or with the flour in the grocery store)

1 1/2 cups warm chicken stock

1 tablespoon baking powder

1/2 tablespoon salt

ADOBO SAUCE

1 ounce cascabel chili peppers

1 ounce ancho chili peppers

2 tablespoons vegetable oil

2 tablespoons chopped garlic

1 tablespoon whole cloves

2 tablespoons whole black pepper

1 stick cinnamon

1/2 teaspoon ground cumin

1/2 tablespoon chopped fresh oregano

1/2 tablespoon chopped fresh thyme

1 tablespoon chicken base (similar to chicken concentrate and found in the soup section of the grocery store)

1/2 cup brown sugar

4 cups chicken stock

GARNISH

Salsa (see the recipe on page 84)

Slice the venison into very thin strips, then finely dice the strips. Heat the oil in a skillet until lightly smoking and sauté the onion over medium to high heat for about 2 minutes or until clear. Add the venison and continue cooking for about 4 more minutes, stirring occasionally. Add the red wine and reduce to a glaze. Add the stock and reduce again to a glaze consistency. Season with salt. Set aside.

If using dried corn husks, soak them in water for 30 minutes. Using an electric mixer, beat the shortening on medium speed for 5 minutes or until light and fluffy. Gradually add the masa harina alternately with the chicken stock, adding the stock in a slow steady stream. If the stock is too warm, the dough will separate. Stir in the baking powder and salt. The mixture will be quite sticky.

Place the corn husks on a work surface. Tear 36 strips 1/6-inch wide from six of the husks to use in tying the tamales. Spread the dough on the wider half of each of the remaining husks, leaving a 1-inch border on one long side and both ends. Spoon the filling down the center of the dough. Fold in the long side of the husk and roll until the filling is completely enclosed. Tie each end with a 1/6-inch strip of corn husk.

Arrange the tamales upright in a steamer with a tight-fitting lid. Cover with a dish towel, then the steamer lid, and steam over gently boiling water for 30 to 35 minutes or until done.

Remove the seeds and cut the chilies into pieces. Heat the vegetable oil and sauté the chilies, garlic, cloves, peppercorns, cinnamon stick and cumin for 5 minutes or until the garlic is golden. Add the oregano, thyme, chicken base and brown sugar. Stir in the chicken stock. Bring to a boil and simmer for 20 minutes. Puree in a blender. Season to taste with salt.

When the tamales are ready, slice the husks from one end to the other with a knife. Press the ends together gently (like a baked potato) and transfer the tamales to a serving platter. Pour the sauce over the top. Serve with a bowl of salsa and the extra adobo sauce.

SOUTHWESTERN VENISON

Five great French chef were brought to Houston for a charity dinner. While in town they were proclaimed official Texans, visited a real ranch for the first time, rode horses, also for the first time and were given real cowboy hats! They attended a "Haut Barbeque" where this wonderful dish, which blends all the flavors of the southwest, was served.

— Mary Nell Reck

SERVES 8-10

MARINADE

2 carrots, peeled and chopped

1 red onion, chopped

2 stalks celery, finely chopped

4 tablespoons chopped shallots

4 tablespoons olive oil

3 cups dry white wine

1/2 cup red wine vinegar

2 jalapeños, split, seeded and chopped

3 tablespoons coarsely chopped cilantro

1 tablespoon chopped rosemary

2 cloves garlic, chopped

1 teaspoon thyme leaves

2 bay leaves

1 tablespoon salt

2 teaspoons freshly ground black pepper

VENISON AND SAUCE

2 venison back straps (pork loin, leg of lamb or top sirloin steak may be substituted)

3 cups rich beef stock

2 teaspoons chili powder

Beurre manie (equal parts soft butter and flour mixed)

Sauté the carrots, onions, celery and shallots in the olive oil over high heat for 5 to7 minutes or until they become aromatic and begin to color. Combine the sautéed vegetables with the white wine and vinegar. Add the chopped jalapeño, cilantro, rosemary, garlic, thyme, bay leaves, salt and pepper.

Using a small, sharp knife, trim the silver skin from the back strap. Place the trimmed meat into the marinade. Turn to completely coat and refrigerate for at least 4 hours or overnight. Remove the meat and set aside.

Place the stock in a saucepan along with 4 cups of the marinade and all its herbs and vegetables. Add the chili powder. Boil for 30 minutes to reduce the liquid. Pass through a sieve and return to the saucepan. Taste and adjust the seasoning. If you need to thicken the sauce, whisk in 1 to 2 teaspoons of beurre manie.

Slice the venison into 1/2 to 3/4-inch pieces on the diagonal for optimum tenderness. Grill over high heat on a rack 2 to 3 inches from the heat until reaches medium doneness. Let rest in a warm place for 5 minutes. Serve immediately with the sauce.

BEURRE MANIE

❋

Beurre manie translates to "hand butter" in French. Take equal parts of cold butter and flour and work them into a paste. You can then drop pieces of the paste directly into whatever you are trying to thicken. Use it in sauces rather than broths because it can cloud the final result. For unclouded thickening, cornstarch dissolved in cold water is best. In either case, bring the liquid back to a full boil to achieve the full thickening potential.

RABBIT IN WHITE WINE

*Rabbit meat has the delicate flavor of chicken's white meat, combined
with the juiciness of its dark meat. It is tender, sweet and mild.*

— *Mary Nell Reck*

SERVES 4-6

RABBIT

✳

*As the cliché goes, "It
tastes like chicken."
Rabbit also smells and
looks like chicken.
However, pieces of rabbit
tend to be smaller and
thinner. It is also said to
be softer and easier to
digest than chicken.*

*Rabbit meat may be
found in the form of
cutlets and Italian-style
sausage as well.*

DREDGING

✳

*To dredge means to coat
something lightly,
usually using flour, cornmeal or bread crumbs.
This creates a crunchy,
browned surface on
sautéed or fried foods.
You can also season your
flour to add flavor as
well as crunch.*

*To help the coating stick,
you can first dredge the
food in flour, then dip it
into an egg wash and
finally roll it in the cornmeal or bread crumbs.
This creates a thicker
coat called a breading.*

2 rabbits (2 pounds each)

1 teaspoon salt

1/2 teaspoon freshly ground
   white pepper

All-purpose flour for dredging

4-6 tablespoons olive oil

4 cups dry white wine

3 tablespoons finely chopped
   fresh rosemary

Pinch of crushed red pepper

3-4 tablespoons lemon juice

If necessary, cut the rabbit in pieces the same way you would
cut up a chicken. Sprinkle the meat lightly with salt and white
pepper. Dip each piece into the flour to thoroughly coat. Shake
off the excess.

Heat half the olive oil in a frying pan over moderately high
heat. Lightly brown the pieces of rabbit on both sides. Add the
remaining oil as needed. Transfer the rabbit to a large soup pot.
Add the wine, rosemary and red pepper. Bring to a boil. Reduce
the heat, cover and simmer gently for about 30 minutes or until
the meat is tender when pierced with a fork.

Transfer the cooked rabbit to a warm serving platter. Reduce the
liquid in the pot to a sauce consistency and add the lemon
juice. Taste and adjust the seasoning.

Pour the sauce over the rabbit and serve immediately.

. . . .

SERVE WITH RICE AND A GREEN VEGETABLE.

. . . .

FIRE DEVIL CHILI

SERVES 8-10

CHIPOTLE PUREE

5 chipotle chilies

2 tablespoons chopped garlic

2 tablespoons chopped shallots

1/4 teaspoon ground cumin

1/4 teaspoon freshly ground
   black pepper

Salt

ANCHO CHILI PUREE

2 ancho chilies

1 cup boiling water

CHILI

1 1/4 pounds wild boar Italian
   sausage, chopped

1 1/4 pounds venison, ground for chili

1 1/4 pounds beef chuck roast, cubed

1 1/4 pounds buffalo sirloin, cubed

1 1/2 yellow onions, chopped

1 tablespoon chopped garlic

1/2 cup masa harina (found in the
   Mexican section or with the flour
   in the grocery store)

3/4 cup tomato paste

3/4 cup water

1 tablespoon chili powder

1 tablespoon ground cumin

2 tablespoons chopped fresh oregano

1 tablespoon chopped fresh thyme

2 tablespoons chopped jalapeños

1/4 cup chili powder

3 tablespoons ground cumin

1 tablespoon paprika

1 tablespoon freshly ground
   black pepper

Salt and cayenne pepper (up to 1
   1/2 teaspoons cayenne)

Place the chipotle chilies in a pot. Pour boiling water over just to cover. Boil for 20 minutes. Add the garlic, shallots, cumin, pepper and salt. Puree in a blender. Return the hot puree to a frying pan and pan sear for 8 to 10 minutes to reduce and develop the flavors. Set aside.

Stem and seed the ancho chilies. Cover with the boiling water and let stand for 30 minutes. Put in a blender or food processor and blend, adding a little of the water to make a smooth puree. Set aside.

Place a large, heavy stockpot over high heat. One at a time, brown the different meats well on all sides, then remove. Leave the drippings in the pot. Add the onions to the drippings and sauté for 6 to 8 minutes or until tender. Add the garlic. Return the browned meat to the pot and sprinkle with the masa harina. Stir to evenly distribute. Cook for 2 to 3 minutes, stirring to prevent sticking.

Combine the tomato paste with the water and add to the pot along with the chili powder and cumin. Add the oregano and thyme, and cover the chili with additional water. Bring to a boil, reduce to a simmer, cover and continue to cook for 2 hours, stirring occasionally.

Add the remaining ingredients along with 1 tablespoon each of the chipotle puree and the ancho chili puree. Cook for another hour. Taste and adjust the seasoning.

MASA HARINA

✳

Masa harina is the Mexican term for corn flour. It is like corn meal but much finer, and it can be found in most supermarkets. In the South, it is readily available in large bags in the flour section. In other regions, it may be found in smaller packages in the Mexican food section.

Masa harina is also used as a thickener in many recipes and as a roux ingredient in soups.

WILD BOAR ITALIAN SAUSAGE

✳

Wild boar Italian sausage is a classical Italian sausage reminiscent of Tuscany.

STUFFED TENDERLOIN OF BEEF

Recipe on page 116

MEAT

STUFFED TENDERLOIN OF BEEF

SERVES 10-12

BEEF

*

The rib, short loin, and
sirloin render the most
delicate cuts of beef.
Broiling, grilling,
sautéing and roasting
reign supreme here. Rib
steaks, (also known as
delmonico or prime rib),
rib eye steaks, (without
the bone), and rib roasts,
naturally come from the
rib. The sirloin provides
a variety of sirloin steaks
differing on where in the
sirloin they are cut from.
Sirloin can also be
ground and mixed with
ground chuck for primo
hamburgers.

Finally, the crème de la
crème of beef: the short
loin. Picture a porter-
house or T-bone steak.
The larger side is
referred to by the names
top loin, strip, New York
strip, shell steak, etc.
The smaller side is the
tenderloin or filet mignon.
The porterhouse and the
T-bone are the same
except that the porter-
house is cut from the
larger end of the short
loin and thus provides
more of the filet mignon.
Both the top loin and the
tenderloin can be cut
into individual steaks, or
larger roasts. In the case
of the top loin, the steaks
may or may not be
attached to the bone.
The tenderloin is always
boneless except when
part of a porterhouse or
T-bone steak.

TENDERLOIN

1 whole beef tenderloin
   (4-5 pounds), trimmed
Virgin olive oil for coating
Freshly ground black pepper

STUFFING

4 tablespoons (1/2 stick)
   unsalted butter
1 medium yellow onion, peeled
   and chopped
2 cloves garlic, crushed and
   finely chopped
1 pound fresh mushrooms,
   coarsely chopped
1/4 cup dry Madeira wine
1 cup bread crumbs
1/2 cup freshly grated
   Parmesan cheese
Dash of salt and freshly ground
   black pepper
1-2 tablespoons melted butter

BROWN SAUCE

3 tablespoons butter
3 tablespoons all-purpose flour
2 cups good beef stock,
   preferably homemade
Salt and freshly ground pepper
1/2 cup chopped shallots
1/2 cup dry Madeira wine
3/4 cup diced tomatoes
2 teaspoons fresh thyme leaves or
   1/2 teaspoon dried thyme

GARNISH

Sprigs of fresh watercress

Trim away the small end of the tenderloin, which tapers to a point. Do not throw this piece of meat away. It will be added to the stuffing later. Rub the meat with olive oil, then crushed black pepper to taste. Heat a heavy, flat-bottomed frying pan until very hot. Quickly brown the meat on all sides, turning only when a side has fully browned. Remove from the pan and set aside to cool. Browning seals in the juices and gives the meat a rich flavor. Set the pan aside without washing. It will be used to prepare the stuffing.

Preheat the oven to 500 degrees. Heat the butter in the same frying pan used to brown the meat. When the bubbling subsides, stir in the chopped onion. Cook for 4 to 5 minutes, then add the garlic and mushrooms. Sauté, shaking the pan constantly, until the onions are soft and the mushrooms have a moist appearance. Add the Madeira wine and quickly evaporate over high heat for about 2 minutes.

Place the sautéed mixture in a bowl. Add the bread crumbs and Parmesan cheese. Chop the reserved end of the tenderloin into 1/2-inch pieces and add to the stuffing. Add salt and crushed black pepper to taste. Add a little melted butter, if necessary, until the mixture is just moist enough to hold together.

Cut the browned tenderloin at 3/4 to 1-inch intervals almost all the way through. Place the stuffing into each of the cuts.

Place the stuffed tenderloin in a roasting pan. Spoon any excess stuffing around the meat and loosely cover with aluminum foil. Roast in the preheated oven for 12 to 15 minutes for medium rare. Test the meat for doneness using an instant read ther- mometer stuck into the center of one of the slices. For medium rare the temperature should read 130 degrees. Transfer the cooked tenderloin to a warm platter and allow to rest while preparing the sauce. Surround with the extra stuffing and garnish with sprigs of watercress.

Melt the butter in a saucepan and stir in the flour. Cook on medium low heat until the flour has turned a nice golden brown. Be careful not to burn the mixture. Add the beef stock, stirring with a whisk until the mixture is smooth and thick. Season with salt and pepper. Set aside.

Return the roasting pan to high heat. Sauté the shallots for 2 to 3 minutes in the pan drippings. Add the brown sauce, Madeira wine, and more salt and pepper to taste. Boil until reduced by about one-fourth. Strain into a sauce boat and add the diced tomatoes and fresh thyme. Pass at the table with the stuffed tenderloin. Serve immediately.

GRILLED TENDERLOIN OF BEEF
WITH ANCHO CHILE SAUCE

SERVES 8

MARINATED BEEF

1/2 cup virgin olive oil

1/2 cup molasses

4 tablespoons balsamic vinegar

*2 cloves garlic, peeled, crushed and
    finely chopped*

1/4 teaspoon ground cumin

1 teaspoon crushed red pepper

2 teaspoons salt

*2 tablespoons freshly ground
    black pepper*

*2 beef tenderloins
    (3 pounds each), trimmed*

ANCHO CHILE SAUCE

2 ancho chilies

1 cup boiling water

1/4 cup finely chopped shallots

2 teaspoons virgin olive oil

1 cup cabernet wine

1 cup beef stock

1/2 cup diced Roma tomatoes

In a small bowl, combine the olive oil, molasses, vinegar, garlic, cumin, red pepper, salt and black pepper. Coat the meat on all sides with the marinade. Cover and refrigerate at least 1 hour or overnight. Reserve the marinade after removing the beef.

Stem and seed the chilies. Cover with the boiling water and let stand for 30 minutes. Put the chilies in a blender or food processor and blend, adding a little of the water to make a smooth puree. Set aside.

Sauté the shallots in the hot olive oil in an 8-inch frying pan for about 1 minute. Add the cabernet and stock to the hot pan, and boil to reduce by about a half cup. Add the reserved marinade and simmer for a few minutes. Add 1/4 cup of the ancho chili puree. Stir in the tomatoes. Taste and adjust the seasoning. Set aside until ready to serve.

Preheat the oven to 300 degrees. Grill the meat over very hot coals until well marked on all sides. Place in the preheated oven to rest, allowing the juices to dissipate as it continues cooking. Use an instant read thermometer to check for doneness. Medium rare should read 130 degrees. To serve, thinly slice the beef and serve with the ancho chili sauce.

**ANCHO
CHILIES**

✳

Ancho chilies are broad, dried chilies that are 3 to 4 inches long. A deep reddish brown, they range in flavor from mild to pungent. The rich, slightly fruit-flavored ancho is the sweetest of the dried chilies. In its fresh green state, it is called a poblano chili.

PEPPER STEAK WITH COGNAC SAUCE

SERVES 8

COGNAC SAUCE

1 tablespoon white peppercorns

1 tablespoon clarified butter

1/2 bay leaf

1/2 cup chopped shallots

1/2 cup red wine vinegar

1 quart veal stock

1 tablespoon demi-glace (found at gourmet food markets)

1 cup heavy cream

2 tablespoons brandy

Dash of salt

STEAKS

4 teaspoons whole white peppercorns

8 tenderloin fillets (8 ounces each), trimmed

2 tablespoons or more olive oil

GARNISH

Parsley sprigs

Place the peppercorns in a large, dry sauté pan over high heat. Cook, shaking the pan, until they develop a toasty aroma. Add the butter, bay leaf and shallots. Sauté for 3 to 4 minutes or until the shallots are soft. Add the red wine vinegar and veal stock. Boil for 10 minutes to reduce. Add the demi-glace to thicken the sauce, then add the cream. Simmer for 5 minutes. Add the brandy and a dash of salt. Strain the sauce. Place in a bain-marie (a hot water bath) and keep warm.

Crush the whole white peppercorns with the bottom of a saucepan. Spread out on the counter and press into the steaks. Use about 1/2 teaspoon per steak.

Heat a sauté pan until very hot. Add the olive oil and pan grill the tenderloin steaks until very brown outside and cooked to order inside. Turn the meat only once during cooking.

To serve, place 4 tablespoons of the cognac sauce on each warm plate. Place the grilled meat on top of the sauce. Serve with new potatoes, mushrooms and two vegetables. Garnish with parsley sprigs.

STEAK MADAGASCAR

SERVES 8

6 tenderloin steaks (1 1/2-inch
   thick, 8 ounces each)

2 tablespoons whole green
   peppercorns

Beef fat (request beef trimming from
   the local butcher)

2 tablespoons virgin olive oil

4 tablespoons finely chopped shallots

1 1/2 cups drained and halved
   artichoke hearts

1/4 cup chopped tomatoes

Dash of salt and freshly ground
   black pepper

1/2 cup port wine

4 tablespoons cognac

1/4 cup heavy whipping cream

2 tablespoons green peppercorns

2 tablespoons finely chopped chives

Using the tip of a small, sharp knife, make a pocket in each steak by cutting through one side. The cut needs to go only to the center. Place about 1 teaspoon of whole green peppercorns in each pocket and press closed. The meat may be prepared several hours in advance to this point and refrigerated until ready to cook. The flavor of the peppercorns will permeate the meat.

Close to serving time, heat a heavy, flat-bottomed frying pan over high heat. When the pan is extremely hot, add some pieces of chopped fat. When the oils have cooked out and the pan is coated, remove the fat with a slotted spoon and discard. Place the steaks in the pan and cook without touching or turning until brown on one side. When the top of the steak becomes moist and iridescent, the meat is ready to turn for medium rare. For medium, wait until a small amount of blood seeps to the surface. The cooking time will vary depending on the intensity of the heat, thickness of the meat and desired taste. To test the temperature, use an instant read thermometer. Medium rare should read 130 degrees. When the meat is done, transfer to a warm serving platter and allow to rest for 5 minutes in a warm place while preparing the sauce.

Return the hot frying pan to the heat. Add the olive oil and sauté the shallots for 2 minutes. Add the artichoke hearts and continue cooking for about 1 minute or until heated through. Add the tomatoes and cook for 1 or 2 minutes longer or until they begin to exude their liquid. Sprinkle with salt and black pepper.

Add the port and cognac to the pan. Quickly reduce to half its volume while scraping and loosening the meat juices that have adhered to the bottom. This contributes to the flavor of the sauce. Stir in the cream and green peppercorns. Continue boiling for about 2 minutes or until thick. Return to the pan any juices that have come out of the meat as it rests.

To serve, place the steaks on individual plates. Spoon the sauce along the sides of the meat, but not on top. Sprinkle the steaks with the finely chopped chives. Serve immediately.

STEAK
THICKNESS

✳

Cooked over high heat, only thick steaks remain pink and juicy inside as they develop a rich, brown surface. If a steak is too thin, the meat overcooks internally before the outside has a chance to brown thoroughly.

Beef Short Ribs
Braised in Zinfandel

BEEF SHORT RIBS BRAISED IN ZINFANDEL

SERVES 6

RIBS

6 pounds beef short ribs

Dash of salt and fresh black pepper

Virgin olive oil

1 yellow onion, quartered

3 carrots, quartered

1 1/2 stalks celery with leaves,
    quartered

3 bay leaves

3 sprigs of fresh thyme

3 sprigs of fresh oregano

1 sprig of rosemary

1/2 bottle zinfandel wine

2 cups veal stock

2 tablespoons veal demi-glace
    (found at gourmet food markets)

1/4 cup tomato paste

3 cloves garlic

SAUTÉED VEGETABLES

1 cup chopped yellow onions

2 cups chopped carrots

1/2 cup chopped celery

Virgin olive oil

2 cups sauce from the meat

1 cup diced tomatoes

1 tablespoon chopped parsley

Preheat the oven to 325 degrees.

Season the ribs with salt and pepper, and brown on all sides in a frying pan over very high heat. After browning each rib, transfer to a large roasting pan. Place the remaining ingredients in the roasting pan on top of the browned short ribs. Cover with aluminum foil. Place in the preheated oven. Roast for 2 1/2 to 3 hours.

Sauté the chopped onions, carrots and celery in the olive oil until the onions are tender. Add 2 cups of the sauce from the braised meat and simmer gently for 10 minutes or until the carrots are tender. Taste and adjust the seasoning. Stir in the diced tomatoes and parsley. Set aside.

Test the ribs for tenderness. When done, remove from the roasting pan and transfer to a platter. Strain the sauce in the pan and discard the roasted vegetables. Boil the sauce for several minutes to reduce to the desired consistency. Add the sautéed vegetables, tomatoes and parsley. Spoon the sauce over the meat and serve.

Serve with mashed potatoes and fresh green vegetables.

DEMI-GLACE

✳

A rich brown sauce, demi-glace begins as a meat stock mixed with Madeira or sherry and slowly cooked until it is reduced by one-half. The intense flavor is used as a base for many other sauces and stews.

STEAK CHARNIGAN

SERVES 6

PORT SAUCE

1/2 cup chopped shallots

4 tablespoons (1/2 stick) butter

2 tablespoons raspberry preserves

1 tablespoon tomato paste

3/4 cup port wine

2 1/2 cups veal stock

1 tablespoon demi-glace (found at gourmet food markets)

Salt and freshly ground black pepper to taste

STEAK

6 tenderloin steaks (8 ounces each), trimmed

Virgin olive oil

Dash of salt and freshly ground white pepper

18 artichoke heart halves, rinsed and drained

3/4 cup peeled and diced tomatoes

GARNISH

Parsley sprigs

Sauté the shallots in the butter for 4 to 5 minutes or until soft. Stir in the raspberry preserves and tomato paste. Stir to combine. Add the port and veal stock, and boil for about 12 minutes to reduce. Stir in the demi-glace to enrich. Add salt and black pepper to taste. Set aside.

Brush the steak with the olive oil. Place on a hot grill and sprin-kle with salt and white pepper to taste. Grill to medium rare.

To serve, place each steak on a warm plate. Place 3 artichoke hearts on top. Ladle the port sauce over the artichoke hearts and sprinkle with the diced tomatoes.

Serve with new potatoes, sautéed mushrooms and two vegeta-bles. Garnish with parsley sprigs.

ROASTED RED PEPPER SAUCE

This sauce is also a wonderful accompaniment to Grilled Tenderloin of Veal with Grilled Portabello Mushrooms or any grilled meat.

YIELDS ABOUT 2 CUPS

4 large red bell peppers

2 cloves garlic

1 tablespoon virgin olive oil

1 cup chicken stock

Dash of salt and freshly ground white pepper

Pinch of cayenne

Grill the whole peppers until blackened and blistered on all sides. Place in a bowl and cover with plastic wrap to sweat. When the peppers are cool enough to handle, peel, split, and discard the seeds and veins. Meanwhile, sauté the peeled garlic in the olive oil over a low flame until golden on all sides. Place the peppers in a blender along with the garlic, chicken stock and seasonings. Puree until smooth. Taste and adjust the seasoning.

GRILLED TENDERLOIN OF VEAL
WITH GRILLED PORTOBELLO MUSHROOMS

SERVES 12

VEAL

3 pounds veal tenderloin, trimmed
    and tied

2 tablespoons virgin olive oil

Salt and freshly ground black
    pepper to taste

3 tablespoons chopped fresh rosemary

1 tablespoon crushed, chopped garlic

MUSHROOMS

4 tablespoons balsamic vinegar

2 tablespoons soy sauce

4 tablespoons white wine

1 tablespoon minced garlic

Salt and freshly ground black
    pepper to taste

2 tablespoons virgin olive oil

6 medium portobello mushrooms

CHIANTI SAUCE

1/2 cup chopped shallots

1 tablespoon virgin olive oil

2 cloves whole garlic

2 sprigs of fresh thyme

3 bay leaves

1 sprig of fresh rosemary

4 cups veal stock

2 cups Chianti wine

1/2 teaspoon freshly ground
    black pepper

2 tablespoons honey

2 tablespoons cognac

Dash of salt

GARNISH

Sprigs of thyme

Sprigs of rosemary

Rub the tenderloin with the olive oil, salt, pepper, rosemary and garlic. Set aside until ready to grill.

Combine the marinade ingredients for the mushrooms. Taste and adjust the seasoning. Remove the stems from the mushrooms. Marinate the mushroom caps for 30 minutes to 1 hour. Grill the mushrooms until well marked. Set aside.

Sauté the shallots in the olive oil in a saucepan over moderately high heat until brown. Add the garlic, thyme, bay leaves and rosemary. Cook for 1 minute to develop the flavors. Add the veal stock, Chianti, pepper and honey. Bring to a boil. Reduce the heat and simmer, uncovered, for 30 to 45 minutes or until reduced to sauce consistency. Remove from the heat, strain and return to the saucepan. Add the cognac and a dash of salt. Set aside until ready to serve.

Preheat the oven to 300 degrees. Place the seasoned veal tenderloin on a hot grill until marked well on all sides. Finish cooking in the preheated oven for 6 to 8 minutes or until half-firm to the touch. Set aside to rest for 5 minutes.

To serve, slice the grilled mushrooms and place on 12 hot plates. Spoon 3 ounces of the sauce over the mushroom slices. Top with 1/4-inch thick slices of the veal. Garnish with a sprig of fresh thyme or rosemary.

"Veal is the meat of a young calf, and the best or prime quality comes from an animal 10-12 weeks old fed on milk or milk by-products. It is of the palest pink in color and has both texture and flavor—although the flavor of veal is never robust, like that of lamb or beef."

—JULIA CHILD

VEAL PAILLARD

MADEIRA SAUCE

1 cup chopped shallots

1 tablespoon chopped garlic

2 tablespoons clarified butter

3 cups veal stock

1 cup Madeira wine

1/2 teaspoon salt

*1/2 teaspoon freshly ground
    black pepper*

VEAL

2-3 pounds veal scaloppini

Extra virgin olive oil

*Salt and freshly ground white
    pepper to taste*

1/2 cup chopped shallots

*4 tablespoons (1/2 stick)
    clarified butter*

2 pounds fresh spinach leaves

1 cup quartered mushrooms

Salt and white pepper

MADEIRA
SAUCE

✳

*Madeira sauce may also
be made with dry sherry.
It is a nice complement
to game or fillet of beef.*

Sauté the shallots and garlic in the clarified butter for 3 minutes or until soft. Add the veal stock, Madeira, salt and pepper. Boil to reduce by one-fourth or to the desired sauce consistency. Strain. Keep warm in a bain-marie (a hot water bath).

Brush the veal with olive oil and place on a hot grill. Sprinkle lightly with salt and white pepper. Grill to mark, for no more than 2 minutes total. The veal can also be sautéed in a skillet. Sauté the shallots in the hot clarified butter for 30 seconds. Add the spinach and mushrooms, and sauté for about 1 minute or until the spinach is wilted. Season with salt and white pepper.

To serve, divide the spinach into 8 equal portions and place in a tall mound on the warm dinner plates. Top with the grilled veal scaloppini. Ladle the Madeira sauce over the veal.

Serve with potatoes and vegetables.

VEAL POMMERY

SERVES 6

CREAM SAUCE

2 tablespoons butter

2 tablespoons all-purpose flour

1 1/4 cups milk, heated

Dash of salt and freshly ground
   white pepper

POMMERY SAUCE

1/2 cup chopped shallots

2 tablespoons butter

1 tablespoon brandy

2 tablespoons veal demi-glace (found
   at many gourmet food markets)

1/4 cup old-fashioned grainy mustard

1/2 cup diced Roma tomatoes

Dash of salt and freshly ground
   white pepper

1 tablespoon chopped fresh rosemary

1 cup veal stock (found frozen at
   specialty markets)

VEAL

1 1/2 pounds veal scaloppini

All-purpose flour seasoned with salt
   and freshly ground black pepper

Clarified butter

GARNISH

6 tablespoons chopped walnuts

Mix the flour and butter together over medium heat. Stir for 3 to 4 minutes to cook the flour so the sauce does not taste floury, but do not brown. Add the heated milk and stir with a whisk until thickened. Add the salt and pepper. Set aside.

Sauté the shallots in the butter. Add the rest of the ingredients along with 1 cup of the cream sauce. Simmer for a few minutes to develop the flavors. Remove from the heat but keep warm.

Coat the veal with the seasoned flour. Pat off the excess. Sauté in the hot clarified butter for about 2 minutes or until golden.

To serve, place the veal scalloppini on warmed plates. Add a ribbon of the Pommery sauce across the veal and to the side. Sprinkle with the chopped walnuts.

Serve with new potatoes, sautéed mushrooms and two vegetables.

VEAL SCALLOPS

*

Scallops of veal come from the rump roast of a young calf. Cutlets and scallops are very versatile and quick to cook. Because they are so thin, there is little need to test for doneness when sautéing—take them out of the pan when they are brown on both sides.

Smoked Tenderloin of Jerk Pork with Jamaican Barbecue Sauce

SERVES 12

JERK

*

Jerk is a traditional Jamaican style of cooking that uses a paste-like rub. The jerk spice marinade also works well on chicken.

JERK MARINATED PORK

1 bottle dark beer

1 tablespoon olive oil

1 tablespoon chopped garlic

4 bay leaves

1/4 cup soy sauce

2 tablespoons molasses

1 1/2 tablespoons chopped lime zest

2 tablespoons lime juice

1/2 cup chopped cilantro

1/2 teaspoon allspice

1/2 teaspoon juniper berries

1/2 teaspoon salt

1/2 teaspoon freshly ground black pepper

4 whole pork tenderloins

JAMAICAN BARBECUE SAUCE

2 tablespoons chopped garlic

1/2 cup tomato paste

1/2 cup water

1/4 cup Worcestershire sauce

1/2 cup honey

1/2 cup lime juice

1/4 cup virgin olive oil

4 bay leaves

1 tablespoon fresh thyme leaves

2 teaspoons paprika

1/2 teaspoon Tabasco® sauce

1 teaspoon crushed red pepper

2 teaspoons salt

2 teaspoons freshly ground black pepper

1/2 cup finely chopped parsley

1/2 cup finely chopped scallions

1 cup diced mango

Combine the marinade ingredients in a mixing bowl. Rub over the pork. Marinate in the refrigerator for 1 to 2 hours.

Combine all the ingredients for the barbeque sauce except the parsley, scallions and mango. Place in a saucepan and simmer gently for 20 minutes to develop the flavors. Just before serving, stir in the remaining ingredients. Taste and adjust the seasoning.

Smoke the marinated pork tenderloins slowly over hardwood, such as pecan or hickory, for 30 minutes to develop a mild smoky flavor. You may also use a stovetop smoker, following the manufacturer's directions. Place the smoked pork over a hot grill until well marked on all sides. Remove and let rest in a warm place for 10 minutes to finish the cooking and allow the juices to dissipate.

To serve, spoon the Jamaican barbeque sauce onto the plates. Slice the jerk pork and arrange on top of the sauce.

ROAST LOIN OF PORK WITH ROSEMARY

SERVES 8-10

PORK

1 center-cut pork loin (4-5 pounds)

1/4 cup chopped garlic

1/2 cup chopped fresh
 rosemary leaves

1 1/2 tablespoons salt

2 tablespoons freshly ground
 black pepper

4 tablespoons virgin olive oil, divided

SAUCE

1 cup chopped shallots

2 bay leaves

3 tablespoons olive oil

1 cup white wine

1 cup Madeira wine

3 cups veal stock (found at
 gourmet markets)

2 tablespoons all-purpose flour

Drippings from the pan

2 tablespoons white wine

Salt and freshly ground white
 pepper to taste

Preheat the oven to 350 degrees. Lay one hand firmly and flatly on top of the meat. Butterfly the meat in thirds horizontally, cutting down the entire length.

In a small bowl, mix the garlic, rosemary, salt, black pepper and 2 tablespoons of the olive oil. Spread half of the mixture over the inside of the roast and roll it up. Tie with cotton string at 1-inch intervals.

Rub the remaining mixture over the outside surface of the roast. Place in the preheated oven and roast for about 12 to 15 minutes per pound. After 1 hour of roasting, turn the meat over, and for the last 10 minutes of roasting, increase the oven temperature to 400 degrees to brown the outside of the meat. The reading on an inserted instant read meat thermometer should be 150-155 degrees. Remove and set aside but keep warm.

Sauté the shallots and bay leaves in the olive oil for 1 minute or until soft. Add the white wine and Madeira, and reduce by one-fourth. Combine the stock and flour, and add to the pan. Boil until the liquid is reduced by one-fourth again. Pour the fat off the pan drippings from the roast pork. Deglaze the drippings with 2 tablespoons of wine and add to the sauce.

Slice the pork loin and serve with the warm sauce.

DEGLAZING

✳

Deglazing allows you to recover the drippings and flavorful bits left on the bottom of a roasting pan once the meat has been removed. Pans can be deglazed using a stock, wine or vegetable cooking liquid.

BUTTERFLYING

✳

Butterflying meat allows you to stuff the roast with flavor-enhancing ingredients. The roast will also cook a bit faster.

COOKING PORK

✳

It is no longer necessary to cook pork until it is well done. Modern methods of raising swine have just about eradicated trichinae from the swine population. Also, trichinae are destroyed at 138 degrees. Most professional chefs feel that pork is at its best when cooked between 145 and 150 degrees. Chops and loins are quite lean, and when cooked to medium rather than well-done, they remain juicy and succulent. Remove the cooked pork from the oven when a meat thermometer reaches 145 degrees, cover loosely with foil and let rest for 10 minutes. As it rests, it will cook another 5-10 degrees.

ALLSPICE CRUSTED LAMB CHOPS
WITH ROASTED RED PEPPER SAUCE

SERVES 8

LAMB CHOPS

1/4 cup whole allspice

1/4 cup whole black peppercorns

2 tablespoons whole cumin seed

2 tablespoons brown sugar

1 tablespoon salt

18 lamb chops

1 tablespoon virgin olive oil

ROASTED RED PEPPER SAUCE

1/2 cup chopped yellow onion

1/4 cup chopped carrots

1/4 cup chopped shallots

1 tablespoon virgin olive oil

1 tablespoon chopped garlic

*1 cup chopped or pureed roasted
   red bell pepper*

1/2 cup white wine

1/2 cup chicken stock

1 cup heavy cream

Pinch of cayenne

*Dash of Cholula® sauce (found at
   most grocery stores)*

*Dash of salt and freshly ground
   black pepper*

GARNISH

Finely chopped parsley

Finely chopped chives

Grind the allspice, peppercorns, cumin and sugar in a coffee grinder. Add the salt. Rub the lamb chops with the olive oil, then coat with the allspice mixture. Set aside until ready to grill.

Sauté the chopped onions, carrots and shallots in the olive oil. Add the garlic and the chopped or pureed red bell pepper. Cook for 5 minutes. Add the wine and stock. Boil to reduce by half. Add the cream, cayenne and Cholula® sauce. Boil for 5 minutes or until thick. Remove from the pan and puree in a blender. Add a dash of salt and pepper.

Grill the lamb chops to medium rare.

To serve, place several tablespoons of the roasted red pepper sauce in the bottom of each plate. Top with two to three chops. Garnish with finely chopped parsley or chives.

LAMB CHOPS

Rib lamb chops or loin chops about 1-inch thick are the best type for grilling because they brown on the outside well while remaining pink and tender on the inside.

Allspice Crusted Lamb Chops with Roasted Red Pepper Sauce

LAMB CIPRIANI

> *"You can make a wonderfully healthy broth out of lamb bones and meat scraps. Brown bones and scraps in a 450° oven in a roasting pan with a quartered onion and carrot. Drain off fat and dump contents into a large saucepan. Add water to cover. Deglaze the roasting pan, and pour contents into the saucepan. Simmer, skim, and add two celery ribs, salt, an herb bouquet and a clove of garlic. Simmer three hours, strain and degrease."*
>
> — JULIA CHILD

STUFFED LAMB CHOPS

2 whole racks of lamb (7-8 ribs each)

3-4 tablespoons virgin olive oil

1 medium yellow onion, chopped

2 cloves garlic, crushed and finely chopped

2 medium ripe tomatoes, peeled and diced

1/2 pound crumbled feta cheese

1/2 cup chopped fresh mint leaves

Dash of salt and freshly ground black pepper

GRILLED VEGETABLES

2 large red onions

2 medium eggplants

1 cup virgin olive oil

1/4 cup fresh lime juice

1/4 cup chopped parsley

1/4 cup chopped fresh mint leaves

Dash of salt and freshly ground black pepper

SAUCE

2 cups lamb, beef or veal stock

1 tablespoon fresh lime juice

1/2 cup fruity white wine

1/4 cup honey

2 tablespoons beurre manie: 1 tablespoon soft butter mixed with 1 tablespoon all-purpose flour

1/4 cup chopped fresh mint leaves

Dash of salt and freshly ground black pepper

With a small, sharp knife, trim off all the fat surrounding the lamb racks. Since the lamb fat has a strong, unpleasant taste, remove as much as possible. Cut between each rib, separating the rack into 7 or 8 individual chops. Scrape all the fat and connective tissue off the ribs so they are lean and more delicate in appearance (you may also have a butcher do this). Set aside in the refrigerator while preparing the stuffing.

Heat the olive oil in a 10-inch frying pan and sauté the onions for 4 to 5 minutes or until tender. Add the garlic and diced tomatoes, and cook for 5 minutes. Remove the pan from the heat and stir in the crumbled feat cheese, mint leaves, salt and freshly ground black pepper to taste. Cut pockets in the side of each of the lamb chops and stuff with about 2 tablespoons of the stuffing. Press closed. You may tie the chops with butcher's twine if desired. The dish may be prepared a day in advance to this point and refrigerated until close to serving time.

Peel the red onions and slice about 3/8-inch thick into 8 perfect slices. Wash and trim the eggplants and slice (unpeeled) about 1/2-inch thick into 19 perfect slices. Combine the olive oil, lime juice, parsley, mint, salt and black pepper in a small bowl, and pour over just the onions. (The eggplant does not marinate because it would absorb the oil and become greasy tasting when grilled.) Refrigerate until ready to grill.

Grill the vegetables and lamb, placing the marinated onion slices first on a rack 2 to 3 inches from the hot coals. After 6 to 7 minutes, when they have dark grill marks on one side, turn the onions. Brush the stuffed lamb chops and eggplant slices with the marinade and place on the grill. Cook the eggplant for 6 to 8 minutes or until soft with dark grill marks. Cook the lamb for 3 to 4 minutes or until brown outside and pink inside. Remove from the grill and keep warm.

Place the stock, lime juice, white wine and honey in a saucepan. Boil for 10 minutes or until it has reduced and the alcohol has evaporated. Whisk in the beurre manie to thicken slightly. Remove from the heat and stir in the chopped mint leaves, salt and black pepper.

To serve, arrange the grilled eggplant and onions on a large warm platter. Arrange the lamb chops on top. Serve the sauce at the table.

PORTUGUESE LAMB CHOPS WITH PORT SAUCE

SERVES 8-10

LAMB

1/2 cup olive oil

2 tablespoons chopped garlic

1/4 cup chopped fresh oregano

1 tablespoon freshly ground
    black pepper

1/2 tablespoon salt

4 whole lamb racks, rib bones
    frenched (have your butcher do
    this for you)

CABERNET SAUCE

2 tablespoons olive oil

1 cup sliced shallots

2 tablespoons crushed fresh garlic

1/2 cup chopped dried prunes

2 bay leaves

2 sprigs of thyme

2 slices orange with rind

4 cups beef stock

2 cups cabernet wine

Salt and freshly ground pepper

1 tablespoon julienned lemon zest

PORT SAUCE

1/4 cup chopped shallots

1 tablespoon chopped fresh garlic

1/2 bay leaf

1/2 tablespoon olive oil

1/2 cup port wine

1 tablespoon French Dijon-style
    whole grain mustard

1/2 cup heavy cream

Dash of salt and black pepper

Juices from grilled meat (if any)

Prepare the lamb rub by combining all the ingredients to achieve a paste-like consistency. Spread over the lamb racks and allow the lamb to marinate for at least 2 hours and as long as overnight in the refrigerator.

Heat the olive oil in a large saucepan. Sauté the shallots, garlic, prunes, bay leaves and thyme for 3 to 4 minutes or until the shallots are tender and beginning to brown. Add the orange slices, beef stock and wine. Boil rapidly for 10 minutes to reduce and to develop the flavors. Season to taste with salt and black pepper.

Strain the sauce through a sieve, forcing the pulp through with a spoon. Return to low heat. Add the lemon zest and set aside until ready to serve. (Do not be afraid to make the entire recipe. This sauce is wonderful with any red meat and freezes well.)

Sauté the shallots, garlic and bay leaf in the olive oil until tender. Add the port and boil for 4 minutes. Add 2 cups of the cabernet sauce and bring to a boil again. Stir in the mustard and cream. Season with salt and pepper.

Grill the lamb racks to medium rare. Remove and let rest for 5 minutes. Carve into double-rib chops. If the ribs produce any juices while resting, add those to the port sauce for additional flavor. Serve the lamb chops with the port sauce.

LAMB

✳

Four types of lamb are available: baby lamb, which is from lambs six to ten weeks old, is very tender, delicate and hard to find. The meat from lambs five to six months old is light red, still young and tender, and delicious. The French favorite, pré-salé, is from lambs fed on the salt meadows near the coast of France. The oldest and strongest flavored lamb is mutton, from lambs over two years old. Most stores carry the younger lamb and the pré-salé.

CHIPOTLE BARBEQUE SAUCE

CHIPOTLE PUREE

10 chipotle chilies

Boiling water

1/4 cup chopped garlic

1/4 cup chopped shallots

1/2 teaspoon ground cumin

1/2 teaspoon freshly ground
     black pepper

Salt to taste

BARBEQUE SAUCE

1/2 cup diced red onion

1/4 cup diced shallots

2 tablespoons chopped garlic

1 bay leaf

2 sprigs of thyme

1/2 cup chipotle puree

1/2 cup brown sugar

1/2 cup white wine

1/2 cup orange juice

2 cups chicken stock

1/4 cup catsup

1/4 cup balsamic vinegar

1 cup canned roasted tomatoes,
     pureed in a food processor
     or blender

2 tablespoons Worcestershire sauce

1/4 teaspoon crushed
     red pepper flakes

1 tablespoon dry mustard

1/4 tablespoon freshly ground
     black pepper

Dash of salt to taste

1/2 tablespoon cornstarch

1/2 tablespoon water

CHIPOTLE CHILIES

❊

Chipotles are actually dried, smoked jalapeño peppers. They have a wrinkled, dark-brown skin and a smoky, sweet, almost chocolate flavor. They are generally added to stews and sauces. They can be found dried, pickled and canned in adobo sauce.

WORCESTERSHIRE SAUCE

❊

Worcestershire sauce, developed in 1835, originally purported to make "hair grow beautiful" as well as taste great on meat.

Place the chipotle chilies in a pot. Pour boiling water over to cover. Boil for 20 minutes. Add the garlic, shallots, cumin, pepper and salt. Remove from the pot and puree in a blender. Return the hot puree to a frying pan and pan sear for 8 to 10 minutes to reduce and develop the flavors. Set aside.

Sauté the onion in a large sauté pan for 5 minutes. Add the shallots and sauté for 3 minutes. Add the garlic, bay leaf, thyme, 1/2 cup of the chipotle puree and the sugar. Sauté for 5 minutes more. Add the remaining ingredients except the cornstarch and water. Boil, stirring, for 10 minutes. Combine the cornstarch and water in a small bowl and stir into the boiling sauce. Continue boiling until the sauce thickens slightly. Store in the refrigerator for up to 10 days.

Serve with pork, beef, buffalo, venison or chicken.

ADOBO SAUCE

YIELDS 3 CUPS

1 ounce cascabel chilies

1 ounce ancho chilies

2 tablespoons chopped garlic

1 tablespoon whole cloves

2 tablespoons whole black
  peppercorns

1 cinnamon stick

1/2 teaspoon ground cumin

1/2 tablespoon chopped fresh oregano

1/2 tablespoon chopped fresh thyme

1 tablespoon chicken base
  (found in the soup section of
  most grocery stores)

1/2 cup brown sugar

1 quart chicken stock

Salt

Remove the seeds from the chilies and cut into pieces. Sauté the chilies, garlic, cloves, peppercorns, cinnamon stick and cumin for 5 minutes or until the garlic is golden. Add the oregano, thyme, chicken base and brown sugar. Stir in the chicken stock.

Bring to a boil and simmer for 20 minutes. Puree in a blender. Season with salt and store in the refrigerator for up to 10 days.

Serve with veal, pork, buffalo or venison.

....

WEAR DISPOSABLE GLOVES WHEN WORKING WITH
CHILIES AND DO NOT TOUCH YOUR EYES!

....

ADOBO SAUCE

*

Adobo sauce is Mexican in origin. This dark-red sauce is used as a marinade as well as a serving sauce.

SOUTH AMERICAN BARBECUE SAUCE

YIELDS 4 CUPS

2 tablespoons olive oil

1/2 cup chopped onions

2 ancho chilies, chopped

1 pasilla chili, chopped

1 tablespoon chopped garlic

1 tablespoon ground cumin

1 1/2 tablespoons chopped thyme

1/2 bottle dark beer

2 tablespoons white vinegar

1/2 cup chicken stock

2 tablespoons soy sauce

1/4 cup lemon juice

2 tablespoons Dijon mustard

2 tablespoons Worcestershire sauce

1/4 cup molasses

1 cup catsup

1 cup chopped tomatoes

2 tablespoons chopped basil

2 tablespoons chopped cilantro

Salt and freshly ground black pepper

Heat the olive oil and sauté the onions and chiles for about 2 minutes or until soft. Add the garlic, cumin, thyme, beer, vinegar, stock, soy sauce, lemon juice, Dijon mustard, Worcestershire and molasses. Cook until reduced by half. Add the catsup, tomatoes, basil, cilantro, salt and pepper, and simmer for 1 hour. Taste and adjust the seasoning. Remove from the pan and puree in a food processor. Store in the refrigerator for up to 10 days.

Serve with meat, chicken or fish.

**BARBECUE
SAUCE**

*

Because barbecue sauces contain sugars and can burn easily, they are usually brushed on during the last 15 to 20 minutes of grilling and are used for dipping at the table.

SEAFOOD

Grilled Yellow Fin Tuna with
Blackberry Lime Zest Sauce

Recipe on page 153

TROUT PIÑÓN WITH
PAPAYA LIME BUTTER SAUCE

This recipe combines a delicately flavored fresh fish with the distinctive taste and crunchy texture of pine nuts from New Mexico and a sauce having the exotic flavor of papaya, the tang of fresh lime juice and the openness of garlic.

— *Mary Nell Reck*

SERVES 8

PAPAYA LIME BUTTER SAUCE

1/2 medium red onion, finely diced

2 tablespoons virgin olive oil

2 cloves garlic, finely diced

1 medium ripe papaya, peeled, seeded and finely diced

1/2 teaspoon granulated sugar

1/2 cup white wine

1/4 cup fresh lime juice

6 tablespoons unsalted butter, softened

Dash of salt and freshly ground white pepper

TROUT

8 trout fillets (6 ounces each)

1 1/2 cups all-purpose flour seasoned with salt and freshly ground pepper

Egg wash: 2 large eggs mixed with 1/2 cup water

1 cup coarsely ground pine nuts

Virgin olive oil and butter for sautéing

Sauté the onion in the olive oil. After about 4 minutes, add the garlic and the papaya. Cook for 1 to 2 minutes more or until soft. Sprinkle with the sugar. Add the wine and lime juice, and bring the mixture to a boil, scraping the bottom of the pan to free any of the sautéed mixture that may have adhered. Allow to reduce slightly, then beat in the soft butter, bit by bit, until you have a creamy sauce. Remove from the heat and add salt and white pepper. Keep the sauce warm while preparing the fish.

Check the trout fillets for bones, removing any with small pliers. Place the seasoned flour in a shallow bowl. In another shallow bowl, make an egg wash by beating the eggs and water together. Place the coarsely ground pine nuts in another shallow dish. Dip the trout fillets in the flour to completely coat. Shake off the excess and dip into the egg wash. Then coat with the coarsely ground pine nuts. The trout may be prepared to this point 2 to 3 hours in advance.

When ready to cook, heat a 12-inch frying pan over moderate heat. Add 1 to 2 teaspoons of mixed olive oil and butter, just enough to coat the bottom of the pan. Sauté a few fillets at a time until golden on each side. Shake the pan gently as each fillet is added to prevent the coating from sticking. Serve immediately with the papaya lime butter sauce.

GRILLED RED SNAPPER WITH
CRABMEAT AND PINK PEPPERCORN SAUCE

SERVES 8

SNAPPER

8 red snapper fillets (6 ounces each)

Virgin olive oil

*Dash of salt and freshly ground
white pepper*

CRABMEAT

2 tablespoons chopped shallots

2 tablespoons unsalted butter

1/2 pound fresh lump crabmeat

2 tablespoons chopped dill

*Salt and freshly ground white
pepper to taste*

PINK PEPPERCORN SAUCE

*1 cup lemon butter: 4 tablespoons
lemon juice and 1 cup
melted butter*

2 tablespoons pink peppercorns

1 tablespoon chopped fresh dill

An hour before serving, stir the pink peppercorns into the lemon butter. Set aside and keep warm.

Check the snapper fillets for bones. Lightly coat with olive oil and season to taste with a sprinkling of salt and white pepper. Place on the grill for about 2 to 3 minutes or until well marked. Set aside and keep warm.

Sauté the shallots in hot butter in a 10-inch frying pan. Add the crabmeat and heat through. Add the dill, salt and white pepper.

To serve, place a mound of the sautéed crabmeat on top of each of the grilled snapper fillets. Just before spooning the pink peppercorn sauce over the crabmeat, stir in the chopped dill. Serve immediately.

COURT BOUILLON

This bouillon is perfect for poaching fish or blanching vegetables.

YIELDS 3 QUARTS

2 leek tops

2 carrots

1 yellow onion

3 ribs celery with leaves

6 bay leaves

4 sprigs of thyme

3 sprigs of parsley

1 tablespoon white peppercorns

2 tablespoons salt

6 lemon slices

3 quarts water

Medium chop the leeks, carrots, onion and celery. Place in a stockpot with the remaining ingredients. Bring to a rapid boil. Cover and boil for 20 minutes to develop the flavors. Taste and adjust the saltiness. Strain.

SAUTÉED CRABMEAT WITH
FRESH CHIVES AND BEURRE BLANC

SERVES 8

CRABMEAT

1/2 cup chopped shallots

3 tablespoons unsalted butter

1/2 pound mushrooms, sliced

2 pounds fresh lump crabmeat

Salt and freshly ground white pepper

3 tablespoons chopped chives

2 tablespoons cognac

BEURRE BLANC SAUCE

1 tablespoon white wine

1/4 cup white wine vinegar

3/4 teaspoon salt

1/4 teaspoon freshly ground
    white pepper

1 1/2 tablespoons minced shallots

2 cups (4 sticks) butter, chilled and
    cut into 1-inch pieces

Sauté the shallots in the butter in a 12-inch frying pan for 3 to 4 minutes or until soft. Add the mushrooms and cook until barely moist. Add the crabmeat and season with salt and white pepper. Toss the pan instead of stirring to avoid breaking up the delicate pieces of crabmeat. Add the chives and flame with the cognac. Set aside.

Combine the wine, vinegar, salt, pepper and shallots in a small saucepan. Bring to a boil and reduce until approximately 2 tablespoons of liquid remain. Over very low heat, whisk in the butter, a piece or two at a time, using the chilled butter to keep the sauce between 100 and 130 degrees. If the sauce gets any warmer, it will separate. Once all the butter is incorporated, remove from the heat and strain. Hold the sauce in a water bath at 100 to 130 degrees.

To serve, transfer the crabmeat mixture to 8 warm plates and surround with a ribbon of sauce. Serve immediately.

CRAB MEAT TERMINOLOGY

✳

"Lump crabmeat" refers to the largest pieces of meat, adjacent to the back fin. "Back fin" refers to the white body meat, including both lump crabmeat and large flakes—good for crab cakes. "Claw meat" is brownish and best for soups and dips.

SAUTÉED CRABMEAT
WITH TOMATILLO SAUCE

SERVES 8

PASTRY

1/2 pound sheet of puff pastry

1 large egg

1 tablespoon water

TOMATILLO SAUCE

8 tomatillos

1 fresh jalapeño pepper, split

1 1/2 cups chicken stock

Dash of cumin

Salt and freshly ground white pepper

1 cup chopped cilantro

CRABMEAT

1/2 cup chopped shallots

*4 tablespoons (1/2 stick)
    unsalted butter*

1 pound fresh lump crabmeat

Salt and freshly ground white pepper

4 tablespoons tequila liquor

2 tablespoons chopped chives

GARNISH

Cilantro sprigs

Preheat the oven to 400 degrees. Roll out the sheet of puff pastry on a lightly floured surface to a thickness of about 3/16-inch. Cut the dough into 2 1/2-inch squares. Place on a baking sheet lined with parchment paper. Beat the egg and water together, and lightly brush on the surface of each pastry square. Bake for 8 to 10 minutes or until puffed and golden. Set aside.

Remove the outer leaves from the tomatillos. Rinse. Place in a saucepan with the split jalapeño. Add the chicken stock, cumin, salt and white pepper. Boil gently for 6 to 8 minutes or until the tomatillos are tender.

Puree the contents of the pan along with half the cilantro and pass through a food mill to remove the seeds. Finely chop the remaining cilantro and stir into the sauce. Taste and adjust the seasoning. Set aside.

Just before serving, sauté the shallots in the butter until soft. Add the crabmeat. Season with salt and white pepper. When the crabmeat is heated through, add the tequila and ignite. When the flames die, toss in the chopped chives.

To serve, place portions of the sauce on 8 plates. Top with a hot pastry square and spoon the hot crabmeat over the pastry. Some of the crabmeat will fall down into the sauce. Garnish with a sprig of fresh cilantro. Serve immediately.

TEQUILA

✳

Contrary to popular belief, tequila is not made from cactus but from the blue agave, a member of the lily family. When alcohol is added and flamed near the end of preparation, about 75 percent of the alcohol is retained.

CRABMEAT REMICK

SERVES 8

REMICK SAUCE

1 teaspoon dry mustard

1/2 cup dry white wine

2 cups mayonnaise

5 tablespoons chili sauce

1 teaspoon Tabasco® sauce

1 tablespoon Worcestershire sauce

CRABMEAT

4 tablespoons chopped shallots

1/2 cup (1 stick) butter

2 pounds fresh lump crabmeat

Salt and freshly ground white pepper

1 cup white wine

TOPPING

3 tablespoons chopped, cooked bacon

Dissolve the dry mustard in the white wine; set aside. In a mixing bowl, combine the mayonnaise, chili sauce, Tabasco® and Worcestershire. Whisk together until smooth. Slowly add the wine-mustard mixture, whisking constantly. Set aside.

Sauté the shallots for 30 seconds in the butter. Add the crabmeat, season with salt and white pepper to taste, and heat through. Add the wine and quickly evaporate.

To serve, transfer the crabmeat mixture to an au gratin dish. Top with 2 cups of Remick sauce and sprinkle with the bacon. Place under the broiler for 2 minutes.

Alternatively, divide the mixture between 8 scallop shells or individual ramekins, top with the sauce and bacon, and broil.

FAUX CRAB

✳

The flaky, red-edged "faux crab" commonly found in less expensive seafood salads and California rolls is most likely Alaska pollock, also called walleye pollock, snow cod or whiting.

TABASCO® SAUCE

✳

The U.S. Territory of Guam is the world's largest per capita consumer of Tabasco® sauce, according to the McIlhenny Company, which produces the fiery drops, made from capsicum peppers, vinegar and salt.

STUFFED CRAB

SERVES 8

2 cups chopped onions

1 cup chopped celery with leaves

6 tablespoons clarified butter

2 cloves garlic, crushed and chopped

1 cup dry white wine

2 cups freshly grated
   Parmesan cheese

1 cup 1/2-inch Monterey Jack
   cheese cubes

1/2 cup chopped fresh sage or 2
   teaspoons dried

1/4 cup chopped parsley

1-2 jalapeño peppers, seeded,
   deveined and finely chopped

1 pound fresh lump crabmeat

Dash of salt and freshly ground
   white pepper

TOPPING

Melted butter

Freshly grated Parmesan cheese

Preheat the oven to 375 degrees.

Sauté the onions and celery in the butter until completely soft. Add the garlic and wine. Boil for 1 minute to evaporate the alcohol. Remove the pan from the heat and stir in the remaining ingredients. Taste and adjust the seasoning.

Stuff the mixture into 8 buttered crab shells or scallop shells. Sprinkle with additional grated Parmesan cheese and drizzle with melted butter. Place in the preheated oven and bake for 10 to 12 minutes or until golden and heated through. Serve immediately.

PADRE ISLAND SHRIMP

SHRIMP

24 extra large shrimp (12 or less to the pound)

2 tablespoons unsalted butter

1 medium yellow onion, chopped

2 medium jalapeño peppers, seeded and deveined

8 ounces fresh crabmeat

2 tablespoons gold tequila liquor

1/4 cup chopped cilantro

Salt and freshly ground white pepper to taste

8 ounces Monterey Jack cheese, cut into 1/4-inch cubes

2 cups fresh bread crumbs

1/2 to 3/4 cup whipping cream

4 tablespoons (1/2 stick) unsalted butter, melted

LEMON BUTTER SAUCE

1 1/2 cups fish stock (found at most gourmet food markets) or chicken stock

3 tablespoons cornstarch

1/2 cup lemon juice

1 cup (2 sticks) butter, cut into 1-inch pieces

Dash of salt and freshly ground white pepper

Dash of Worcestershire sauce

Dash of Tabasco® sauce

GARNISH

Chopped dill

Peel the shrimp, leaving on the last section of shell and tail. Remove the vein if it is visibly dark by cutting along the backside. Turn the shrimp over and cut a deep incision along the underside. Flatten the shrimp on a tray. Refrigerate while preparing the stuffing.

Preheat the oven to 400 degrees. Heat a 10-inch frying pan over moderately high heat. Add the butter and sauté the onions until soft, stirring so they do not overbrown. Add the jalapeños. Stir in the crabmeat. Heat through, shaking the pan. Add the tequila and quickly ignite to burn off the alcohol. When the flames die, remove from the heat. Add the cilantro. Season with salt and white pepper.

Stir in the cheese and bread crumbs. Add enough cream to barely hold the mixture together in a mass when squeezed in the palm of your hand. Taste and adjust the seasoning.

Place a small, compressed mound of the stuffing mixture in each shrimp. Drizzle lightly with the melted butter and bake in the preheated oven for 10 to 12 minutes or until the shrimp are opaque and the stuffing is golden.

While the shrimp are cooking, combine the cold stock and cornstarch in a saucepan with a whisk. Bring to a boil over a high flame. Stir in the lemon juice and return to a boil. While boiling, add half the butter, piece by piece, while beating with a whisk.

Remove from the heat and whisk in the remaining butter until thick and creamy. Add the salt, pepper, Worcestershire and Tabasco® to taste. Do not keep too warm or the sauce will break down—hold in the pan off the heat, warming very gently just before using.

Serve the shrimp immediately from the oven. Top with 4 tablespoons of lemon butter sauce and a sprinkling of chopped fresh dill.

SHRIMP

✳

Shrimp has often been called the favorite shell-fish in the United States. Indeed it is the most valuable commercial crustacean to come from the Texas Gulf Coast waters. Fresh shrimp are highly perishable but freeze beautifully. Place newly purchased shrimp in a heavy duty plastic storage bag and cover the shrimp with water. Close the bag securely, pushing out as much air as possible before closing and put in the freezer. When thawed, shrimp frozen in this manner will taste as good as fresh shrimp.

SHRIMP AND CRABMEAT IMPERIAL

COGNAC

✳

"All cognacs are brandies, but not all brandies are cognacs". Cognac is a brandy produced in the region of Cognac, France. Grapes grown in this region are picked and pressed to extract the juice. The juice is fermented to make wine that is weak in alcohol (6 to 8% alc./vol.) and very acidic. The wine is then distilled twice to become young cognac. The young cognac is aged in oak casks, for a period of time, before being bottled and sold.

There are 6 sub-regions in cognac: Bois Ordinaire, Bon Bois, Fins Bois, Borderies, Petite Champagne and Grande Champagne. (The latter two should not be confused with "Champagne" the french sparkling wine produced in the region of Champagne in France.)

On certain bottles of cognac the words "Fine Champagne" may appear. It means that this product is a blend of Grande Champagne cognac and Petite Champagne cognac. Fine Champagne cognac must contain at least 50% Grande Champagne cognac.

Cognac is light to medium amber (never judge a cognac by its color). Best enjoyed straight up at room temperature in a cognac snifter, in mixed drinks,tall drinks and cocktails. Blends well with fruit juices, dairy products, carbonated drinks, coffee and most liqueurs.

SHRIMP

48 large shrimp (21 or 25 to the pound), peeled and with tail removed

6 large tomatoes, cut into 3/8-inch thick slices

Virgin olive oil

Dash of salt and freshly ground white pepper

CRABMEAT

4 tablespoons chopped shallots

3 tablespoons butter

1 pound fresh large lump crabmeat

2 tablespoons cognac

Salt and freshly ground white pepper to taste

LEMON BUTTER SAUCE

(See page 141)

GARNISH

Chopped chives

Coat the shrimp and tomato slices with olive oil. Place over hot coals and grill until marked and the shrimp are opaque. Sprinkle lightly with salt and white pepper. Meanwhile, sauté the shallots in the butter in a 10-inch frying pan until tender. Add the crabmeat and gently toss in the pan until heated through. Flame with the cognac. Season to taste with salt and white pepper. Set aside.

Prepare the lemon butter sauce according to the recipe on page 141. Do not keep too warm or the sauce will break down. To hold it for a couple of hours, put it in a thermos.

To serve, arrange 3 to 4 slices of grilled tomatoes in an overlapping row on 8 warm plates. Top with 6 shrimp per person. Top the shrimp with a mound of sautéed crabmeat. Spoon the lemon butter sauce over the crabmeat and garnish with a sprinkling of fresh chives. Serve immediately.

PECAN SHRIMP

SERVES 6

SHRIMP

1 1/2 cups all-purpose flour

12 ounces beer

1/2 teaspoon salt

24 extra large shrimp, peeled and
    butterflied with tail on

All-purpose flour seasoned with salt
    and freshly ground white pepper

3/4 cup chopped pecans

4 cups peanut or vegetable oil

SAUCE

2 cups water

1/4 cup catsup

1/2 cup red wine vinegar

1/2 cup brown sugar

1/2 teaspoon cayenne

1 tablespoon grated fresh ginger

Salt and freshly ground white
    pepper to taste

3 tablespoons cornstarch mixed
    with 1/4 cup water

Combine the flour, beer and salt. Let the batter stand at least
an hour.

Dip the shrimp in the seasoned flour to completely coat. Dip
into the batter and lay out on paper-lined sheet pans with the
cut side down. Sprinkle with the chopped pecans. Freeze the
trays until time to cook.

In a saucepan, combine all the ingredients for the sauce except
the cornstarch-water mixture. Bring to a boil. Taste and adjust the
seasoning. Slowly add the cornstarch and water until the mixture
thickens enough to coat a spoon. Set aside and keep warm.

Heat the peanut or vegetable oil to 360 degrees. Fry the shrimp
for 4 to 5 minutes or until the coating is golden brown. Do not
overcook the shrimp. Serve with the sweet and sour sauce.

GINGER

❋

*The flavor of fresh ginger
on a final dish depends
on when it is added.
Added early in the cook-
ing, it will confer a
subtler flavor. Added
near the end, it will
deliver more pungency.*

SNAPPER ALMONDINE

SERVES 6

SNAPPER

6 red snapper fillets (6 ounces each)

1 cup all-purpose flour seasoned with
    salt and freshly ground pepper

Egg wash: 1 egg combined with 1/4
    cup water

1 cup sliced raw almonds

1/2 cup (1 stick) clarified butter

GARNISH

Lemon butter sauce (see the recipe
    on page 141)

Chopped chives

Lemon halves

Preheat the oven to 350 degrees.

Coat the snapper fillets with the seasoned flour. Pat off the
excess. Dip into the egg wash, then into the almonds to coat
one side only. Be sure to coat the side of the flesh that was next
to the bones.

In an ovenproof pan, sauté the almond-coated side of the snapper fillets in the clarified butter. When the almonds are golden,
turn the snapper and transfer to the oven for a few minutes
until opaque and tender. Transfer each snapper fillet to a warm
dinner plate.

Top with a ribbon of lemon butter sauce and a sprinkling of
chives. Garnish with a wrapped lemon half. Serve with rice and
two vegetables.

RED SNAPPER

❋

*Recent demand for red
snapper has been so high
that many imposters are
now turning up on the
market. "Pacific red
snapper" is really red
rockfish, for example.
Purchase red snapper
from a knowledgeable
fishmonger.*

LOBSTER WITH CRABMEAT STUFFING

LOBSTER

Stockpot of salted water

4 live Maine lobsters (1 1/2 pounds each)

CRABMEAT STUFFING

1/2 cup diced red onions

1 jalapeño, seeded and diced

1/2 cup each diced red, green and yellow bell peppers

2 tablespoons olive oil

1/2 teaspoon chopped, crushed garlic

1/4 cup chopped cilantro

1/2 cup bread crumbs

1/4 cup grated Parmesan cheese

1/4 cup grated Monterey Jack cheese

1/3 cup heavy cream

Salt and freshly ground white pepper to taste

1 pound fresh lump crabmeat

Bread crumbs

Melted butter or olive oil

GARNISH

1 tablespoon chopped fresh chives (optional)

"A woman should never be seen eating or drinking, unless it be lobster, salad and champagne. The only true feminine and becoming viands."

— LORD BYRON
(1788-1824)

Prepare a large bowl of ice water. Bring the salted water to a boil. Drop the live lobsters into the rapidly boiling water. Cook for about 4 minutes or until bright red in color. Remove from the pot and plunge immediately into the ice water. The lobster will not be completely cooked.

When the lobster is cool enough to handle, remove the claws and split the bodies down the center using kitchen scissors. Remove the meat from the tail and the claws. For the tail, cut along the backside; for the claws, crack them open. Keep the end of the tail, the tail shell and the head for presentation purposes.

Sauté the onions, jalapeño and bell peppers in hot olive oil in a skillet until soft. Add the garlic and cook another minute. Remove from the heat and stir in the cilantro, bread crumbs, cheeses, cream, salt and white pepper. Toss together lightly. Taste and adjust the seasoning. Add additional cream if necessary to barely hold the mixture together.

Very gently stir in the crabmeat, being careful not to break the pieces. Shape 2- to 3-ounce portions in your hand and gently press into the split meat of the lobster tail.

Arrange the stuffed lobster tails in a single layer on a baking sheet. Sprinkle with more bread crumbs and drizzle lightly with melted butter or olive oil.

Place under a preheated broiler for about 3 minutes or until the stuffing is brown and the lobster is opaque. Be careful-it is important to not overcook the lobster.

Place a stuffed lobster tail on each plate and arrange the meat removed from the claws on each side of the stuffed tail where they would be on the live lobster. Place the end of the lobster tail and the head in their proper places. Garnish with chopped fresh chives if desired.

Alternatively, you may place the saved tail shell carefully around and over the cooked lobster tail as shown in the photograph.

. . . .

SERVE WITH SAFFRON BEURRE BLANC (SEE THE RECIPE ON PAGE 152) OR LEMON BUTTER SAUCE (SEE THE RECIPE ON PAGE 141).

. . . .

BLACKENED REDFISH

SERVES 6

BLACKENED HERB MIXTURE

1/4 cup paprika

1 tablespoon cayenne

1 cup dried basil leaves

1 cup dried oregano leaves

1/2 cup dried thyme leaves

2 tablespoons salt

*1/2 tablespoon freshly ground
    white pepper*

REDFISH

6-7-ounce redfish or red snapper fillet

3/4 cup clarified butter

GARNISH

Chopped fresh dill

Lemon wedges

Parsley sprigs

Combine the ingredients for the blackened herb mixture. Store in a plastic container at room temperature to use as needed.

Dip the fish in the herb mixture to coat both sides. Quickly pan fry in the clarified butter in a very hot pan.

Place on a warm plate. Sprinkle with chopped fresh dill. Garnish with lemon wedges and parsley sprigs. Serve with rice and two vegetables.

FAVORITE FRIED CATFISH

SERVES 6

*2 cups all-purpose flour seasoned
    with salt and freshly ground
    white pepper*

1 cup buttermilk

2 cups cornmeal

1/4 cup white sesame seeds

1/2 teaspoon paprika

Dash of cayenne

Salt and white pepper

2 1/2 pounds catfish fillets

Vegetable oil for deep frying

GARNISH

Pico de gallo (see page 17)

Cocktail sauce (see page 147)

Tartar sauce (see page 147)

Lemon wedges

Place the seasoned flour in a shallow dish. Place the buttermilk in another shallow dish. Place the cornmeal in a third shallow container. Add the sesame seeds, paprika and cayenne to the cornmeal. Season to taste with salt and white pepper.

Check the catfish fillets for bones. Trim to six 8-ounce portions. Set aside in the refrigerator.

When ready to serve, heat the vegetable oil to 360 degrees in a large, deep pan. Dredge the catfish, one fillet at a time, in the flour. Shake off the excess. Dip into the buttermilk, then into the cornmeal mixture to form a uniform coat. Gently lower the breaded fillet into the hot oil. Cook for 2 to 3 minutes or until golden brown. Remove, drain and serve immediately.

Serve with lemon wedges, pico de gallo, cocktail sauce and tartar sauce.

SEAFOOD COCKTAIL SAUCE

2 3/4 cups chili sauce

3/4 cup horseradish sauce

3 1/2 tablespoons lemon juice

2 1/2 teaspoons Worcestershire sauce

1/4 teaspoon Tabasco® sauce or
   to taste

Combine the ingredients. Store in a covered container in the refrigerator. Serve with fried or cold boiled seafood.

TARTAR SAUCE

2 cups mayonnaise

1/2 cup finely chopped red onions

1/2 cup dill pickle relish, drained

1/4 cup capers

1/4 cup finely chopped parsley

2 tablespoons lemon juice

1/2 teaspoon salt

1/8 teaspoon white pepper

Combine all the ingredients. Place in a covered container and refrigerate.

HORSERADISH

✻

Horseradish is related to the mustard family, hence its biting flavor and aroma. At one time, it was known as "German mustard."

SOLE MONTEREY
WITH CRABMEAT STUFFING

SERVES 8

8 sole fillets (6 ounces each)

1 pound fresh lump crabmeat

1/2 cup chopped fresh basil

1 1/4 cups diced tomatoes

1 1/2 cups grated Monterey
    Jack cheese

Dash of salt and freshly ground
    white pepper

1/2 cup dry white wine

1/2 cup (1 stick) unsalted
    butter, melted

1/2 cup lemon butter sauce
    (see the recipe on page 141)

Cut the sole fillets in half crosswise. Arrange 8 of the fillets on a baking sheet in a single layer. Cut the remaining 8 fillets in half lengthwise and set aside.

Make a mound of crabmeat on each of the 8 fillets on the baking sheet. Top with a sprinkling of fresh basil, a mound of diced tomatoes, the Monterey Jack cheese, and salt and white pepper to taste. Place the two small fillet strips on top of the crabmeat mixture, leaving it exposed in the center. Sprinkle the fish with the white wine and drizzle with the melted butter.

The dish may be prepared in advance to this point and refrigerated several hours. When ready to serve, preheat the oven to 375 degrees. Place the fish in the preheated oven and bake for 10 to 12 minutes or until the sole is opaque and firm to the touch, and the cheese is melted. Transfer to a warm plate and serve immediately with the lemon butter sauce.

SOLE

✳

Unlike any other fish except skate, sole is said to improve with a little age—a day or two— after catching. Cynics say that this is why it is so popular with restaurateurs. Be that as it may, it is the most delectable of the flatfish.

SOLE PARMESAN

SERVES 6

6 lemon sole fillets (6 ounces each)

1 1/2 cups seasoned all-purpose flour

Egg wash: 2 large eggs mixed
    with water

1 1/2 cups finely grated Parmesan
    cheese (parmigiana reggiana)

3/4 pound (3 sticks) clarified butter

1/2 cup lemon butter sauce
    (see the recipe on page 141)

GARNISH

Chopped fresh chives

Lemon wedges

Parsley sprigs

Coat both sides of the sole with the seasoned flour. Pat off the excess. Dip into the egg wash, then into the finely grated Parmesan cheese to completely coat. Sauté over a moderate flame in the clarified butter. This must be done in a non-stick pan.

When golden on both sides, place on a warm plate. Drizzle with a ribbon of lemon butter sauce and a sprinkling of fresh chives. Garnish with lemon wedges and a parsley sprig.

Serve with rice and two vegetables.

SOLE WITH SCALLOPS

SERVES 8

CREAM SAUCE

2 tablespoons butter

2 tablespoons all-purpose flour

1 1/4 cups milk, heated

Salt and freshly ground white
pepper to taste

PESTO SAUCE

3 cloves garlic, crushed and chopped

1/4 teaspoon salt

1/2 teaspoon freshly ground
black pepper

2 cups firmly packed basil leaves

1/2 cup parsley

1/3 cup raw pine nuts

1/2 cup freshly grated
Parmesan cheese

1/4 cup virgin olive oil or more
if needed

SOLE

8 sole fillets (6 ounces each)

1/2 cup all-purpose flour seasoned
with salt and freshly ground pepper

Egg wash: 1 egg beaten with 4
tablespoons water

1/2 cup clarified butter

8 ounces mushrooms, sliced

1/2 cup (1 stick) butter, softened
and mixed with 1 teaspoon each
fresh basil, oregano and thyme

1 pound bay scallops

Salt and freshly ground pepper

GARNISH

Chopped parsley

Melt the butter in a saucepan and add the flour. Mix until bubbly and the flour cooks a bit. Do not brown. Add the heated milk all at once, stirring with a whisk. Cook until thickened and bubbly. Season to taste with salt and white pepper. Set aside.

Place the garlic, salt, pepper, basil leaves, parsley, pine nuts and Parmesan cheese in the bowl of a food processor. Process until the mixture is thoroughly ground. Gradually add the olive oil while continuing to process. Taste and adjust the seasoning. The pesto may be tightly covered and refrigerated for 2 weeks.

When ready to serve, dip the sole fillets into the seasoned flour, then the egg wash. Sauté in the clarified butter in a hot pan. Set aside. In another pan sauté the mushrooms in the herb butter. Add the scallops and sauté for 1 minute more. Add 1 cup of the cream sauce and 1/2 cup of the pesto sauce. Toss and season with salt and pepper.

Place each sautéed fillet of sole on a warm plate and top with the scallop mixture. Sprinkle with chopped parsley.

SCALLOPS

✽

The edible portion of the scallop, a mollusk with two beautifully scalloped shells, is the muscle that opens and closes the two shells. It is also called the "nut."

GRILLED SALMON WITH LIME CAPER SAUCE

SERVES 8

GRILLED SALMON

8 salmon fillets (7 ounces each)

Olive oil

Dash of salt and freshly ground white pepper

LIME CAPER SAUCE

2 cups lemon butter sauce (see the recipe on page 141)

Zest of 2 limes, finely chopped

2 tablespoons capers

GARNISH

Chopped dill

Prepare the lemon butter sauce. (The sauce may be made with lime juice instead of lemon juice.) Add the lime zest and capers. Set aside.

Coat the salmon with olive oil. Sprinkle with salt and white pepper to taste. Grill until well-marked on both sides and tender to the touch.

Place on a warm plate. Cover with the lime caper sauce. Sprinkle with chopped dill.

(see the recipe on page 141)

STEAMED MUSSELS PROVENÇAL

SERVES 8-10

MUSSELS

5 pounds fresh mussels

1 quart white wine

1/2 cup chopped shallots

4 cloves garlic, crushed and chopped

6 bay leaves

4 sprigs of thyme

4 sprigs of oregano

Salt and freshly ground white peppercorns

SAUCE

1 cup heavy cream

2 cups finely diced Roma tomatoes

1 cup basil leaves

GARNISH

1/4 cup chopped chives

Scrub the mussels with a wire brush and remove the beards. Keep chilled until ready to steam.

Combine the remaining ingredients in a large pot. Boil for 5 minutes to develop the flavors. Add the mussels to the boiling liquid. Cover and steam for 3 to 4 minutes or until they open. Do not overcook or they will become rubbery.

Remove the mussels from the pan and transfer to warm bowls. Add the cream to the steaming broth and bring to a boil. Stir in the tomatoes and basil leaves. Taste and adjust the seasoning as needed. Ladle the sauce over the mussels. Sprinkle with the chopped chives and serve immediately with crusty bread.

Grilled Salmon with Lime Caper Sauce

POACHED ATLANTIC SALMON WITH JULIENNED VEGETABLES AND SAFFRON BEURRE BLANC

SERVES ABOUT 8-10

BELL PEPPERS

✳

Red bell peppers are sweet, juicy, colorful and surprisingly nutritious. By weight, red peppers are said to have three times as much Vitamin C as citrus fruit. Red bell peppers also are a good source of beta-carotene, fiber and Vitamin B6.

The bell pepper is said to be the most popular sweet pepper in the United States and accounts for more than 60 percent of the domestic pepper crop. Bell peppers have little "bite" since they contain a gene that eliminates capsaicin. Instead they have a mild tang and a crunchy texture that makes them suitable for eating raw; they are also good to stuff whole because of their shape, size and firmness. Sweet bell-shaped peppers are green, red, yellow, orange or purple, depending on the variety and the ripeness stage. The mature green pepper is fully developed, but not ripe, turning red and becoming sweeter as it ripens on the vine.

SALMON

3 quarts court bouillon (see the recipe on page 137)

1 whole salmon (4-5 pounds)

Salt and freshly ground white pepper to taste

2 tablespoons chopped, crushed garlic

1/2 bottle champagne

JULIENNED VEGETABLES

1/2 cup julienned red bell peppers

1/2 cup julienned zucchini

1/4 cup julienned leeks, green part

1/4 cup julienned leeks, white part

1/4 cup julienned carrots

SAFFRON BEURRE BLANC

1 cup chopped shallots

1 tablespoon olive oil

1 cup white wine

1/2 cup rice wine vinegar

1 tablespoon all-purpose flour

Dash of salt and freshly ground white pepper

2 cups heavy cream

1 cup (2 sticks) unsalted butter, cut into pieces

Generous pinch of saffron

GARNISH

1/4 cup fresh tarragon leaves

Prepare the court bouillon.

Fillet the salmon. Cut into 5-ounce portions or leave whole, depending on the desired presentation. Rub with salt, pepper and garlic. Place the salmon in a single layer in a shallow baking dish. Cover and refrigerate until close to serving time.

Preheat the oven to 350 degrees. Bring the court bouillon to a boil. Add the champagne and boil again. Carefully ladle enough boiling liquid over the salmon to cover and place in the preheated oven. Poach in the oven for 5 to 8 minutes, depending on the thickness of the fish, or until medium firm to the touch. Remove from the oven. Leave in the warm liquid until ready to serve.

Place the julienned vegetables in a sieve and plunge into the boiling court bouillon for 20 seconds. Remove from the liquid, shake and reserve.

Sauté the shallots in the olive oil for 3 minutes or until half soft. Add the wine, vinegar, flour, salt and white pepper. Whisk together. Bring to a boil, then reduce to a simmer and cook gently for 20 minutes to reduce and develop the flavors. Strain through a sieve, pressing firmly with the back of a spoon.

Return the reduction to the saucepan and stir in the cream. Boil for about 2 minutes or until thick. Whisk in the butter, bit by bit. Stir in the saffron. Taste and adjust the seasoning.

To serve, ladle 3 tablespoons of the sauce on each warm plate. Place the poached salmon portion on the sauce. Place a mound of the julienned vegetables on the salmon and sprinkle the vegetables and the sauce with the fresh tarragon leaves.

GRILLED YELLOW FIN TUNA
WITH BLACKBERRY LIME ZEST SAUCE

SERVES 8

TUNA

3 1/2 pounds center-cut
  yellow fin tuna

Salt and freshly ground white pepper

2 tablespoons chopped tarragon

2 tablespoons chopped dill

Virgin olive oil

SAUCE

1 cup fish fumet or chicken stock

1/2 cup white wine

1/4 cup lime juice

1 tablespoon cornstarch

2 tablespoons cassis liqueur

2 tablespoons granulated sugar

Dash of salt and freshly ground
  white pepper

1/2 jalapeño pepper, seeded and
  finely chopped

TOPPING

4 tablespoons julienned lime zest

2 tablespoons granulated sugar

1/4 cup green crème de menthe

1 cup fresh blackberries

Trim and discard the skin from the tuna. Remove any silver skin. Cut into 1-inch thick steaks about 5 ounces each. You may need to cut the loin lengthwise if it is large.

Rub both sides of the tuna steaks with seasonings, herbs and oil. Cover and refrigerate until close to serving time, then grill the tuna steaks to medium rare.

Place the fumet and wine in a small saucepan. Bring to a boil. Combine the lime juice and cornstarch until dissolved. Gradually add to the boiling liquid, stirring. Stir in the cassis and sugar. Season with salt, white pepper and jalapeño. Set aside.

Place the julienned lime zest in a small pan with the sugar and crème de menthe. Simmer gently for about 5 minutes or until tender. Set aside in the liquid.

To serve, place the fish on a warm platter. Place the fresh blackberries on top. Spoon the sauce over the berries. Top with a drizzle of julienne lime zest and its liquid.

FISH FUMET

✳

A fish fumet is a concentrated fish stock, used for enriching and giving body to sauces that accompany fish dishes. Fish stocks have a very different character from classical stocks like beef, chicken, or veal. Rather than a big, robust, long-simmered flavor, a fish fumet has a delicate essence that will enhance and support the flavor of the lighter fish dish, either for poaching or for a sauce.

The key to a good fumet is to quickly extract the flavor of the soft and porous whitefish bones and the shrimp and lobster shells. Fish stock is made from the bones and trimmings of a variety of lean fish such as snapper, halibut, sole, cod or grouper (you can use the heads for more flavor, but make sure the gills and scales are removed). Avoid salmon or trout bones. Fresh fish is always better, but you can still get good results with frozen fish bones, as long as the fish was very fresh, clean and properly packed when frozen. The finished stock should be strained very carefully to be sure that not a single bone, particle of shell or scale gets through.

**PEPPERCORN
SHELFLIFE**

✳

Whole peppercorns will last indefinitely. Ground pepper remains fresh about 3 months. It can be frozen, but that will intensify the flavor.

ROASTED CHERRY TOMATOES

Recipe on page 159

ACCOMPANIMENTS

BLACK BEANS

✳

Black beans are one of
hundreds of varieties of
the common bean. Black
beans are dried after
harvesting (originally the
drying of beans was a
way to ensure a winter
food supply, as beans can
be successfully dried and
stored for up to a year).
Black beans are small,
oval and jet black. They
have cream-colored flesh,
a mild, sweet, earthy
taste, and a soft texture.

LEGUMES

✳

The common bean is a
member of the legume
family which also
includes peanuts, lentils,
and peas. Black beans
are just one of hundreds
of varieties of the
common bean. They are
black in color and small.
Black beans are
commonly sold dried
and can be successfully
stored for a year.

**HARICOTS
VERTS**

✳

French green beans (hari-
cot vert) are smaller than
common green beans and
have a soft velvety skin.
When cooked crisp-
tender, they are bright
green and make a deli-
cious and colorful addi-
tion to the plate.

BLACK BEANS

BEANS

1 pound dried black beans, washed

2 tablespoons salt

1 large yellow onion, quartered

4 bay leaves

2 teaspoons thyme leaves

1/2 teaspoon ground cumin

1 teaspoon freshly ground
   black pepper

OTHER INGREDIENTS

3 tablespoons olive oil

2 cups finely diced carrots

2 cups finely diced yellow onions

2 cups finely diced celery with leaves

2 jalapeño peppers, seeded
   and chopped

Salt and freshly ground black pepper

Place the beans in a large soup pot. Cover with water. Add the salt, onion, bay leaves, thyme, cumin and black pepper. Bring to a boil and simmer gently for about 1 1/2 hours or until tender. Add additional water as needed to keep the beans covered.

Meanwhile heat the olive oil in a large frying pan and sauté the carrots, onions, celery and jalapeños. When bright in color and half tender, remove from the heat.

Remove and discard the onions and bay leaves from the beans when they are almost tender. Stir the sautéed vegetables into the pot of beans for the last 15 minutes of cooking. Remove from the heat.

Season with salt and freshly ground black pepper.

HARICOTS VERTS

2 pounds tiny French green beans

Olive oil or melted butter, optional

Salt

Prepare a large bowl of ice water. Wash the beans in a colander. Trim the stem ends. Drop into a large pot of rapidly boiling salted water. Quickly return water to boil. Boil uncovered for 4 to 5 minutes or until beans are tender, yet firm and bright green. Immediately transfer to the bowl of ice water.

Just before serving, drop the beans into a pot of very hot water or chicken stock to reheat, then drain and drizzle with olive oil or butter and a sprinkling of salt. Alternatively, sauté beans in a small amount of olive oil or butter.

Serve either warm or chilled.

SAUTÉED SPINACH

SERVES 6-8

2 tablespoons olive oil

8 cups spinach leaves, stems removed

2 cloves garlic, crushed and
    finely chopped

Salt and freshly ground black pepper
    to taste

2 tablespoons lemon juice

Heat the olive oil in a pan. Sauté the spinach, turning with tongs until wilted. As it cooks, add the garlic, salt and pepper. Continue turning the spinach and shaking the pan. Sprinkle with lemon juice and serve.

SPINACH

✳

Spinach is a popular garden vegetable that is eaten both cooked and raw. It was cultivated by the English as early as the 16th century and was grown by Americans during the colonial period. Spinach is an excellent source of vitamins A and C and it contains a large amount of fiber.

JULIENNE OF CARROT, RED PEPPER AND ZUCCHINI

SERVES 8-10

2 medium carrots

1 small leek

1 small red bell pepper

3 small zucchini

1/4 cup finely chopped shallots

1 tablespoon extra virgin olive oil

Salt and freshly ground white pepper
    to taste

Peel the carrots and cut into a fine julienne. Trim and halve the leek. Thoroughly wash, and separate the white and green parts. Julienne into 2-inch lengths, keeping the white separate from the green. Halve the red bell pepper; remove the seeds and veins. Cut into julienne strips. Trim the zucchini. Cut into a 2-inch julienne.

Prepare a bowl of ice water. Drop the carrots into a large pot of boiling salted water and cook for 1 minute. Add the green part of the leek and boil 30 seconds longer. Remove and refresh immediately in the bowl of ice water. Drain and set aside.

When ready to serve, heat the olive oil in a pan. Sauté the shallots, carrots and green part of the leek for about 30 seconds. Add the white part of the leek and red pepper; sauté for 30 seconds. Add the zucchini and cook for 30 seconds more or until the zucchini becomes bright green. Season with salt and freshly ground white pepper. Serve immediately.

CARROTS

✳

Carrots are a good source of Vitamin A and beta-carotene, which has been linked to reducing chronic diseases such as cancer and heart disease.

SQUASH

✳

There are more than 40 kinds of gourd-shaped vegetables that make up the squash family. They are native to the Western Hemisphere where Indians introduced them to the first European explorers. The name comes from asku-tasquash, an Indian word meaning "eaten raw or uncooked." Zucchini is the most popular member of the squash family eaten by Americans.

ASPARAGUS BUNDLES

ROASTED CHERRY TOMATOES

SERVES 8

2 cups red cherry tomatoes

2 cups yellow cherry tomatoes

1/4 cup olive oil

1/4 cup chopped fresh basil

1/4 cup chopped parsley

1/4 cup chopped fresh oregano

1 tablespoon granulated sugar

Salt and freshly ground black pepper
to taste

Preheat the oven to 350 degrees.

Gently rinse the tomatoes. Place in a mixing bowl with all the remaining ingredients. Toss gently with your hands to evenly coat. Place in a single layer on a parchment paper-lined baking sheet.

Place in the preheated oven and roast for 5 to 7 minutes or until slightly dehydrated and spotty brown. Remove from the oven and serve immediately.

ASPARAGUS BUNDLES

SERVES 8

2 bunches fresh asparagus

1 leek top (green part only)

2 large, firm zucchini

1 large red bell pepper, split, seeded
and deveined

Olive oil

Salt

Prepare a large bowl of ice water. Trim the bottoms from the asparagus. Drop into a large pot of rapidly boiling water. Boil 30 seconds to 1 minute. Remove and immediately plunge into the ice water to stop the cooking and set the color. When cool, arrange on a towel to dry.

Blanch the leek top by following the same procedure. Cut the blanched leek into long strips 1/4-inch wide.

Flatten the bell pepper on the grill and cook until blistered and blackened. Remove, cool and peel. Cut into strips.

Thinly slice the zucchini lengthwise. Drizzle very lightly with olive oil and sprinkle lightly with salt. Grill on one side only until lightly marked and flexible. Set aside.

Wrap 4 or 5 asparagus and a strip of red pepper with a slice of grilled zucchini. Tie the bundles with the leek strips. Set aside until close to serving time.

Preheat oven to 400 degrees. Place the bundles on a baking sheet. Drizzle lightly with olive oil and place in the preheated oven for 5 to 6 minutes or until heated through. Serve immediately.

ASPARAGUS

SERVES 8

2 pounds fresh asparagus, keep
    bundled

1/2 teaspoon salt

2 tablespoons olive oil

Prepare a large bowl of ice water. Bring 4 inches of salted water to a boil in an 8-quart pot. Without removing the bands that tie the bundles, rinse the asparagus; cut off and discard the tough ends. Drop the bundles into the rapidly boiling water. When the water boils again, cook uncovered over high heat for about 1 minute.

Remove the asparagus from the water and instantly plunge into the bowl of ice water to stop the cooking and set the color. Remove the bands and allow the asparagus to cool. Drain and gently pat dry on a towel. Set aside until ready to serve.

Heat a 12-inch frying pan over moderately high heat. Drizzle olive oil over the asparagus and sprinkle with salt. Toss in the hot pan until heated through. Transfer to a warm platter and serve immediately.

. . . .

AN ALTERNATE METHOD OF HEATING
IS TO DRIZZLE THE ASPARAGUS WITH OLIVE OIL
AND PLACE ON A HOT GRILL FOR 2 MINUTES.
SPRINKLE WITH SALT AND SERVE.

. . . .

ASPARAGUS

✻

Asparagus is a nutritious vegetable, which is an excellent source of protein, vitamins and minerals. A member of the lily family, asparagus is delicious served hot or cold. White asparagus is not commonly eaten in the United States; however, it is very popular in Europe. It is grown under the soil where sunlight cannot penetrate the plant thus preventing the production of chlorophyll. The asparagus fern is also a type of asparagus that is used as an ornamental plant and is inedible.

GRILLED PORTOBELLO MUSHROOM GRATINEÉ

SERVES 8 AS A FIRST COURSE

MARINADE

1/4 cup soy sauce

1/4 cup balsamic vinegar

1/2 cup olive oil

1/2 cup dry sherry

1 tablespoon crushed
  red pepper flakes

1/2 tablespoon crushed black
  peppercorns

1 tablespoon chopped garlic

MUSHROOMS

8 portobello mushrooms

10 ounces chevré (goat cheese) or
  another soft cheese

1 cup pine nuts

1 cup bread crumbs

1 cup grated Parmesan cheese

4 tablespoons balsamic vinegar

Mix together all the ingredients for the marinade. Pour over the mushrooms and marinate for about 1 hour. Grill the mushrooms on both sides to mark. Set aside to cool.

Spread a 1/4-inch layer of chevré on the underside of each mushroom. Coat both sides of the mushroom with a crumb mixture made by grinding the pine nuts, bread crumbs and Parmesan cheese in a food processor.

Place the mushrooms under the broiler until golden brown. To serve, slice the mushrooms, place on a warm plate and sprinkle with balsamic vinegar. Serve warm.

MUSHROOMS

✳

There are thousands of different species of mushrooms growing in the world, which vary greatly in size and color. Mushrooms are classed as fungi and do not need light to grow. They lack chlorophyll and survive mainly by absorbing food material from living or decaying plants in their surroundings. Many are safe to eat and are prized by chefs everwhere. However others are extremely toxic and can be fatal if eaten. Portobello mushrooms are large, crimini-like mushrooms with tops that are circular and flat. They have a dense, chewy texture and are great for grilling or roasting.

LEMON RISOTTO

SERVES 12

2 cups chopped yellow onions

1/2 cup chopped shallots

2 tablespoons olive oil

1 tablespoon chopped garlic

5 sprigs fresh thyme

5 bay leaves

Zest of 1 lemon

3/4 pound Arborio rice

1/2 cup white wine

1 1/2-2 quarts chicken stock

1 cup grated Parmesan cheese

In a large heavy saucepan, heat the olive oil and sauté the onions and shallots over medium heat. After 3 minutes, add the garlic, thyme, bay leaves and lemon zest. Continue cooking for 2 minutes. Stir in the rice and sauté for about 6 minutes, stirring constantly to prevent sticking or browning.

Stir in the wine and stock, and bring to a boil. Cover and reduce heat to a simmer. Cook for 20 to 25 minutes or until tender. Stir frequently, adding more stock as needed. When the risotto is cooked, remove the bay leaves and thyme sprigs. Add the Parmesan cheese and serve immediately.

ARBORIO RICE

✳

Arborio rice is a short grain rice, which is grown in northern Italy and eastern Spain. It has a high starch content, which makes it perfect for risotto. The starch being released and incorporated in the broth during the cooking process produces the "creaminess" of a risotto. It is important to not rinse the rice prior to cooking as that would remove the starch that is needed when preparing the dish.

GRILLED BELGIAN ENDIVE

4 whole heads Belgian endive
8 cups well-seasoned chicken stock
Olive oil

Bring the chicken stock to a boil. Drop the Belgian endive into the boiling stock. Blanch for 1 minute. Remove, drain and cut in half lengthwise. Just before serving, sprinkle lightly with olive oil. Place, cut side down, on the grill to mark and heat thoroughly. Serve immediately.

OYSTERS AND ARTICHOKE STUFFING

SERVES 12

ARTICHOKES

✳

The artichoke was known to the ancient Greeks and Romans. Wealthy Romans ate artichokes seasoned with cumin and prepared in honey and vinegar. A close relative of the this-tle, artichokes are actu-ally a bud which has not been allowed to flower. Not grown in the United States until the early 20th century, all commercially grown artichokes today are grown in California.

STUFFING

1 tablespoon olive oil
3 tablespoons chopped shallots
3/4 cup bread crumbs
1/3 cup grated Parmesan cheese
1/3 cup chopped parsley
1 1/2 tablespoons chopped
  fresh tarragon
1/2 teaspoon salt
1/2 teaspoon freshly ground
  white pepper
1/2 cup heavy cream

OYSTERS AND ARTICHOKES

3 dozen oysters
18 artichoke hearts, well drained
  and halved
1 1/2 cups white wine
1/4 cup bread crumbs
1/4 cup grated Parmesan cheese
3/4 cup melted butter

Preheat the oven to 400 degrees.

Heat the olive oil and sauté the shallots. When soft, remove from the heat and stir in the remaining ingredients. Adjust the seasonings to taste. Set aside.

Partially cook the oysters by boiling them in wine over high heat. Poach a few oysters at a time in the wine, cooking for 30 seconds before lifting out with a skimmer. Set aside. Add the remaining wine to the stuffing until it reaches a moist, thick consistency that barely holds its shape in a spoon.

Place the oysters and artichoke hearts in a buttered 9 x 12-inch baking dish and spoon the stuffing over to cover. Sprinkle lightly with Parmesan cheese and bread crumbs. You may prepare the dish to this point the day before. Cover and refrig-erate overnight. Bring to room temperature before baking.

Drizzle with melted butter. Bake uncovered for 25 to 30 minutes.

GRILLED BELGIAN ENDIVE

GRILLED SWEET POTATOES

SERVES 8

4 medium sweet potatoes

Olive oil

Dash of salt and freshly ground
   white pepper

Peel and slice the sweet potatoes lengthwise about 1/4 inch thick. Drizzle lightly with olive oil and sprinkle with salt and white pepper.

At serving time, grill the sweet potato slices over high heat until well marked and tender on one side. Keep warm in a slow oven until ready to serve.

PARMESAN SWEET POTATOES

*This is my favorite way to serve sweet potatoes. It is a break from
the tradition of adding sweet ingredients and offers my guests the security
of the expected with the surprise of a taste that's new.*

— Mary Nell Reck

SERVES 8

POTATOES

2 1/2 pounds sweet potatoes

2 tablespoons unsalted butter, softened

1/4 cup heavy cream

1/2 tablespoon salt

1/2 teaspoon freshly ground
   white pepper

1 tablespoon grated fresh ginger

TOPPING

1 cup heavy cream

1/4 teaspoon salt

1/8 teaspoon cayenne

1 cup grated Parmesan cheese

Preheat the oven to 400 degrees.

Place the potatoes on a baking sheet in the preheated oven. Bake about 1 hour or until soft when squeezed. Remove from the oven. Cut in half and scoop the pulp from the skins while hot.

Place the potato pulp in a mixing bowl with the butter, cream, salt, pepper and ginger, and beat until smooth and combined. Do not overbeat or the potatoes will become gummy. Place the potato mixture in a 2-inch deep casserole.

Combine the cream, salt and cayenne in a mixing bowl. Whip until half stiff; it should have a fluffy sauce consistency. Pour over the potatoes. Sprinkle with the Parmesan cheese. Cover with plastic wrap and refrigerate until ready to cook.

Preheat the oven to 400 degrees. Place the potatoes, uncovered, on the top shelf of the oven. Bake until heated through, about 30 minutes. If necessary, brown the topping by placing under the broiler for 2 to 3 minutes until bubbly and golden brown.

OVEN-ROASTED NEW POTATOES

SERVES 8

3 pounds small new potatoes

1/2 teaspoon salt

1 teaspoon freshly ground
    black pepper

3 tablespoons virgin olive oil

2 tablespoons chopped oregano leaves

2 tablespoons chopped rosemary

2 cloves garlic, crushed and
    finely chopped

Preheat the oven to 400 degrees.

Wash the potatoes. Place in a pot and cover with cold salted water. Bring to a boil; cover and simmer until tender, but resistant when pierced with a small, sharp knife.

Drain. Halve or quarter the potatoes, depending on size. Combine with the remaining ingredients and place in a shallow baking dish. Roast in the oven for 15 minutes or until aromatic and lightly brown around the edges.

ROASTED GARLIC MASHED POTATOES

SERVES 8

ROASTED GARLIC

1 whole pod of garlic

2 tablespoons olive oil

1 teaspoon thyme leaves

Salt and freshly ground white
    pepper to taste

1 tablespoon olive oil

MASHED POTATOES

3 pounds Idaho baking potatoes,
    peeled

Heavy cream or yogurt to taste

Butter or chicken stock to taste

Salt and freshly ground black
    pepper to taste

Preheat the oven to 350 degrees.

Cut the top one-fourth off the garlic. Place on a 10-inch square of aluminum foil. Drizzle with 2 tablespoons of olive oil and sprinkle with the thyme, salt and pepper. Wrap tightly in the aluminum foil. Place on a baking sheet in the preheated oven for 40 to 50 minutes or until very tender. Using a small butter knife, scoop out the roasted garlic cloves. Chop into 1/4-inch pieces. Sauté in 1 tablespoon of olive oil until golden brown. Drain and set aside.

Place the potatoes in a pot and cover with cold water. Bring to a boil. Reduce to a simmer, cover and cook for 25 to 30 minutes until the potatoes are tender. Remove from the water and press through a potato ricer or mash while very hot. Stir in the cream or yogurt, the butter or chicken stock, and the salt and black pepper. Stir in the roasted garlic. Set aside until ready to serve.

DESSERTS

PEAR TART WITH
THREE CREAMS

Recipe on page 171

GORGONZOLA PEAR TART

YIELDS 2 TARTS

MUSCAT WINES

❊

Moscato d'Asti is a slightly sparkling wine made from the muscat grape grown near the wine-producing town of Asti, which lies south of Turin in Italy's Piedmont region. The muscat grape has existed for centuries and is one of the oldest known varieties of grape. Muscat wines are noted for their musky, fresh grape flavors and range from fine light whites (often sparkling) to sweet dark versions (often fortified). Wines made from the muscat grape should be drunk young and fresh.

RIESLING WINES

❊

The riesling is considered one of the world's great white wine grapes; it produces some of the very best white wines. A native of Germany, it has been cultivated for at least 500—and possibly as many as 2,000—years. Riesling wines are delicate but complex, characterized by a spicy, fruity flavor, sometimes reminiscent of peaches and apricots, with a flower-scented bouquet and a long finish.

TART

1 1/2 cups toasted, peeled hazelnuts
  (see helpful hint on page 169)
3/4 cup granulated sugar
2 cups all-purpose flour
1/4 teaspoon salt
1 cup (2 sticks) unsalted butter, cold
2 large egg yolks
1 teaspoon vanilla extract

POACHED PEARS

2 bottles white wine (Moscato d'Asti
  or Riesling)
1 teaspoon whole black
  peppercorns, lightly crushed
1 cup freshly squeezed lemon juice
1/2 cup granulated sugar
1 vanilla bean, split and scraped
8 Bosc pears

FILLING

1/2 cup granulated sugar
3/4 cup mascarpone cheese
1/2 cup crumbled Gorgonzola
  Dolce cheese
1 tablespoon chopped lemon zest
1 large egg yolk
3/4 cup chilled thick pastry cream
  (see the recipe on page 195)

APRICOT GLAZE

12 ounces apricot preserves
3 tablespoons water

Preheat the oven to 325 degrees.

Finely chop the hazelnuts in a food processor. Place in a mixing bowl with the sugar, flour and salt. Mix with your hands. Cut the butter into small pieces. Add the butter pieces, egg yolks and vanilla to the bowl. With the mixer set on low, work the butter, eggs and vanilla into the flour and nuts until the mixture just comes together.

Press into the bottom of two unbuttered 9-inch tart pans with removable bottoms. Bake for 30 minutes. Do not let the crust brown too much, as it will be cooked again with the topping. Cool completely and chill.

In a large stainless steel or enamel saucepan, combine the wine, peppercorns, lemon juice, sugar and vanilla bean. Peel, core and halve the pears, placing each piece in the pear poaching liquid as you go. Add water if needed to completely cover the pears.

Bring the liquid to a boil, then reduce it to low. Place a clean, wet kitchen towel or wet paper towels over the pears to keep them submerged in the liquid. Simmer on low until the pears are tender, but not mushy, from 15 minutes to 1 hour. When the pears are just tender, turn off the heat and let them cool in the liquid. If they are very soft, drain them and refrigerate immediately.

Strain the poaching liquid and refrigerate; the poaching liquid can be reused. The pears can be poached a day ahead.

Prepare the pastry cream as directed on page 195. Whisk together with the sugar, cheeses, lemon zest, and egg in a mixing bowl. Divide into the two chilled tart crusts. Slice the poached pears crosswise into 1/8-inch slices. Arrange on top. Bake for 15 minutes in the preheated oven. Chill.

Put the apricot preserves and water in a saucepan. Bring to a boil. Remove from the heat and strain out the apricot pieces. Return the strained mixture to the saucepan and simmer until the jelly thickens slightly. Using a thin pastry brush, coat the pear tarts with the warm glaze. Refrigerate until ready to serve. Warm in the oven for 4 to 5 minutes before serving.

TORTUGA PIE

Tortuga pie is one of those decadent, exquisite desserts for indulging in on rare occasions or at important holiday celebrations. Your guests are guaranteed to swoon, especially if you serve it with a Brut Champagne.

— *Mary Nell Reck*

SERVES 12-16

CHOCOLATE COOKIE CRUST

1/2 cup toasted and skinned
   hazelnuts

2 1/2 cups fine chocolate
   wafer crumbs

3 tablespoons unsalted butter, softened

CARAMEL LAYER

3 tablespoons unsalted butter

3/4 cup granulated sugar

3/4 cup toasted, skinned and
   coarsely chopped hazelnuts

3/4 cup heavy cream

CHOCOLATE MOUSSE LAYER

8 ounces semisweet chocolate

1/4 cup coffee

2 large egg yolks

3 large egg whites

1 1/2 tablespoons granulated sugar

1 cup heavy cream

GARNISH

Crème anglaise sauce (see the recipe
   on page 193) flavored with 2
   tablespoons of Frangelico® liqueur

Preheat the oven to 350 degrees.

Place the toasted hazelnuts in a food processor and process until finely ground. Add the cookie crumbs and softened butter. Process until combined. Press the crumb mixture firmly into the bottom and sides of an unbuttered 10-inch tart pan with removable bottom. Place on a baking sheet in the center of the preheated oven for 10 to 12 minutes or until aromatic and crusty. Remove from the oven to cool.

Place the butter in a small heavy saucepan along with the granulated sugar. As the butter melts, stir only enough to combine. Allow to boil and caramelize over moderately high heat. When it is a rich, golden amber, add the hazelnuts and cream. Allow to boil for 3 minutes more. Pour the caramel mixture into the crust. Refrigerate until well chilled, 1 hour or more.

Place the chocolate and coffee in a mixing bowl and melt slowly over a pan of simmering water. Place the egg yolks in another mixing bowl. Slowly add the warm chocolate to the egg yolks while whisking. Cool. Whip the egg whites in a copper bowl with a large bulb wire whip. When frothy, add the sugar and whip a minute more. Whip one-fourth of the egg whites into the cooled chocolate mixture, then fold in the remainder. Whip the cream in the same bowl used for the egg whites. Fold the whipped cream into the mousse. Mound the chocolate mixture on top of the caramel layer in the crust. Chill.

Serve the pie with the crème anglaise sauce flavored with Frangelico® liqueur.

(see the recipe on page 193)

HAZELNUTS

✳

Hazelnuts are usually packaged whole, though some producers are now also offering them chopped. Hazelnuts have a bitter brown skin that is best removed, usually by placing them in an oven preheated to 350 degrees for 10 to 15 minutes or until the skins begin to flake. Remove the skins by placing a handful of nuts at a time in a dishtowel, then folding the towel over the warm nuts and rubbing vigorously.

COFFEE

✳

When deciding on what type of coffee to use, keep in mind that flavored coffees may compete with other ingredients in your dessert. Choose a roast that reflects your palate objective, whether a mild roast or a bold one.

WHITE FRENCH SILK

White French silk offers its share of decadence, that is utterly veiled by its delicacy and lightness.

— *Mary Nell Reck*

SERVES 12

WHITE CHOCOLATE

✳

White chocolate is not technically chocolate. It contains no chocolate liquor, which is what gives chocolate its color and bitter flavor. White chocolate does contain cocoa butter, the fat extracted from cocoa beans during the chocolate-making process. The cocoa butter is mixed with sugar, milk solids, flavorings and lecithin, and then formed into bars. It is important to use high-quality white chocolate when cooking as it can be difficult to work with. It should be melted at a very low temperature, over hot water, as it turns grainy and unusable quickly.

SPRINGFORM PANS

✳

A springform pan is a round pan with straight sides 2 1/2 to 3 inches in height. They are available in a number of sizes, 9 and 10-inch pans being the most common. The side of the pan has a spring or clamp that allows you to loosen and remove the side from the bottom of the pan. Cheesecakes baked in this type of pan can be served easily once the side of the pan is removed.

GRAHAM CRACKER CRUST

3/4 cup graham cracker crumbs

1/4 cup (1/2 stick) unsalted butter, melted

4 tablespoons unsweetened cocoa

3 tablespoons granulated sugar

FILLING

8 ounces best quality, imported white chocolate (do not use white chocolate chips)

1 cup (2 sticks) unsalted butter, softened

1 cup granulated sugar

6 ounces cream cheese, softened

4 whole eggs

1 egg yolk

2 teaspoons vanilla

2 tablespoons white crème de cacao

2 teaspoons unsweetened cocoa

Preheat the oven to 350 degrees.

Combine the cracker crumbs, melted butter, cocoa and sugar. Mix lightly with your hands until the ingredients are well combined and uniformly moist. Press the crumb mixture firmly into the bottom of a 9-inch springform pan. Place on a baking sheet and bake on the center shelf of the oven for 10 minutes or until it develops a toasty aroma. Remove from the oven and chill while preparing the filling.

Melt the chocolate over a pan of simmering water. When it is three-fourths melted, remove from the heat and stir until completely melted. Do not let the chocolate get too hot or it will become granular and you will be unable to use it. Place the softened butter in a mixing bowl and beat until light and fluffy. Gradually add the sugar and cream cheese, and continue to beat for 5 to 6 minutes at medium high speed until light and white in color. Add the melted chocolate. Add the eggs one at a time, beating for about 2 minutes after each addition. If the eggs are added too fast, or if the mixture becomes too warm from overbeating, it will separate and the dessert will lose its desired lightness. Stir in the vanilla and the crème de cacao, and pour into the chilled crust.

Refrigerate for 2 hours or overnight. Before serving, remove the sides of the pan and dust the surface lightly with unsweetened cocoa.

PEAR TART WITH THREE CREAMS

SERVES 8

CRUST

See the sweet pie crust recipe on page 194.

FILLING

6 ounces mascarpone cheese

6 ounces cream cheese

1/3 cup sour cream

1/4 cup granulated sugar

1 large egg yolk

1 tablespoon chopped lemon zest

4 ripe pears, peeled

Juice of 1 lemon

2 tablespoons granulated sugar for sprinkling on top

GARNISH

Chilled whipped cream

Fresh mint sprigs

Prepare the piecrust as directed on page 194.

Preheat the oven to 425 degrees.

Soften the mascarpone and cream cheese. Stir in the sour cream until smooth. Add the sugar, egg yolk and lemon zest. Stir.

Cut each pear in half and remove the core. Place the cut side on a cutting board and very thinly slice crosswise. Keep the pears in their original shape. Sprinkle with lemon juice. Set aside while rolling out the pastry.

Roll out the dough to a 1/8-inch thickness. Cut out eight ovals that are 1 inch larger than the pears. Place ovals on two baking sheets lined with parchment paper. Place one tablespoon of the cheese mixture in the center of each pastry oval and spread out to cover an area 3 inches long and 1 inch wide. Separate the slices of each pear half, spread about 1/2 teaspoon of the cheese mixture between each slice and reassemble the pear half on a pastry oval.

Spread about 2 teaspoons of the filling over the top of each pear, making no effort to cover completely. Sprinkle with granulated sugar and bake in the preheated oven for 12 to 15 minutes or until both pastry and pears are golden. Serve hot with fresh, chilled whipped cream. Garnish with sprigs of fresh mint.

ZEST

Zest is the perfumed outermost skin layer of citrus fruit, usually oranges or lemons, which is removed with the aid of a citrus zester, paring knife or vegetable peeler. Only the colored portion of the skin (not the white pith) is considered the zest. The aromatic oils of citrus zest are what add so much flavor to food. Zest can be used to flavor raw or cooked foods and sweet or savory dishes.

PEARS

*

More than 5,000 varieties of pears are grown throughout the world. Most of the U.S. crop comes from California, Oregon and Washington. Unlike most fruit, pears improve in both texture and flavor after being picked. Pears are in season from late July to early spring, depending on the variety. Choose pears that are fragrant and free of blemishes and soft spots. Store pears at room temperature until the desired ripeness is attained.

MIXED BERRY TART

A favorite for summer gatherings.

SERVES 8

PASTRY

1 1/4 cups unbleached pastry or
   all-purpose flour, plus extra
   for dusting

1/4 cup granulated sugar

1/2 cup (1 stick) unsalted butter,
   chilled and cut into small pieces

1 extra large egg yolk

2 tablespoons heavy cream, plus
   extra as needed

2 ounces semisweet chocolate,
   chopped

FILLING AND GLAZE

1 cup fresh raspberries

1 cup fresh blackberries

1/2 cup fresh blueberries

1 cup fresh strawberries, quartered

3/4 cup raspberry preserves

2 tablespoons water

2 tablespoons granulated sugar

Using an electric mixer fitted with a paddle attachment or a food processor with a metal blade, combine the flour and sugar until mixed completely. Add the small pieces of butter and mix just to a coarse cornmeal-like consistency.

In a small mixing bowl, whisk together the egg yolk and heavy cream. Pour into the flour mixture and mix just until the cream and eggs bring the dough together into a ball. It may be necessary to add as much as 1 tablespoon of extra cream to make the dough moist enough to form a ball. Lightly dust your hands and a smooth work surface with flour. Place the dough on the surface. Knead a few times to distribute the fat. Form a ball and chill for at least 1 hour.

Preheat the oven to 450 degrees. Roll out the dough to a 1/8-inch thickness. Place in a 9-inch tart pan and bake in the preheated oven for 10 to 12 minutes until golden. Remove the crust from the oven and place the chocolate pieces on the hot crust. Spread to melt. Cool completely.

Place all the berries in a mixing bowl and mix gently using your hands. Place in the cooled, chocolate-coated crust.

Place the raspberry preserves, water and sugar in a small saucepan and boil for 5 minutes. Gently brush the glaze on the berries. Remove the sides of the springform pan and serve the tart at room temperature.

The crust may be made in advance, and the finished tart may be made up to 4 hours before serving.

. . . .

NOW THAT FRESH FRUIT IS SHIPPED
AROUND THE WORLD, WE CAN ENJOY LUSCIOUS FRUIT
YEAR-ROUND. USE THE FRUITS SUGGESTED HERE
OR YOUR OWN COMBINATION FOR A VARIETY
OF COLORS AND SHAPES.

. . . .

CARROT CAKE

Throw all other carrot cake recipes away. This is the only one worth saving. This version of the all-American favorite is simple to make and impossible to mess up. It has been a family favorite for 30 years and the most frequently requested cake for birthdays. The texture is light, moist and flavorful. The cake will stay fresh for a week in the refrigerator. The cake layers, before being iced, may be wrapped in plastic wrap and frozen for up to 6 weeks.

— *Mary Nell Reck*

SERVES 16

CAKE

2 cups granulated sugar

1/2 cup vegetable oil

4 large eggs

2 cups all-purpose flour

2 teaspoons cinnamon

1 tablespoon baking soda

1/4 teaspoon salt

3 cups finely grated carrots

1 cup chopped walnuts

FROSTING

16 ounces (2 packages) cream
cheese, softened

1 cup (2 sticks) unsalted
butter, softened

1 tablespoon vanilla extract

1 cup confectioners' sugar

1 cup finely chopped walnuts

Preheat the oven to 350 degrees. Line three 9-inch round cake pans with parchment. Lightly coat with butter and a sprinkling of flour. Refrigerate while preparing the cake.

Place the sugar and vegetable oil in a large mixing bowl. Using a wooden spoon, stir to combine. Add the eggs one at a time while continuing to beat with the spoon. Sift the flour, cinnamon, baking soda and salt into the contents of the bowl. Stir until the flour is barely combined with the egg mixture. Do not overbeat or the cake will not be soft and moist. Stir in the grated carrots and walnuts.

Pour the batter into the three prepared cake pans. Place on a baking sheet and bake in the center of the preheated oven for 25 to 30 minutes or until the cakes are springy when touched.

Remove the cakes from the oven. Allow to cool for 5 minutes. Run a knife around the edges and invert onto a rack to completely cool. When cool, place the bottom layer onto a 9-inch round of cardboard covered with aluminum foil to make handling easier.

Place the cream cheese and butter in a mixing bowl and beat together until light and fluffy, about 5 minutes. Stir in the vanilla and confectioners' sugar. Spread the cream cheese frosting between the three cake layers, then over the top and sides. Stack and smooth the frosting on the sides. With your hands, press the finely chopped walnuts around the sides of the cake.

Refrigerate until close to serving time. This cake may be made 2 days in advance. Bring to room temperature before serving.

. . . .

FOR BEST RESULTS, USE SHINY METAL BAKING PANS.
ALUMINUM AND TIN ARE THE BEST METALS
FOR BAKING PANS. HOWEVER, INSULATED, DARK-
SURFACED AND NONSTICK PANS ARE BECOMING
INCREASINGLY POPULAR. FOODS BAKED IN INSULATED
PANS REQUIRE MORE BAKING TIME AND
TAKE LONGER TO BROWN. FOODS BAKED IN DARK-
SURFACED PANS REQUIRE A SHORTER BAKING
TIME AND BROWN MORE QUICKLY.

ONE 8-INCH SQUARE PAN MAY BE SUBSTITUTED FOR
ONE 9-INCH ROUND CAKE PAN.

. . . .

*"Only in dreams
are carrots as big
as bears."*

— YIDDISH SAYING

MN's Outrageous Chocolate Cake

This cake was served at Mary Nell's birthday celebrations. It was one of her favorite cakes.

SERVES 16

CHOCOLATE CAKE

3 ounces unsweetened, best
   quality chocolate

1/2 cup (1 stick) unsalted butter

2 cups granulated sugar

2 large eggs

1 cup sour cream

1 teaspoon vanilla extract

2 cups all-purpose flour

1 1/2 teaspoons baking soda

1 cup boiling water

RASPBERRY GLAZE

1 cup raspberry preserves

1/2 cup granulated sugar

2 tablespoons water

1 tablespoon cognac

NUT LAYER

1 cup walnut halves

1 cup pecan halves

1 cup slivered almonds

1 cup whole hazelnuts, peeled

CREAM CHEESE FROSTING

3 tablespoons unsweetened cocoa

3 tablespoons hot, strong coffee

8 ounces (1 package) cream cheese

1/2 cup (1 stick) unsalted
   butter, softened

1 cup sifted confectioners' sugar

1 teaspoon vanilla extract

**CHOCOLATE SOUR CREAM
FROSTING**

1 1/2 cups granulated sugar

1/2 cup unsweetened cocoa

1/4 cup strong coffee

1/2 cup light corn syrup

1 cup sour cream, room temperature

1 teaspoon vanilla extract

GARNISH

Raspberries and strawberries

Fresh mint sprigs

Preheat the oven to 350 degrees. Lightly butter the bottom and sides of two 9-inch round cake pans. Sprinkle with a light coating of flour.

Place the unsweetened chocolate and butter in a mixing bowl over a pan of simmering water. Heat, stirring occasionally, until melted. Set aside to cool slightly.

Place the sugar in a mixing bowl. Stir in the chocolate mixture and mix well. Add the eggs, one at a time, beating after each. Stir in the sour cream and vanilla.

Carefully measure the flour and place in a sifter along with the baking soda. Sift over the liquid ingredients. Stir until the flour is barely combined. Stir in the boiling water.

Divide the cake batter evenly into the prepared cake pans. Place in the preheated oven and bake for 30 minutes or until the cake is springy to the touch. Remove the pans from the oven. Cool for 5 minutes, then remove the cakes from the pans.

Place the raspberry preserves, sugar and water in a small saucepan. Boil until large shiny bubbles form on the surface and the syrup forms a string when tested between two fingers (240 degrees on a candy thermometer). Remove from the heat and stir in the cognac. Place the cake layers on a baking sheet and spread the warm syrup over the warm cake layers.

When the cake layers are cool, transfer them to 9-inch cardboard rounds, covered with foil. They can then be moved easily without cracking.

Preheat the oven to 300 degrees. Spread all the nuts on a baking sheet and place in the preheated oven. Bake, shaking the pan occasionally, for 15 minutes or until the nuts are aromatic and the almonds are light brown. Set aside to cool.

Dissolve the cocoa in a small bowl with the hot coffee. Using an electric mixer, process the cream cheese, butter and confectioners' sugar until light and fluffy. Stir the cocoa/coffee into the creamed mixture. Add the vanilla. Make sure all the ingredients are well combined.

Spread the frosting evenly over the bottom layer of the cooled chocolate cake. Then press 2 cups of the mixed toasted nuts lightly into the frosting. Transfer the layer to the serving platter. Top with the second layer. Frost the top and sides, then press 2 cups of the nuts into the top layer. Chill in the freezer while preparing the chocolate sour cream frosting.

Place the sugar and cocoa in a heavy saucepan over low heat. Stir until completely combined and lump free. Stir in the coffee to form a paste, then stir in the corn syrup. Place over a moderate heat and bring to a boil. Do not stir. Cook until the mixture forms large, shiny bubbles on the surface and forms a soft ball

(Recipe continues on to next page)

**"Forget love ...
I'd rather fall in
chocolate!"**

— ANONYMOUS

CHOCOLATE

✳

The word "chocolate" comes from the Aztec word xocolatl, meaning "bitter water." The Aztec king Montezuma believed so strongly that chocolate was an aphrodisiac that he purportedly drank 50 golden goblets of it each day. Chocolate comes from the tropical cocoa bean, Theobroma ("food of the gods") cacao.

The first chocolate house opened in London in 1657, advertising "this excellent West India drink."

MN's Outrageous Chocolate Cake

when dropped into a bowl of cold water. Remove from the heat. Stir in the vanilla. Set aside about one-third of the frosting. Whisk the sour cream into the remaining two-thirds.

Spoon the chocolate sour cream frosting over the nut-covered cake, letting it fall in uneven globs, half covering the nuts. Allow it to run down the sides. Chill the cake again.

When the chocolate sour cream frosting has set, drizzle the remaining chocolate frosting over the entire cake. Refrigerate. Just before serving, garnish with fresh raspberries and strawberries, and sprigs of fresh mint.

WARM CHOCOLATE SOUFFLÉ CAKES

SERVES 12

CAKES

12 ounces semisweet chocolate

3/4 cup (1 1/2 sticks) unsalted butter

8 eggs, separated

1/3 cup granulated sugar

4 teaspoons vanilla extract

1/4 teaspoon salt

1/4 teaspoon cream of tartar

GARNISH

Vanilla ice cream

Preheat the oven to 350 degrees.

Coat twelve 6-ounce ramekins with butter and sprinkle with granulated sugar.

Place the chocolate and butter in a mixing bowl and melt over simmering water.

Place the egg yolks in a mixing bowl and gradually add the sugar while beating. Add the vanilla. Stir in the warm melted chocolate.

Combine the egg whites, salt and cream of tartar in a mixing bowl. Whip until stiff peaks form. Quickly fold into the chocolate mixture.

Spoon into the prepared ramekins. Bake in the preheated oven for 10 to 12 minutes. Cool for 10 minutes. Unmold onto a paper-lined sheet pan.

When ready to serve, place the soufflé cakes in the oven for 4 minutes to reheat. Transfer to a dessert plate and serve with a scoop of vanilla ice cream.

ITALIAN CREAM CAKE

SERVES 16

CAKE

1 cup (2 sticks) unsalted
    butter, softened

2 cups granulated sugar

5 large eggs, separated

1 teaspoon vanilla extract

2 cups all-purpose flour

1 teaspoon baking soda

1 cup buttermilk

1 cup chopped pecans

1 cup sweetened grated coconut

1/8 teaspoon cream of tartar

Dash of salt

FROSTING

1 package (8 ounces)
    cream cheese, softened

1 cup (2 sticks) unsalted
    butter, softened

2 teaspoons vanilla extract

1 3/4 pounds (about 7 cups)
    confectioners' sugar

1 cup chopped pecans

1 cup sweetened grated coconut

GARNISH

1/2 cup sweetened grated coconut

Preheat the oven to 350 degrees. Lightly butter and flour the bottom and sides of three 9-inch round cake pans.

Place the butter in a mixing bowl. Beat on medium speed until light in color. Gradually add the sugar while continuing to beat. Beat in the egg yolks one at a time (reserve the whites for later). Stir in the vanilla extract.

Remove the bowl from the mixer and sift in one-third of the flour and the baking soda. Gently stir to combine. Do not beat or the cake will be heavy. Stir in half the buttermilk, then one-third more flour. Finally, stir in the remaining buttermilk and flour.

Stir in the pecans and coconut. Whip the reserved egg whites with the cream of tartar and gently fold into the batter.

Divide the batter into the three prepared cake pans. Place on a baking sheet and bake in the preheated oven for 35 minutes or until they spring back to the touch. Remove from the oven and cool.

 Beat together the cream cheese and butter until light and fluffy. Add the vanilla extract, then gradually add the confectioners' sugar. Stir in the pecans and coconut.

Toast the coconut in the preheated oven for 3 to 5 minutes or until lightly browned. Frost the cakes with the cream cheese frosting, and garnish the sides with the toasted coconut.

FLOUR

✳

Flour provides the structure for baked goods. It is the fine meal produced during the grinding of various edible grains. The most common flours are made from hard and soft wheat, blended during milling to produce different kinds of flour. All-purpose flour is a blend milled from the inner part of the wheat kernel. This versatile flour is appropriate for all uses and is available bleached or unbleached. All-purpose flour should be used within 18 to 24 months of purchase; self-rising flour should be used within 12 to 18 months.

WALNUT SOUFFLÉ CAKE
WITH KENTUCKY BOURBON MOUSSE

SERVES 8

CAKE

4 ounces semisweet chocolate

6 large eggs, separated

1/2 cup granulated sugar

1/2 cup all-purpose flour, sifted

1 cup finely ground toasted walnuts

1 teaspoon vanilla extract

1/8 teaspoon salt

KENTUCKY BOURBON MOUSSE

6 ounces imported
   bittersweet chocolate

1/4 cup strong coffee

1/4 cup brown sugar, packed

3 large eggs, separated

2 tablespoons bourbon

1 teaspoon vanilla extract

1 cup heavy cream

1/8 teaspoon salt

GARNISH

Confectioners' sugar

Fresh mint sprigs

Raspberries or strawberries

Crème anglaise sauce (see the
   recipe on page 193)

Preheat the oven to 375 degrees.

Line a half sheet (12 x 18-inch) pan with aluminum foil. Butter and flour the bottom and sides. Chill.

Place the chocolate in a small bowl over a pan of simmering water to gently melt. Separate the eggs, placing the whites in a clean copper bowl and the yolks in a large mixing bowl. Beat the yolks with a whisk while gradually adding the granulated sugar. Stir in the flour, toasted walnuts and melted chocolate. Add the vanilla and salt.

Whip the egg whites until stiff. Quickly whip a small amount into the chocolate mixture and fold in the remaining. Pour the batter into the prepared pan. Spread evenly and place in the preheated oven. Bake for about 10 minutes or until lightly puffed and dry-looking. Remove from the oven and cool.

Place the chocolate, coffee and sugar in a mixing bowl over a pan of simmering water. When nearly melted, remove from the heat and stir until completely smooth.

Next, separate the eggs. Place the yolks in a mixing bowl and the whites in a copper bowl. Very slowly add the melted chocolate to the yolks while beating with a whisk. Stir in the bourbon and vanilla, and refrigerate to cool.

Whip the cream to form soft peaks. Then whip the egg whites with the salt to form stiff peaks. Quickly fold both into the cooled chocolate. Chill.

Cut the cake into sixteen 3-inch rounds using a biscuit cutter. Spread or pipe the mousse on half the rounds and top with the remaining rounds of cake. Dust the surface with a sprinkling of sifted confectioners' sugar. Garnish with sprigs of fresh mint and fresh raspberries or strawberries. Serve with crème anglaise sauce.

BOURBON

✳

Bourbon, an all-American liquor distilled from fermented grain, is named for Bourbon County, Kentucky.

Walnut Soufflé Cake with Kentucky Bourbon Mousse

PUMPKIN CHEESECAKE

This pumpkin cheesecake could compete with traditional pumpkin pie as a new holiday favorite.

— *Mary Nell Reck*

SERVES 12-16

CRUST

3/4 cup walnuts

2 cups graham cracker crumbs

1/3 cup granulated sugar

1/2 teaspoon cinnamon

4 tablespoons (1/2 stick) unsalted
butter, softened

CHEESECAKE

3 packages (8 ounces each) cream
cheese

1 cup granulated sugar

1 tablespoon cornstarch

1 cup sour cream

4 large eggs

1 cup pumpkin puree

1/2 cup (1 stick) unsalted
butter, melted

1 2-inch piece ginger root, peeled
and grated

1/2 teaspoon nutmeg

1/4 teaspoon ground cloves

TOPPING

3/4 cup sour cream

3/4 cup pumpkin puree

1/2 cup granulated sugar

1 tablespoon vanilla extract

1/4 teaspoon cinnamon

Preheat the oven to 375 degrees.

Place the walnuts in a food processor and finely grind. Place them in a mixing bowl with the graham cracker crumbs, sugar and cinnamon. Using the back of a wooden spoon or your hands, work the butter into the crumb mixture. The crust will remain crumbly but the butter will be evenly distributed, leaving the crumbs moist looking. Using your hands, very firmly press the crust into the bottom and sides of a 9-inch springform pan. Line the crust with a sheet of aluminum foil, pressing it firmly over the bottom and up the sides of the crust. Fill with 2 cups of raw rice or beans. Place on a baking sheet and bake for 8 minutes in the preheated oven. Remove the foil and its contents, and return the crust to the oven for 3 minutes. Remove from the oven and set aside while preparing the filling.

Reduce the oven temperature to 325 degrees. Place the cream cheese and sugar in the bowl of an electric mixer. Using the wire whip attachment, beat for 3 to 4 minutes until fluffy and smooth. Beat in the cornstarch and sour cream. Add the eggs, one at a time, beating well after each egg is added. Stir in the pumpkin puree and butter.

Measure 2 teaspoons of the grated ginger and add to the cheesecake filling along with the nutmeg and cloves.

Pour the batter into the prepared crust. Place the pan on a baking sheet and bake in the center of the preheated oven. Bake the cheesecake for 1 hour and 15 minutes or until the cake is set but still a little shaky. If the top of the cake has large, deep cracks or if there is a deep valley in the center, your oven is too hot.

While the cake is baking, combine the sour cream, pumpkin puree, sugar, vanilla and cinnamon. Mix well. Spread the topping over the hot cheesecake and return to the oven for 5 minutes. Remove the cake and cool at room temperature for 1 hour. Cover with plastic wrap and refrigerate overnight or until ready to serve.

PUMPKINS

❋

The pumpkin is a member of the gourd family, which also includes muskmelon, watermelon and squash. Fresh pumpkins are available in the fall and winter. The flesh from smaller sizes will be more tender and succulent. Choose pumpkins that are free from blemishes and heavy for their size.

GINGER

❋

Fresh ginger is available in two forms: young and mature. Young ginger, sometimes called spring ginger, has a pale, thin skin that requires no peeling. It is very tender and has a milder flavor than its mature form. Young ginger can be found in most oriental markets during the springtime. Mature ginger has a tough skin that must be carefully peeled away to preserve the delicate flesh just under the surface. Look for mature ginger with smooth skin (wrinkled skin indicates that the root is dry and past its prime). It should have a fresh, spicy fragrance. Fresh unpeeled ginger root, tightly wrapped, can be refrigerated for up to 1 week and frozen for up to 2 months. Dried ginger is very different from fresh ginger and is not an appropriate substitute for dishes specifying fresh.

APPLE BLACKBERRY COBBLER

SERVES 8

FRUIT FILLING

1/2 pound Granny Smith apples, peeled, cored and chopped

1/2 pound blackberries or blueberries

1/2 cup granulated sugar

2 tablespoons lemon juice

1 tablespoon cornstarch

1/2 teaspoon cinnamon

CRUMB TOPPING

3/4 cup all-purpose flour

3/4 cup granulated sugar

1/4 teaspoon cinnamon

6 tablespoons unsalted butter, chilled

GARNISH

Vanilla ice cream

Confectioners' sugar

Fresh mint sprigs

Preheat the oven to 375 degrees.

Place the apples, berries, sugar, lemon juice, cornstarch and cinnamon in a large mixing bowl and gently toss with your hands to combine. Set aside.

Place the flour, sugar and cinnamon in a mixing bowl. Cut the butter into the dry ingredients, using your fingertips, until it has a coarse but uniform texture.

Place the fruit mixture and all its juices in a serving casserole. Sprinkle with the crumb mixture.

Place the casserole on a baking sheet in the preheated oven and bake for 30 minutes or until golden and crisp on top. Check the juices in the center. They should be clear and hot. Remove from the oven.

Serve with a scoop of vanilla ice cream.

Decorate the plate with a sprinkling of confectioners' sugar and a sprig of fresh mint.

PANDOWDIES

✳

Pandowdies were first made in the 1600s. Similar to a cobbler, a pandowdy is a fruit mixture covered with a layer of soft biscuit dough. It was customary for the server to "dowdy the pan," or cut into the dessert with a spoon, stirring the top and bottom together a bit, before serving.

CHOCOLATE MIXED BERRY SHORTCAKE

SERVES 8-10

"There are two kinds of people in the world. Those who love chocolate and communists."

— LESLIE MOAK MURRAY
IN "MURRAY'S LAW"
COMIC STRIP

COCOA
POWDER

✳

Cocoa powder is the least fatty form of chocolate. It is made by crushing roasted cocoa beans and removing the cocoa butter. This leaves behind a powdery substance that can range in color from tan to red to black. Most chefs prefer to use Dutch process cocoa, a process developed in The Netherlands by C.J. Van Houten. This process involves neutralizing the natural acidity of the cocoa with lye.

CHOCOLATE CAKE

3 1/2 cups all-purpose flour

1/2 cup unsweetened cocoa

2 teaspoons baking powder

1/2 teaspoon salt

1 1/4 cups vegetable oil

1 1/4 cups buttermilk

2 cups granulated sugar

5 large egg yolks

2 teaspoons vanilla extract

1 1/4 cups boiling water

WHIPPED CREAM FILLING

2 cups heavy cream

1/4 cup confectioners' sugar

1/2 teaspoon vanilla extract

RASPBERRY SAUCE

3 cups frozen raspberries

1/4 cup granulated sugar

2 tablespoons cornstarch

2 tablespoons lemon juice

BERRIES AND GARNISH

3 pints mixed berries, stems removed

Unsweetened cocoa

Confectioners' sugar

Chocolate sauce

Preheat the oven to 350 degrees. Line a half sheet (12 x 18-inch) pan with parchment paper; spray with vegetable oil and coat with flour. Refrigerate.

Sift together the flour, cocoa, baking powder and salt. Set aside. Combine the oil and buttermilk, using an electric mixer, and beat well. Add the sugar and continue mixing. Slowly add the egg yolks, then the vanilla. Stir in the dry ingredients, mixing until just combined. Add the boiling water and pour into the prepared baking pan.

Bake in the center of the preheated oven for 20 minutes or until springy to the touch. Remove from the oven. Cool for 5 minutes. Invert and remove the paper. Cut into circles or ovals with a 3-inch biscuit cutter. Cut two rounds per person.

Whip the cream, sugar and vanilla in a chilled mixing bowl on medium speed until it forms soft peaks. Set aside and refrigerate until ready to use.

Place the raspberries and their juice in a small heavy saucepan. Sprinkle with the sugar and cornstarch. Stir to combine. Bring to a boil, uncovered. Boil gently, stirring until thickened and clear. Stir in the lemon juice to taste. Remove from the heat and pass through a food mill fitted with a fine sieve. Set aside until ready to serve.

When ready to serve, place the mixed berries in a mixing bowl. Add 1 1/2 cups of the raspberry sauce and gently toss with your hands until lightly coated.

Place a chocolate cake round in the center of a plate. Top with the whipped cream, then the berries. Layer again with the cake, cream and berries, allowing the juice to run onto the plate. The plate may be sprinkled with cocoa or confectioners' sugar or drizzled with a chocolate sauce.

CHOCOLATE MIXED BERRY SHORTCAKE

CHOCOLATE BREAD PUDDING

Bread pudding has graduated from the "poor man's dessert" of years past.
This spectacular soufflé-like bread pudding is a chocolate lover's fantasy.

SERVES 6-8

CHOCOLATE

✳

The cocoa bean, native to the New World, was brought to Spain by Columbus. However, its use remained largely unknown until Cortez conquered the Aztec Indians. He observed the Indians roasting the beans, grinding them into a fine powder and adding hot water to make a bitter drink. Cortez took the beans and the process back to Spain where cream and sugar were added, making a delicious drink. The Spanish kept the process for making hot chocolate a secret for over 100 years. Eventually the secret got out and hot chocolate became a huge fad throughout Europe.

It wasn't until the 19th century that solid chocolate was produced, and the Swiss are credited with inventing the many processes for making chocolate bars, including the technique of milk chocolate production.

PUDDING

6 cups 1-inch cubes French bread, crusts removed

1/2 cup (1 stick) unsalted butter, melted

1 3/4 cups whole milk

1 cup heavy cream

4 ounces best quality unsweetened chocolate, chopped

1 cup granulated sugar

4 large egg yolks

1 teaspoon vanilla extract

GARNISH

Whipped cream or vanilla ice cream

Preheat the oven to 350 degrees.

Grease an 8-inch square glass dish. If the bread is fresh, place the cubes on a baking sheet and dry out in a 300 degree oven for 15 to 20 minutes. Watch carefully; do not let the bread get very brown. Place the bread cubes in a large bowl, drizzle with the melted butter and toss.

Bring the milk and cream to a simmer in a large saucepan. Remove from the heat and add the chopped chocolate, whisking until smooth and the chocolate is melted.

In a large bowl, whisk together the sugar and egg yolks, then whisk in the chocolate mixture. Add the vanilla, then pour the custard over the bread. Stir. Cover with plastic wrap, refrigerate and let stand for 1 hour. Some of the custard will not be absorbed by the bread. This may be prepared up to 2 hours ahead.

Pour the bread mixture into the greased baking dish. Bake for 35 minutes in the preheated oven until set; the center should jiggle slightly when the dish is shaken. Serve warm or at room temperature with whipped cream or vanilla ice cream.

TIRAMISU

SERVES 8-10

LADYFINGERS

3 large eggs, separated

1/3 cup granulated sugar

1 teaspoon vanilla extract

1/3 cup cake flour

1/3 cup all-purpose flour

Pinch of salt

Confectioners' sugar for dusting

ZABAGLIONE

8 large egg yolks

1 cup granulated sugar

1 cup dry Marsala wine

4 tablespoons dark rum

1 1/2 cups whipping cream

SUGAR SYRUP

2 cups granulated sugar

1 cup instant espresso coffee

3 tablespoons dark rum

FILLING AND GARNISH

10 ounces mascarpone cheese, at
room temperature

1 ounce semisweet chocolate

Preheat the oven to 300 degrees. Butter and lightly flour two baking sheets.

Put the egg yolks in a mixing bowl over a pan of simmering water until lukewarm. Gradually whisk in the sugar. Remove from the heat and beat with a whisk or a mixer until the mixture falls from the beater in a flat ribbon. Stir in the vanilla.

Sift the two flours directly into the yolk and sugar mixture, and stir with a rubber spatula until well combined. In another bowl whip the egg whites with a pinch of salt until stiff peaks form. Using a whisk, beat a fourth of the egg whites into the yolk mixture, which lightens the heavy mixture and makes it easier to fold in the rest of the whites. Using a rubber spatula, fold in the remaining egg whites.

When the mixtures are barely combined, place the batter in a pastry bag fitted with a 1/2-inch plain tip. Pipe the batter onto the baking sheets to a length of about 3 inches. Leave about 1 inch between each ladyfinger for expansion while baking. Sift a liberal coating of powdered sugar on the ladyfingers. Bake in the oven for 15 to 18 minutes or until lightly golden on the surface.

Beat the egg yolks vigorously with a wire whip. Gradually add the sugar until the mixture is very thick and light in color. Stir in the Marsala wine. Place the bowl over a pan of boiling water. Beat the yolk mixture vigorously until the custard becomes thick and foamy. Once thick, add the rum and place in the refrigerator to chill completely. Chill another mixing bowl in the freezer, pour in the cream and whip. Fold the whipped cream into the chilled custard. If the custard has separated, stir before adding the whipped cream. Chill.

Put the sugar and espresso into a saucepan and boil for 5 minutes without stirring. Brush down the sides of the pan with water as crystals form around the edges. Remove from the heat and add the rum.

Spoon one-fourth of the warm, espresso-flavored syrup into the bottom of an 9 x 13 inch rectangular dish.. Place a single layer of ladyfingers on the syrup. Spoon another fourth of the syrup over the ladyfingers. Whip the mascarpone cheese with a rubber spatula until soft and easy to spread. Spread half of the softened cheese over the ladyfingers. Now spread half of the zabaglione over the cheese.

Make another set of layers on top of the first. When completed, you will have two layers of espresso-soaked ladyfingers and two layers each of mascarpone and zabaglione.

Grate the semisweet chocolate over the top of the dessert. Refrigerate for at least 2 hours or overnight.

. . . .

PURCHASED LADY FINGERS MAY BE USED INSTEAD OF
MAKING YOUR OWN.

. . . .

MASCARPONE

✳

Hailing from Italy's Lombardy region, mascarpone is a buttery rich double-cream to triple-cream cheese made from cow's milk. This ivory-colored, soft and delicate cheese ranges in texture from that of light clotted cream to that of room temperature butter.

ZABAGLIONE

One of Italy's great gifts to the rest of the world, zabaglione is an ethereal dessert made by whisking together egg yolks, wine (traditionally Marsala wine) and sugar. This beating is done over simmering water so that the egg yolks cook as they thicken into a light, foamy custard. The warm froth can be served either as a dessert by itself or as a sauce over cake, fruit, ice cream or pastry. In France it is called sabayon sauce.

WALNUT CREAM CHEESE BROWNIES

It is amazing what delicious things can result from disasters. As we were loading a catering van with 200 uncut brownies, I noticed that the cook was moving swiftly so I wouldn't get too close a look at the trays. Upon quick examination, I discovered that he had overcooked them. They were not burned, just on the far-from-delicious dry side. We brought them back into the kitchen and exercised eleventh-hour emergency procedures, which resulted in spreading a chocolate cream cheese frosting over the top. The brownies, which became moist and chewy, took on a whole new taste. There are seldom any left over and guests tend to lose all dietary dignity when they taste them.

— *Mary Nell Reck*

YIELDS 60 BROWNIES

BAKING WITH CREAM CHEESE

✳

Always use blocks of cream cheese in baking recipes. Soften the cream cheese block by removing the wrapper, placing the cheese in a plastic dish and microwaving it for 15 seconds on high.

BROWNIES

1 cup (2 sticks) unsalted butter

6 ounces semisweet chocolate

6 tablespoons unsweetened cocoa

4 cups granulated sugar

4 large eggs

2 teaspoons vanilla extract

2 cups all-purpose flour, plus some for dusting

1/4 teaspoon salt

2 cups walnut halves

CREAM CHEESE FROSTING

1 package (8 ounces) cream cheese, softened

1/2 cup (1 stick) unsalted butter, softened

2 tablespoons unsweetened cocoa

3 tablespoons hot, strong coffee

1 cup sifted confectioners' sugar

1 teaspoon vanilla extract

1/4 cup Droste unsweetened cocoa or processed unsweetened cocoa

Preheat the oven to 325 degrees. Prepare a 12 x 18-inch jellyroll pan by lining it with aluminum foil. Brush the foil and sides of the pan with melted butter and dust lightly with flour. Set aside.

Place the butter, semisweet chocolate and cocoa in a saucepan over low heat. Slowly melt while stirring. Remove from the heat and transfer to a large mixing bowl. Beat in the sugar. When thoroughly combined, beat in the eggs one at a time. Stir in the vanilla.

Sift in the flour and salt, and stir with a wooden spoon to barely combine. Pour the batter into the prepared pan and spread evenly. Evenly distribute the walnuts on the surface. Place in the middle of the oven. Bake for 40 to 45 minutes or until set but still soft. Transfer to a rack to cool.

Beat together the cream cheese and butter until light and fluffy. Dissolve the cocoa and the hot coffee in a small bowl. Stir into the creamed mixture. Sift in the confectioners' sugar and stir in the vanilla. When all the ingredients are well combined, spread the frosting evenly over the pan of cooled brownies. Sift the remaining 1/4 cup cocoa over the surface.

Using a large, sharp knife, cut the brownies into 1 to 2-inch squares.

Rugelach

YIELDS 40 PIECES

PASTRY

1 cup (2 sticks) unsalted
   butter, softened

8 ounces (1 package) cream
   cheese, softened

2 cups all-purpose flour

FILLING

1/2 cup granulated sugar

1/2 cup raisins

1 teaspoon cinnamon

1 cup chopped pecans

4 tablespoons sour cream

TOPPING

1/2 cup granulated sugar

1 teaspoon cinnamon

Place the butter and cream cheese in a mixing bowl. Beat with a dough paddle on medium speed until fluffy. Reduce the speed to low and gradually mix in the flour. Turn the dough out onto a work surface and knead the dough until all the flour is incorporated. Divide the dough into four parts. Cover each part with plastic wrap and chill for 1 hour.

Preheat the oven to 350 degrees. Combine the sugar, raisins, cinnamon and pecans in a bowl and set aside. Roll out each piece of dough onto a floured board into a rectangle approximately 3 x 20 inches. Spread a thin coating of sour cream lengthwise down half of each rolled pastry. Spoon one-fourth of the filling down the center of each. Using a large knife, fold the dough over lengthwise, into thirds, making one long roll. Cut each roll into 2-inch pieces.

Place the rugelach pieces on a cookie sheet lined with parchment paper. Bake in the preheated oven for 20 to 25 minutes or until puffed and golden.

Combine the sugar and cinnamon, and sprinkle on the warm ruglach as they come out of the oven.

RUGELACH

✳

A Hanukkah tradition, rugelach are bite-size, crescent-shaped cookies with any of several fillings, including raisins or other fruit, nuts, poppy-seed paste or jam.

CINNAMON

✳

Cinnamon was once used in love potions and as a perfume by wealthy Romans. Cinnamon comes from the inner bark of a tropical evergreen tree. The bark is harvested during the rainy season when it is more pliable. When dried, it curls into long quills, which are either cut into lengths to be sold as cinnamon sticks or ground into powder.

LEMON MOUSSE CAKE WITH A BROWNIE CRUST

A dish with a delicate lemon flavor is the perfect way to end a meal.

SERVES 10-12

MOUSSE

❋

The word mousse *comes from a French word meaning "froth." Commonly used to describe a cold, fluffy sweet dessert, a mousse may also be savory, made with pureed fish, chicken or vegetables. Sweet mousses are often made with pureed fruit or chocolate lightened with whipped cream and/or stiffly beaten egg whites. Savory mousses are most often made with beaten egg whites and stabilized with gelatin. A hot mousse, which is made with beaten egg whites and then baked, is called a soufflé. If done properly, a hot soufflé will rise several inches above its pan, but must be served immediately as it falls as it cools.*

CARAMEL FUDGE BROWNIES

1 cup (2 sticks) unsalted butter

4 ounces unsweetened chocolate

2 ounces semisweet chocolate

1/2 cup granulated sugar

1 pound dark brown sugar

4 large eggs

2 teaspoons vanilla extract

2 cups all-purpose flour

1/4 teaspoon salt

1/2 teaspoon baking powder

2 1/4 cups toasted and coarsely chopped walnuts or pecans

LEMON MOUSSE

1 cup granulated sugar

1/4 cup water

1/4 cup chopped lemon zest

6 large egg yolks

1/4 cup lemon juice

1 envelope Knox gelatin

1 3/4 cups whipping cream

RASPBERRY SAUCE

2 (10-ounce) packages frozen raspberries in syrup

Juice of half a lemon

1/4 cup granulated sugar

2 tablespoons cornstarch

1/2 cup cold water

1 tablespoon Grand Marnier® or other liqueur (optional)

GARNISH

Lemon slices

Fresh mint sprigs

Fresh raspberries

Preheat the oven to 350 degrees. Line a 12 x 17-inch pan (half sheet) with foil. Rub with butter, then sprinkle with flour to completely coat. Invert the pan and bang it over the sink to remove any excess flour. Set aside.

Place the butter and both chocolates in a large heavy saucepan. Melt over low heat, being careful that the chocolate does not burn. When three-fourths melted, remove from the heat and stir until completely melted. Stir in the sugars. Beat in the eggs one at a time. Stir in the vanilla.

Measure the flour, salt and baking powder into a sifter and sift directly over the pot. Gently stir until the dry ingredients are barely combined. Stir in the nuts. Pour the batter into the prepared pan and smooth the top with a spatula. Place in the preheated oven and bake for 25 to 35 minutes or until done. Allow the brownies to cool in the pan.

Place the sugar, water and lemon zest in a small saucepan. Simmer for 5 minutes without stirring until it forms a syrup. Do not let the sugar caramelize. Remove from the heat and set aside. Place the egg yolks in a mixing bowl and beat on medium speed for 5 minutes. Change the mixer setting to low and gradually add the hot syrup to the egg yolks. Change the mixer setting back to medium and beat for 10 minutes until the mixture is thick and fluffy.

Place the lemon juice in a small shallow pan and place the gelatin on top to soften. When soft, place pan over low heat to dissolve. Stir the warm gelatin mixture into the egg mixture.

Place the whipping cream in a mixing bowl and set in the freezer to completely chill before mixing. Whip the cream until it forms soft peaks and fold into the lemon mixture. Set aside.

Combine the undrained berries and lemon juice in a food processor or blender and puree. Strain, pressing with the back of a spoon. Add the sugar, cornstarch, water, and liqueur; blend well. Place in a saucepan over medium heat and bring to a boil, stirring frequently. Reduce the heat and continue stirring for 1 minute. Remove from the heat and allow to cool until ready to use.

Cut the brownies with a biscuit or other cutter to fit the individual molds or ramekins. Place in the molds. Spoon the mousse over each brownie. Place a lemon slice on top of each mold and freeze or refrigerate overnight.

Before serving, drizzle raspberry sauce over the top and garnish with lemon slices, fresh mint, and fresh raspberries.

· · · · · · FLAVORS *of* LIFE · · · · · · 189 · · · · · · DESSERTS · · · · · · · · · · · · · · · · · ·

THIS MAY ALSO BE MADE IN AN 8-INCH SPRINGFORM PAN. USE THE BOTTOM OF THE PAN AS A GUIDE TO CUT OUT THE BROWNIE CRUST. PLACE THE BROWNIE IN THE BOTTOM OF THE SPRINGFORM PAN. USING PARCHMENT PAPER CUT TO FIT, MAKE A COLLAR INSIDE THE PAN THAT IS AT LEAST 3 TO 4 INCHES TALLER THAN THE PAN. POUR THE FILLING INTO THE PAN AND FREEZE OR REFRIGERATE. WHEN READY TO SERVE, REMOVE THE SIDES OF THE PAN AND THE PAPER COLLAR. TRANSFER THE CAKE TO A SERVING TRAY AND DECORATE THE TOP WITH WHIPPED CREAM, IF DESIRED. SERVE WITH THE RASPBERRY SAUCE.

THE BROWNIES ARE ALSO WONDERFUL ALONE, SERVED WITH A SCOOP OF VANILLA ICE CREAM.

· ·

CUTTING THE PERFECT SLICE

✳

Some cakes may be too delicate to cut even with a very sharp knife. The best way to cut these cakes is with waxed, unflavored dental floss. Use a piece of floss about 1 foot long. Hold it taut with both hands, then bring it straight down through the cake (do not use a sawing motion). To remove the floss from the cake, pull it out by one end; don't try to bring it back up through the cut you have just made. Wipe the floss off with a barely damp cloth after each cut, then dry it before cutting again. Mark out your slices before you remove any from the cake. To do this, first lightly oil the blade of a small, stiff-bladed, metal spatula with neutral-flavored vegetable oil. Then, one at a time, run it underneath the cut slices, between the bottom of each slice and the parchment, to loosen them. After that, very gently transfer the slices to their plates.

Savory soufflés are usually served hot as a main dish; they can be made with a variety of ingredients, including cheese, meat, fish or vegetables. Dessert soufflés may be baked, chilled or frozen, and are most often flavored with fruit purees, chocolate, lemon or liqueurs. Both sweet and savory soufflés are often accompanied by a complementary sauce.

Always bake a soufflé on the middle rack in a preheated oven. Do not open the oven door during the first 25 minutes of baking (at least) or the soufflé may fall.

Passion fruit is a tropical fruit named not for the passionate propensity it promotes but because various parts of the plant's flowers resemble different symbols of Christ's crucifixion. When ripe, it has a dimpled, deep-purple skin and a soft, golden flesh generously punctuated with tiny, edible black seeds. The flavor is seductively sweet and tart, and the fragrance is tropical and perfume-like. Fresh passion fruit is available from March through September in most specialty markets. Choose large, heavy, firm fruit with a deep-purple color.

PASSION FRUIT SOUFFLÉ

SERVES 12

SOUFFLÉ

10 large egg yolks

1 cup granulated sugar, divided, plus extra for dusting

1/4 cup cornstarch

1 teaspoon vanilla extract

1/2 cup passion fruit puree (found at gourmet markets)

2 cups milk

12 large egg whites

1/4 teaspoon cream of tartar

1/4 teaspoon salt

GARNISH

Crème anglaise sauce (see the recipe on page 193) flavored with 2 tablespoons of passion fruit puree

Preheat the oven to 350 degrees. Coat twelve 6-ounce soufflé dishes with butter and sprinkle with sugar. Set aside.

Place the egg yolks, 1/2 cup of the sugar, cornstarch, vanilla and passion fruit puree in a mixing bowl. Beat well with a whisk. Bring the milk to a boil in a saucepan. Remove from the heat and slowly add to the egg yolk mixture until combined. Return to the stove and cook until thick. Remove from the heat.

Whip the egg whites with the cream of tartar and salt. When stiff, gradually add the remaining 1/2 cup of sugar. Fold the stiffly beaten egg whites into the custard mixture.

Pour into the prepared molds. Bake in the preheated oven for 12 to 15 minutes or until puffed and golden. Let rest for 5 minutes. Run a knife around each mold, invert and place on parchment paper-lined sheet pans.

When ready to serve, place the soufflés in the oven to reheat for 3 to 4 minutes. Serve with crème anglaise sauce flavored with passion fruit puree.

HAZELNUT SEMIFREDDO

SERVES 8

HAZELNUTS

1 cup chopped toasted hazelnuts

8 ounces semisweet chocolate, grated

12 crushed Amaretto® cookies

1/4 cup Frangelico® liqueur

SEMIFREDDO

10 large eggs, separated

2 cups granulated sugar, divided

2 teaspoons vanilla extract

1/4 teaspoon salt

1/4 teaspoon cream of tartar

4 cups heavy cream

Line a loaf pan with parchment paper. Spray lightly with pan spray. Set aside.

In a bowl combine the toasted hazelnuts, grated chocolate, crushed cookies and Frangelico®. Set aside.

Place the egg yolks in a mixing bowl. Place over low heat and whip until warm. Gradually add 1 cup of the sugar and beat until thick and lemon yellow. Remove from the heat; add the vanilla and set aside.

Place the egg whites, salt and cream of tartar in a mixing bowl. Whip until stiff. Add the other cup of sugar and continue whipping until it forms stiff peaks. Gently fold the stiff egg whites into the egg yolks.

Whip the heavy cream until it forms soft peaks. Gently fold the whipped cream into the egg mixture. Pour one-third of the semifreddo mixture into the prepared pan. Place half of the hazelnut mixture on top. Add another layer of semifreddo and the other half of the hazelnuts. Then place the remaining semifreddo on top. Smooth with a spatula. Cover with plastic wrap and freeze overnight.

To serve, unmold and cut into thick slices.

Sweet Rolls

ROLLS

7 ounces of puff pastry
  (one 6 x 11-inch sheet)

3 tablespoons butter, melted

3 tablespoons granulated sugar

1/2 teaspoon cinnamon

6 tablespoons chopped pecans

Flour for dusting the rolling pin and
  cutting board

ICING

4 large egg whites

4 cups confectioners' sugar

1/4 cup milk

1/2 cup (1 stick) unsalted
  butter, melted

1/4 teaspoon cinnamon

1 teaspoon vanilla extract

Preheat the oven to 375 degrees.

Place the sheet of pastry on a floured cutting board, rub flour on a rolling pin and roll the puff pastry until it is slightly larger than its original size, about 8 x 14 inches.

Spread the melted butter over the pastry using a pastry brush. Mix the sugar and cinnamon together and sprinkle evenly over the butter. Place the chopped pecans on one half of the pastry.

Fold the other half of the pastry over the chopped pecans. Flour the rolling pin again and roll the puff pastry flat; the pecans will begin to show through the top of the pastry and some will be lost out the side (that's okay).

Using a pastry cutter, slice the pastry into lengths about 1 1/2 inches wide (three fingers), then slice on an angle to make individual pieces.

Place the pieces on parchment paper on a baking sheet and bake in the preheated oven for about 5 minutes. Let cool for 5 minutes before drizzling the icing over the top.

Place the egg whites in a mixing bowl. Beat with a wire whisk until frothy, about 1 minute. Sift the sugar into the bowl and beat until smooth. Gradually add the milk and melted butter while beating. Stir in the cinnamon and vanilla.

Using a fork, drizzle the icing over the sweet rolls before serving.

. . . .

THE ICING CAN BE STORED IN A COVERED PLASTIC
CONTAINER IN THE REFRIGERATOR. TO USE THE
ICING AFTER IT HAS CHILLED, PLACE A SMALL
AMOUNT IN A PLASTIC BOWL AND HEAT IN THE
MICROWAVE ON LOW UNTIL IT FORMS A SOFT LIQUID.

. . . .

PUFF PASTRY

✳

Puff pastry, or pâte feuilletée, is a many-layered, very flaky pastry used to make delectable baked goods such as croissants, turnovers, pastry shells and tarts. The pastry is made by repeatedly layering pastry dough and butter, folding and rolling many times, and then shaping and baking. If done well, the dough will expand and separate into hundreds of flaky layers, rising to over eight times its original thickness. Making puff pastry is a time-consuming activity and must be done to an exacting standard. Fortunately for those of us without the time and patience required to make puff pastry from scratch, there are several excellent commercially made products available. Look for them in the frozen food section in the grocery store.

CRÈME BRÛLÉE WITH GRAND MARNIER®

The contrasting textures of crème brûlée make every bite a sensual experience.

— *Mary Nell Reck*

SERVES 8

CRÈME BRÛLÉE

3 cups milk

1/2 vanilla bean, split

3/4 cup granulated sugar

12 large egg yolks

3 cups heavy cream

ORANGE ZEST

1 large naval orange

2 tablespoons granulated sugar

1 tablespoon Grand Marnier® liqueur

GARNISH

Granulated sugar

Grand Marnier® liqueur

Raspberries

Sprigs of fresh mint

Orange zest

Preheat the oven to 325 degrees.

Place the milk, vanilla bean and sugar in a saucepan and bring to a boil. Remove from the heat, cover and let steep for 2 to 3 minutes. Whisk the egg yolks and cream together in a mixing bowl. Remove the vanilla bean and gradually add the hot milk to the egg yolk mixture.

Strain and pour into eight 6-ounce porcelain molds. Place in a shallow baking pan and fill with boiling water. Bake in the preheated oven for 20 minutes or until set but soft. Remove from the oven and cool to room temperature. Chill until ready to serve.

Using a vegetable peeler, very finely peel the orange. Cut the peel into a very fine julienne. Place in a jar and add the sugar and Grand Marnier®. Mix to combine until the zest is well-coated with sugar. Cover and refrigerate until ready to use.

To serve, sprinkle a very light coating of sugar over the surface of the crème brûlée. Caramelize the sugar with a propane torch or in the broiler until uniformly golden. Sprinkle each serving with about a tablespoon of Grand Marnier® and garnish with raspberries, mint and orange zest.

CRÈME BRÛLÉE

✳

The literal translation of crème brûlée is "burnt cream." It is a chilled, stirred custard that is sprinkled with brown or granulated sugar just before serving. The sugar topping is quickly caramelized under a broiler. The brittle caramelized topping creates a delicious flavor and textural contrast to the smooth, creamy, cool custard below.

CRÈME ANGLAISE

YIELDS 3 CUPS

1/4 cup heavy cream

4 large egg yolks

1/2 cup granulated sugar

1 tablespoon cornstarch

1 1/2 cups milk

1 vanilla bean

Place the heavy cream in a mixing bowl and put in the refrigerator until very cold. Place the yolks in another mixing bowl. While whisking vigorously, gradually add the sugar. Beat until light in color and a ribbon forms. Stir in the cornstarch. Set aside.

Place the milk and vanilla bean in a heavy saucepan and bring to a boil. Remove the vanilla bean from the milk and gradually add the hot milk to the eggs, whisking continuously.

Return the egg and milk mixture to the stove. Cook over medium heat for 5 to 6 minutes or until thickened. Quickly transfer the sauce to the bowl of cold cream. Stir until cool. Cover with plastic wrap and chill until ready to serve.

....

CRÈME ANGLAISE MAY BE FLAVORED BY
ADDING 2 TABLESPOONS OF A VARIETY OF LIQUEURS
(FRANGELICO®, AMARETTO®, COGNAC).

....

CHOCOLATE SAUCE

MAKES ABOUT 4 CUPS

2 1/2 cups heavy cream

1/2 cup light corn syrup

1/2 cup (1 stick) unsalted butter

1/4 teaspoon salt

16 ounces bittersweet chocolate, chopped

2 teaspoons vanilla extract

Place the cream, corn syrup, butter and salt in a saucepan. Bring to a boil for 1 minute.

Remove the pan from the heat and stir in the chocolate. Cover the pan and let stand for 5 minutes. Stir in the vanilla. Serve hot (can be reheated in the microwave) or at room temperature. Store in the refrigerator.

....

FOR AN EYE-CATCHING PRESENTATION, USE A PASTRY
BAG OR LARGE SPOON AND SPIRAL CHOCOLATE SAUCE
ONTO THE PLATE BEFORE PLACING YOUR DESSERT.
YOU CAN ALSO DRIZZLE CHOCOLATE UP AND DOWN,
THEN LEFT TO RIGHT FOR A "CHECKERED" EFFECT.

....

VANILLA

＊

The ancient Totonaco Indians of Mexico were the first keepers of the secrets of vanilla. When they were defeated by the Aztecs, they were forced to relinquish their vanilla pods, the exotic fruit of the Tlilxochitl vine.

One of the most exquisite of all the sweet spices, vanilla has a mellow, fragrant, sweet taste. These tender scented beans come from an orchid, a genus of climbing plants native to the tropics. The long podlike capsules are picked unripe and have a lengthy curing process. Vanilla is one of the three most expensive spices in the world.

To use vanilla beans, cut the bean in half lengthwise. Using your knife, scrape the seeds from the inside of the bean. Don't discard the used bean shell, but make vanilla sugar by storing it in a canister of sugar. The longer the sugar is stored, the more intense the vanilla flavor.

"Strength is the capacity to break a chocolate bar into four pieces with your bare hands— and then eat just one of the pieces."

— JUDITH VIORST
(B. 1931)

Recipes for pie dough are
based on the French
formula for pâte brisée,
or "broken dough,"
meaning the pie crust
should break and flake
apart easily. This flaki-
ness is the hallmark of a
well-made crust and
results when there is a
perfect balance of flour
(both the amount and
type used) to fat and
liquid ingredients.

Evenly dispersed fat and
flour results in a short
crust that is somewhat
cookie-like in texture.
Uneven mixtures of fat
and flour (with a mix of
smaller and larger pieces)
result in a long flaky
dough (sort of like the
flakes in puff pastry used
for milles feuilles and
Napoleons). The latter
type of dough looks
slightly marbleized when
you roll it out. This is fine.
It is far better to err on
the side of under-blend-
ing when cutting in the
fat than overworking it.

ALL-PURPOSE
WHITE FLOUR
VS.
ALL-PURPOSE
UNBLEACHED
FLOUR

✳

Neither all-purpose white
flour nor unbleached
flour has any leavening
agents such as soda.
Although the two are used
interchangeably without
a noticeable difference,
unbleached flour usually
has more of the gluten
protein than white flour,
making it a better flour
for yeast breads.

SWEET PIE CRUST

YIELDS 2 PIE SHELLS OR 1 (2-CRUST) PIE

2 1/2 cups unbleached pastry or
    all-purpose flour, plus additional
    for dusting

1/2 cup granulated sugar

1 cup (2 sticks) unsalted butter,
    chilled and cut into small pieces

2 extra-large egg yolks

1/4 cup heavy cream, plus extra
    as needed

This dough can be made in an electric mixer fitted with a paddle attachment or in a food processor using a metal blade. In either machine, combine the flour and the sugar, and mix completely. Add the small pieces of butter and mix just to a coarse cornmeal-like consistency.

In a small mixing bowl, whisk together the egg yolks and heavy cream, and pour into the flour mixture. It may be necessary to add as much as 2 tablespoons of extra cream to make the dough moist enough to form a ball. Mix just until the cream and eggs bring the dough together into a rough ball. Lightly dust your hands and a smooth work surface with flour and place the dough on the surface. Knead for just a few seconds to distribute the fat. Form a ball and chill for at least 1 hour. Roll out to the desired thickness as needed.

If the pie crust is to be baked before filling, bake in a preheated 350 degree oven for about 10 minutes.

PÂTE BRISÉE (PIE CRUST)

This recipe is appropriate for either sweet or savory dishes.

ONE 9-INCH CRUST

1 1/2 cups all-purpose flour

1/2 cup (1 stick) unsalted butter

4 tablespoons ice water

TWO 9-INCH CRUSTS

3 cups all-purpose flour

1 cup (2 sticks) unsalted butter

1/2 cup ice water

FOUR 9-INCH CRUSTS

6 cups all-purpose flour

2 cups (4 sticks) butter

1 cup ice water

Place the flour on a board. Make a well in the center. Cut the butter into 1/2-inch pieces and place in the well.

Cut the butter into the flour with a pastry cutter. When lumpy but combined, add enough ice water to barely hold the mixture together.

Rub mixture together with the heel of your hand to combine. If making more than one crust, divide into equal portions. Cover and chill.

Preheat the oven to 375 degrees. Roll each pie crust out on a floured pastry board to a 1/4-inch thickness. Fit into a 9-inch pan. Line the crust with parchment paper, then place raw rice on top of the paper and bake in the preheated oven for 20 minutes. Remove the paper and rice, and bake for 10 to 12 minutes more or until golden.

PASTRY CREAM

Pastry cream is a basic staple of dessert making. It is the filling for cream puffs,
éclairs and cream pies. Combined with whipped cream, it becomes a delicious element
in English trifle. Add a little gelatin and it becomes a mousse.

YIELDS ABOUT 3 CUPS

1/2 vanilla bean

2 cups hot milk

4 large egg yolks

1/2 cup granulated sugar

4 tablespoons cornstarch

Split the vanilla bean lengthwise. Place both halves of the vanilla bean with the milk in a heavy 2-quart saucepan. Bring to a boil. Remove from the heat. Cover and set aside to extract the flavor from the vanilla bean.

Place the egg yolks in a medium mixing bowl. Beat with a whisk while gradually adding the sugar. Continue beating until the mixture is very thick and light yellow. When the whisk is lifted, the mixture should fall in a flat ribbon. Stir in the cornstarch.

Remove the vanilla bean from the milk. Very gradually add the hot milk to the egg yolk mixture. The hot liquid tends to splash as it is stirred into the thick egg mixture. Stir the egg mixture with a whisk in a very rapid circular motion until the mixture thins somewhat.

Return the mixture to the saucepan and pause to quickly rinse and dry the mixing bowl. Place the pastry cream over moderately high heat and cook, whisking constantly. As the sauce thickens, whisk vigorously to avoid forming lumps. When thick and smooth, transfer to the clean bowl.

Stir slowly with a wooden spoon for 3 to 4 minutes until it cools slightly. If you are not using the pastry cream right away, cover with plastic wrap, placing the wrap directly on the surface of the pastry cream. Refrigerate until ready to use.

. . . .

ADD FLAVORS WHEN THE PASTRY CREAM IS COOL.
THERE ARE NUMEROUS WAYS TO FLAVOR PASTRY
CREAM. BELOW ARE A FEW VARIATIONS.

STIR IN 2 TABLESPOONS COGNAC, GRAND MARNIER®,
AMARETTO®, FRANGELICO®, RUM OR BOURBON

ADD 1/4 CUP ORANGE ZEST COOKED IN 1/4 CUP
WATER AND 2 TABLESPOONS SUGAR

ADD 2 TABLESPOONS LEMON OR LIME ZEST COOKED
IN 2 TABLESPOONS WATER AND 2 TABLESPOONS
GRANULATED SUGAR

ADD 3 OUNCES MELTED SEMISWEET CHOCOLATE

ADD 1 CUP TOASTED COCONUT

ADD 1 OUNCE MELTED SEMISWEET CHOCOLATE AND 2
TEASPOONS INSTANT ESPRESSO

ADD 1 CUP CHOPPED TOASTED NUTS

. . . .

TO MAKE
CITRUS ZEST

*

Zest is the colored part of a citrus fruit's skin or rind. It is often added to a recipe for a burst of flavor. The white part between the skin and the fruit has a bitter taste, and the objective is to remove the zest without touching it.

Wash your fruit well. Use a vegetable peeler and apply just enough pressure to peel off strips of the rind without including the white cellulose. With a sharp knife, cut the peel into small slices. A special tool, a zester, may be used just for this job.

BENEFICIARIES

MARY NELL RECK CULINARY SCHOLARSHIP FUND

The fund will be used to award scholarships to women seeking to become chefs. Les Dames d'Escoffier's Houston Chapter will administer the scholarship. Les Dames d'Escoffier is an international organization of women leaders who create a supportive culture in their communities to achieve excellence in the food, beverage and hospitality professions. Mary Nell Reck was a member of the Houston Chapter. Les Dames d'Escoffier will publicize the availability of scholarships through the schools in the Houston area that offer accredited culinary programs and through the media. Factors that will be used to evaluate scholarship applicants will include need, previous grades and educational achievements, demonstrated interest in the culinary arts, acceptance to, or enrollment in, an institution offering a legitimate culinary arts curriculum and recommendations from teachers, mentors and employers.

BREAST CENTER AT BAYLOR COLLEGE OF MEDICINE

The major goal of the Breast Center at Baylor College of Medicine is to reduce mortality from breast cancer through research, education and state-of-the-art patient care. The Center is also an important training ground for young researchers and doctors. The Center is divided into two sections: the Breast Care Center and the Breast Research Program. The Breast Care Center offers comprehensive care and includes four sections: breast imaging; breast cancer risk assessment, genetic testing and counseling, and prevention; an evaluation and diagnostic clinic; and a breast cancer clinic. The Breast Research Program carries out both basic and translational breast cancer research. By studying various aspects of the basic biology of mammary gland development, breast disease and breast cancer, researchers can then translate that information into improvement in patient care. The Breast Center has a reputation for research few other centers can match. The Center is currently one of only six recipients of the highly competitive National Institutes of Health Specialized Program of Research Excellence (SPORE) grant in breast cancer.

PINK RIBBONS PROJECT - DANCERS IN MOTION AGAINST BREAST CANCER

Pink Ribbons Project - Dancers in Motion Against Breast Cancer was created in 1995 by four dancers in New York City whose lives had been personally touched by breast cancer. Now based in Houston, the project has raised over $800,000 and continues assisting in the fight against breast cancer through awareness programs, support of proper screening and follow-up care for the medically underserved, and funding research initiatives. It has received national acclaim for its artistic strength, high-quality programming and urgent nature. Now entering its seventh year, the Pink Ribbons Project has rallied some of the nation's most prominent dance artists and professionals to donate their time, services and talent, and it continues to present creative and innovative ways to raise funds and awareness to help in the battle against this disease.

THE ROSE

The Rose is a Houston-based non-profit organization whose mission is to ensure that all women have access to early detection of breast cancer, regardless of their ability to pay. When its first community-based center opened, The Rose offered affordable mammograms to ALL women. Today The Rose offers a full complement of breast cancer diagnostic procedures that include mammography screening, diagnostics, ultrasounds and breast biopsies, plus support services and patient navigators who help ensure the accessibility of treatment for breast cancer. From The Rose's two locations, more than 35,000 women are served annually; additionally, 10,000 women attend breast healthcare programs. The Rose is one of the nation's "Model Programs" listed by the Center for Disease Control, and it won the American Cancer Society's Harold P. Freeman Award for exemplary achievement in bringing cancer control and awareness to traditionally underserved, at-risk communities. Civic and community groups, foundations, corporations and individuals along with the unwavering commitment of employees, physicians and volunteers have helped to create an organization that continues to save the lives of countless women.

ACKNOWLEDGMENTS & SPECIAL THANKS

THE GREATER HOUSTON COMMUNITY FOUNDATION

The Coronado Club is grateful to the Greater Houston Community Foundation for its help and support in making this a nonprofit charitable project. The Greater Houston Community Foundation (GHCF) provides a flexible, cost-effective and tax-efficient way for donors to invest in philanthropic activity in Houston and around the United States. GHCF helps donors fulfill their charitable goals by providing information on important local charitable issues and by matching these donors with the nonprofit organizations that best address their interests. The Foundation began operations in 1995 and has more than 300 charitable family funds. These funds have made more than $68 million in cumulative grants since the founding.

2004 BOARD OF DIRECTORS

V. Scott Kneese
President

Meredith J. Long
Vice President

G. Crawford Moorefield
Secretary

M. Guion Bond, Jr.
Treasurer

John Scott Arnoldy
Director

Ernest H. Cockrell
Director

James T. Edmonds
Director

Drew K. Masterson
Director

Rodney H. Margolis
Director

Charles J. O'Connell
Director

2003 BOARD OF DIRECTORS

Ned S. Holmes
President

V. Scott Kneese
Vice President

G. Crawford Moorefield
Secretary

M. Guion Bond, Jr.
Treasurer

Ernest H. Cockrell
Director

James T. Edmonds
Director

Meredith J. Long
Director

Rodney H. Margolis
Director

Charles R. Ofner
Director

John H. Young
Director

2004 HOUSE COMMITTEE

S. Reed Morian
Chairman

Lorne D. Bain

William M. Hitchcock

Ned S. Holmes

John Wilson Kelsey

V. Scott Kneese

Meredith J. Long

Rodney H. Margolis

2003 HOUSE COMMITTEE

John Wilson Kelsey
Chairman

Lorne D. Bain

Ned S. Holmes

V. Scott Kneese

Kevin J. Lilly

Meredith J. Long

P. Michael Mann

Rodney H. Margolis

S. Reed Morian

Eddy J. Rogers, Jr.

2003-2004 PUBLICATIONS COMMITTEE

Lorne D. Bain
Chairman

G. Clyde Buck

John Wilson Kelsey

David A. Novelli

2003-2004 COOKBOOK SUBCOMMITTEE

Margaret Rochs
Chairman

John Wilson Kelsey
Co-chairman

Thomas N. Amonett

Roni Atnipp

Joe R. Davis

Mary Bendy Eaton

Bryan Emerson

Carla Knobloch

Irwin L. Levy

Crawford Moorefield

Harry C. Pinson

Wick Rowland

Polly Shouse

Anne Stewart

John H. Young

COOKBOOK RECIPE TESTERS

Clair Amonett

Roni Atnipp

Kitty Borah

Nancy Conrad

Babette Dawson

Gary Eaton

Mary Bendy Eaton

Laura Emerson

Jan Greer

Carol Hoppe

Jane McCarroll

Cara Moczulski

Celia Munisteri

Bobby Nau

Victoria Nau

Amy Novelli

Anita O'Shaughnessy

Karen Patrinely

Patty Porter

Cynthia Quill

Elizabeth Reynolds

Margaret Rochs

Wick Rowland

Anne L. Stewart

Anne Stewart

Marian Tindall

Leslie Wade

Nancy Williams

Mary Beth Wimberly

PUBLIC RELATIONS

Rives Carlberg L.P.

The Coronado Club is appreciative of Rives Carlberg for their support and assistance in making this project a success.

THE CORONADO CLUB

Telephone
713.659.2426

Facsimile
713.659.2428

www.coronadoclub.com

SPECIAL THANKS

Kitty Borah

Gary Eaton

Laura Emerson

Patty Porter

Hollie Spessard-Wolfson

Marian Tindall

Leslie Wade

Carlton House Events

Kuhl-Linscomb

Tierra Dulce

David Spaw and Erin Reck

———

The Coronado Club

———

Joe R. Davis/Consolidated Graphics, Inc.
HILL Strategic Brand Solutions
Ralph Smith Photography

———

Andrews Kurth LLP
Clair and Tom Amonett
John Scott Arnoldy
Michelle and Lorne Bain
Mr. and Mrs. A. L. Ballard
Becky and Guy Bond
Cheryl and Philip Burguieres
Baker Botts Club Members
Bracewell & Patterson L.L.P.
Burlington Resources
Central Market
John Daugherty, Realtors
Cherie and Jim Flores
Mr. and Mrs. Michael E. Frazier
Ned S. Holmes
Suzie and Larry D. Johnson
Karen and John Kelsey
Ruth and Scott Kneese
Carla Knobloch
Rolanette and Berdon Lawrence
Mr. and Mrs. Meredith J. Long
Carmelo and Hilary Mauro,
Carmelo's Italian Restaurant
Ann and John E. McFarlane, Sr.
Patrick and Nancy Mendenhall
Laurie and S. Reed Morian
Mr. and Mrs. David A. Novelli
Charles J. O'Connell

Katie and Patrick Oxford
Ellen B. Randall
Sidney C. Roberts, M.D., Lufkin, Texas
Margaret Rochs
Bill and Kathi Rovere
Fayez Sarofim
Polly Shouse
Mr. and Mrs. Earl E. Shouse
Marian Tindall
Bill and Lynda Transier
Susan and Gene Vaughan
Vaughan Nelson Investment Management
Charlotte and Larry Whaley
Keith Williams
Carolyn and John H. Young

———

Mr. and Mrs. Louis K. Adler
Mr. and Mrs. J.D. Bucky Allshouse
Kent and Linda Anderson /
Gerald and Dorothy Smith
Beverly and Dan Arnold
Marshall Ashmore
Roni and Doug Atnipp
David and Judy Beck
Rick and Andrea Behrend
Martin and Kathleen Beirne
Sharon and Joe Bendy
Stuart and Gus Blackshear
Al and Marti Bledsoe
Kitty Borah
Craig C. Brown
Dr. and Mrs. William T. Butler
Margot and John Cater
Bob and Gracie Cavnar
Kimberly and Robert Chambers
Chantal Foundation
Joe and Robin Cunningham
Jim and Diane D'Agostino
Mr. and Mrs. Michael C. Dawson
Nancy and Cletus Dodd
Mike and Yvonne Donohoe

S. Stacy and Tara G. Eastland
Carole and Richard Elledge
Bryan and Laura Emerson
Clayton and Shel Erikson
Carolyn Faulk
Elaine and Marvy Finger
Jerry and Nanette Finger /
Jonathan and Karen Finger
Ann and Peter Fluor
Barbara B. and Peter C. Forbes
Harriet and Joe Foster
Gensler
Alfred C. Glassell III
Mr. and Mrs. Dewey J. Gonsoulin, Jr.
Charles and Sherri Gordon
Cynthia and Ben Guill
Nancy and Barry Harrell
Lauren and Warren Harris
Diana and Russell Hawkins
Robert M. Hopson II
Linda Durant Houssiere
D. Michael Hunter
Grover G. Jackson
Nancy and Dan Japhet
Drs. Blair and Rita Justice
Linda and George Kelly
Clarence F. Kendall II
David W. Kiatta
Albert and Rosemary Kimball
Rita and Randy Kramer
Hal G. Kuntz
Janiece and Stephen Lasher
Locke Liddell & Sapp LLP
Frank Lorenzo
Mr. and Mrs. Rodney H. Margolis
Lanny Martin
Drew and Madeline Masterson
Lisa and Will Mathis
Sharon M. Mattox
Rebecca A. McDonald
Missy and Allen McInnes
Steve and Laurie Mechler
Linda J. Messner
David and Diane Modesett

Nancy and Lucian Morrison

Laura and Roy Nichol

Barbara and William P. O'Connell

Rufus and Kathleen Oliver

Jim and Anita O'Shaughnessy

Mr. and Mrs. Dee S. Osborne

Michael F. Padon

Mr. and Mrs. William E. Penland, Jr.

Harry C. Pinson

Porter and Hedges LLP / Patty and Bill Porter

Charles D. Powell

Estelle and Charles Racusin

Roger A. Ramsey

Christine Eilert Reel

Alison L. Renz

Richard's Liquors and Fine Wine

Liz and Robert Rigney

Eddy and Pat Rogers

Thomas A. Roupe

Walter W. Sapp

Arthur A. Seeligson III

Tommy and Sandy Soriero

N. L. Stevens III and Nancy D. Williams

Anne and Michael Stewart

Kathy and Rey Stroube

Sylvia and John Sullivan

Bette P. Thomas

Tuesday Morning Men's Fellowship-MDPC

Mr. and Mrs. David M. Underwood

Connie and Steve Valerius

Mr. and Mrs. Peter S. Wareing

Raye G. White

Wallace S. and Isabel Wilson

Bill and Marie Wise

WoodRock & Co.

Barbara and Roger Aksamit

Bob and Judy Allen

Maureen Alsup

Michael and Laura Bartolotta

Judy and Ron Bell

Diane B. Biegel

Kelli and Eddy Blanton

Ann and John Bookout

John B. Brent

John and Dianne Brock

Sara Brook, Dessert Gallery Bakery and Café

Robert L. Clarke

Karen and Gus Comiskey, Jr.

Peter Coneway

Diane Connally

George S. Craft

Sanford and Susie Criner

Rose and Harry Cullen

Dr. and Mrs. Clotaire D. Delery

Dr. Nicola Di Ferrante

Cheryl Patton Donaho

Mary Bendy and Gary Eaton

Shelley Edelstein

Linda and Bob Egan

Houston Trust Company

C. Richard Everett

Suzanne Fain

Madelyn and George Farris

Shari and Tom Fish

Steve Folzenlogen/Sandra Lawson

Jennifer and Todd Frazier

David and Anne Frischkorn

Martha and Gibson Gayle Jr.

Rosalie and William M. Hitchcock

Manfred Jachmich

Elaine Jackson

JDA Professional Services, Inc.

Buz and Cindy Jochetz

Josephine and Philip John

Ouisie Jones, Ouisie's Table

Nina Kamin

Diane and Donald Kendall, Jr.

Judith and Irwin L. Levy

Mr. and Mrs. Jeff B. Love

Bud Luther

Mike and Carolyn Mann

Stan and Reinnette Marek

Ed and Gaye McCullough

Marvin McMurrey

Darlene and John McNabb

Bonnie and Bill Miller

Dennis E. Murphree

Shirley Muse

Linwood D. Newman

Flo and Charles Newton

Betty and Stephen Newton

Diane and Charles Ofner

Ann and Bill Olson

Mr. and Mrs. Dean Patrinely

Gary R. Petersen

Cynthia Hesterly Powell

Townes G. Pressler, Jr.

Patti and Steve Raben

Hope and Ed Reh

Ann and Hugh Roff

Wick and Rob Rowland

R.A. "Pete" Seale

Gloria H. and Richard H. Skinner

Peggy and Ashley Smith

Jean and Yale Smith

Dorothy W. Smith

Linda F. Somyak

Lois and George Stark

Steven E. Stern, M.D.

Anne and Bill Stewart

Mike and Anita Stude

J. Kent Sweezey

Leonard and Janet Tallerine

Texas Chef's Association (ACF)

Merrianne J. Timko

Betty and Jess B. Tutor

Mr. and Mrs. Temple Webber

Gerry Odom Williamson

Ken and Gay Wynne

P

PANDOWDY *181*

PAPAYA

papaya salsa, for pheasant enchiladas *100 (illus. 101)*

trout piñón with papaya lime butter sauce *136*

PAPRIKA (pimenton)

about *16, 41*

spicy pork pimenton *16*

PARSLEY *77*

PASSION FRUIT: passion fruit soufflé *190*

PASTA SALAD: pasta salad Genovese *47*

PASTA

basil linguine with salmon *66*

duck ravioli with ginger cream sauce *105*

fettuccine with mussels *62*

fettuccine with shrimp and mushrooms *64*

fresh pasta *69*

grilled breast of quail on rosemary capellini with roma tomato sauce *92*

linguine primavera *67*

lobster quenelles with crawfish sauce *65*

pasta salad Genovese *47*

smoked salmon fettuccine *63 (illus. 60--61)*

venison linguine *109*

PASTIS *29*

PASTRY CREAM *195*

PASTRY, PUFF

about *191*

eggs Juarez *41*

grilled breast of quail en croute with two sauces *93*

sautéed crabmeat with tomatillo sauce *139*

sweet rolls *191*

PÂTE: galantine of pheasant *20 (illus. 21)*

PEANUTS: chicken sate with peanut dipping sauce *22*

PEARS

about *171*

foie gras with a caramelized pear and Courvoisier sauce *28*

Gorgonzola pear tart *168*

pear tart with three creams *171 (illus. 166--67)*

PECANS

Italian cream cake *177*

lemon mousse cake with a brownie crust *188*

MN's outrageous chocolate cake *174 (illus. 175)*

pecan shrimp *143*

rugelach *187*

sweet rolls *191*

PEPPERCORNS

about *99, 118, 137*

grilled red snapper with crabmeat and pink peppercorn sauce *137*

steak Madagascar *119*

storing *153*

PEPPERS, BELL

about *152*

charro bean soup *79*

southwest grilled chicken *86*

Texas seafood stew *74 (illus. 75)*

PEPPERS, JALAPEÑO

black beans *156*

charro bean soup *79*

crabmeat Gruyère tarts *25*

grilled jalapeño quail breast with apple-smoked bacon *14*

jalapeño biscuits *32 (illus. 33)*

jalapeño cornbread *36*

lemon chicken *88 (illus. 80--81)*

Padre Island shrimp *141*

pechuga a la parilla *83*

PEPPERS, RED

allspice crusted lamb chops with roasted red pepper sauce *128 (illus. 129)*

asparagus bundles *159 (illus. 158)*

fettuccine with shrimp and mushrooms *64*

julienne of carrot, red pepper and zucchini *157*

lemon chicken *88 (illus. 80--81)*

poached Atlantic salmon with julienned vegetables and saffron beurre blanc *152*

red pepper ragu *68*

roasted red pepper sauce *122*

southwest chicken salad *45*

see also Sauce, red pepper

PEPPERS, POBLANO

about *79*

charro bean soup *79*

poblano soup *71*

PHEASANT

about *19, 100, 102*

galantine of pheasant *20 (illus. 21)*

grilled breast of pheasant and sun-dried cherry couscous with sauternes sauce *103*

pheasant enchiladas *100 (illus. 101)*

pheasant stew *102*

pheasant stock and cooked pheasant *102*

smoked pheasant spring rolls with sweet and sour sauce *19*

PHYLLOS *25*

PICO DE GALLO *17*

PIE CRUST

about *194*

brownie, for lemon mousse cake *188*

chocolate cookie, for tortuga pie *169*

graham cracker, for white French silk *170*; for pumpkin cheesecake *180*

pâte brisée *194*

sweet pie crust *194*

PIES

tortuga pie *169*

white French silk, *170*

PINE NUTS

about *63, 136*

grilled breast of quail with sour cherry couscous and cassis sauce, *97*

grilled portobello mushroom gratineé *161*

pasta salad Genovese *47*

smoked salmon fettuccine *63 (illus. 60--61)*

spinach and endive salad with blueberry tarragon vinaigrette *56*

trout piñón with papaya lime butter sauce *136*

POBLANO: see Peppers, poblano

PORK

cooking *127*

galantine of pheasant *20 (illus. 21)*

roast loin of pork with rosemary *127*

smoked tenderloin of jerk pork with Jamaican barbecue sauce *126*

spicy pork pimenton *16*

PORT

about *118*

braised duck with port and thyme *106*

Portuguese lamb chops with port sauce *131*

steak Charnigan *122*

PORTOBELLO MUSHROOMS

grilled portobello mushroom gratineé *161*

grilled tenderloin of veal with grilled portabello mushrooms *123*

POTATOES

about *122, 165*

hobo breakfast *38*

oven-roasted new potatoes *165*

roasted garlic mashed potatoes *165*

POTATOES, SWEET

about *164*

grilled sweet potatoes *164*

Parmesan sweet potatoes *164*

POULTRY: see Chicken, Duck, Pheasant, Quail

PUDDING AND CUSTARDS

chocolate bread pudding *184*

crème brûlée with Grand Marnier *192*

hazelnut semifreddo *190*

pastry cream *195*

tiramisu *185*

PUMPKIN: pumpkin cheesecake *180*

PUMPKIN SEEDS: southwest chicken salad *45*

Q

QUAIL

about *14, 15, 93*

chicken fried quail with black pepper gravy *99*

BIBLIOGRAPHY

Berkley, Robert. *Peppers.* New York: Running Heads Incorporated, 1991.

Child, Julia. *Julia Child & Company.* New York: Alfred A. Knopf, 1978.

Conway, Linda Glick. *The New Professional Chef,* 5th ed. New York: Van Nostrand Reinhold, 1991.

Davidson, Alan. *The Oxford Companion to Food.* New York: Oxford University Press Inc., 1999.

Dornenburg, Andrew, and Karen Page. *Culinary Artistry.* New York: John Wiley & Sons, Inc., 1996.

Herbst, Ron, and Sharon Tyler Herbst. *Wine Lover's Companion.* New York: Barron's Educational Series, Inc., 1995.

Herbst, Sharon Tyler. *Food Lover's Companion.* New York: Barron's Educational Series, Inc., 1990.

Rombauer, Irma S., and Marion Rombauer Becker. *Joy of Cooking.* New York: Penguin Books USA Inc., 1973.

Rosso, Julee, and Sheila Lukins. *The New Basics Cookbook.* New York: Workman Publishing, 1989.

Williams, Chuck, and Joyce Goldstein. *Williams-Sonoma Entertaining: Complete Entertaining Cookbook.* San Francisco: Weldon Owen Inc., 1993.

www.happyhour.ca Happy Hour Spirit & Liqueur Dictionary